RUSSIA ABROAD

RUSSIA ABROAD

DRIVING REGIONAL FRACTURE *in* POST-COMMUNIST EURASIA *and* BEYOND

ANNA OHANYAN
Editor

Georgetown University Press / *Washington, DC*

Library of Congress Cataloging-in-Publication Data

Names: Ohanyan, Anna, editor.
Title: Russia abroad : driving regional fracture in post-Communist Eurasia and beyond / Anna Ohanyan, editor.
Description: Washington, DC : Georgetown University Press, 2018. | Includes bibliographical references and index.
Identifiers: LCCN 2018016702 (print) | LCCN 2018033284 (ebook) | ISBN 9781626166219 (ebook) | ISBN 9781626166202 (pbk. : alk. paper) | ISBN 9781626166196 (hardcover : alk. paper)
Subjects: LCSH: Russia (Federation)—Foreign relations. | Russia (Federation)—Foreign relations—Former Soviet republics. | Former Soviet republics—Foreign relations—Russia (Federation) | Regionalism. | Geopolitics.
Classification: LCC JZ1616 (ebook) | LCC JZ1616 .R86 2018 (print) | DDC 327.47—dc23
LC record available at https://lccn.loc.gov/2018016702

♾ This book is printed on acid-free paper meeting the requirements of the American National Standard for Permanence in Paper for Printed Library Materials.

19 18 9 8 7 6 5 4 3 2 First printing

Printed in the United States of America

Cover design by Jeremy John Parker.

CONTENTS

PART III POSTCOLONIAL ROOTS OF REGIONAL FRACTURE BEYOND THE POST-SOVIET SPACE

ACKNOWLEDGMENTS

The idea of regional fracture as a process, and fractured regions as systems, arose in the course of several conversations with academics at International Studies Association conferences and with civil society leaders and scholars in the South Caucasus. In 2015, at the International Studies Association Annual Convention in New Orleans, I presented the findings of my then recently published book, *Networked Regionalism as Conflict Management* (Stanford University Press, 2015). In that work, I focused on the networked dimension of regionalism in conflict areas and argued for the significance of regionalism in cultivating structures and processes in conflict management. The discussant for that panel, Fen Osler Hampson, pointed out that part of the argument seemed to involve the costs of regional fragmentation rather than only the benefits of regional integration. This observation turned out to be immensely helpful. It was the push I needed to start thinking about regional fragmentation as a distinct analytical category.

Still, my struggles with conceptualizing these rather broad ideas at the time persisted, as I started thinking about the costs of missing regional ties in a more systematic manner and quickly realized that as international relations scholars we know more about the value of regional integration than the costs of missing links. Later in the year, this observation from Hampson at ISA 2015 was echoed in a conversation I had with Gevorg Ter-Gabrielyan, the country director of the Eurasia Partnership Foundation in Armenia. Ter-Gabrielyan pointed out how often existing regional ties in the South Caucasus are being strategically undone by Moscow to achieve specific foreign policy goals. Drawing from his expertise as a peacebuilding practitioner, Ter-Gabrielyan proceeded to provide numerous valuable cases of contacts between people in conflict regions being disrupted by governmental establishments from regional powers and national states.

As I proceeded to develop the framework of regional fracture, I moved to identify additional empirical observations beyond the South Caucasus. Hence, the initiative of an edited volume was born. Without the insightful contributions from a team of highly accomplished scholars and analysts, our theory of regional fracture would not be where it is today. I am thankful for invitations to present this book project at various venues, such as the "End of Transition" conference organized by the University of Southern California Institute of Armenian Studies, in Los Angeles in April 2017, and at the "The End of the Region: Future of Spatial Constructs in the Populist Era" conference held in Belgium and jointly organized by Université de Liège, Columbia University, and Cambridge University.

I am deeply appreciative of scholars and practitioners on both sides of the Atlantic. The generosity and insight of my respondents in Armenia, Georgia, Russia, Bosnia and Herzegovina, and the US have been essential for adding much-needed detail to this study. Research grants from Stonehill College and the University of Southern California Institute of Armenian Studies, supported in part by the Calouste Gulbenkian Foundation, allowed me to conduct fieldwork in the South Caucasus and in Russia. I am thankful to my research assistants, Erica Cordatos and Daniel Lavigne, for valuable support and dedication throughout various stages of the research, particularly in conducting the fieldwork in Armenia in 2017. I am grateful to the students in my Russia, the West, and the Rest course for spirited and stimulating discussions on current politics in post-Communist Eurasia. The feedback from anonymous reviewers at Georgetown University Press has been instrumental in structuring the argument of the book and for thinking more broadly about its implications for international relations theory. Susan Allen, Richard Finnegan, Todd Gernes, and David Matz have added greatly to the project with their thoughtful suggestions on structure and content of the book. I am thankful to Donald Jacobs, the senior acquisitions editor at Georgetown University Press, for his early support of this project, his wise counsel, and his professionalism in guiding this project throughout the various stages of the process. Importantly, I credit him with the title of this book.

As always, it is my family that is a constant source of inspiration for my work. They are my toughest critics and the support system for which I am thankful. My twelve-year-old daughter, Elise, challenged me not to hide behind the books about peace that I write and to "actually get out and do something for peace." She has a point. And I dedicate this book to peacebuilders, practitioners, and diplomats that are tasked with the daily work of building connections and ties that will ultimately transform conflict-ravaged and fractured neighborhoods for the better.

Introduction: Margins Matter

Anna Ohanyan

The year 2016 appears to have marked the dawn of a new, centrifugal era in world politics. Britain's departure from the European Union (EU), known as "Brexit," has unsettled the decades-old regional fabric of the European Union while, across the Atlantic, a new American administration has challenged the fundamentals of free trade arrangements from the North American Free Trade Agreement to the aborted Trans-Pacific Partnership. Populist politics is seemingly on the rise wherever one looks. With this as a backdrop, it may appear difficult to remain sanguine about the prospects of regionalism,[1] especially as two of its long-time champions, the US and the UK, pull away from their respective regional groupings.

Ironically, contemporary support for regionalism of sorts comes from an unlikely place: the Kremlin. While seeking to undermine the regional social contract within the EU over the past decade (Contessi 2016), the Kremlin has been working diligently to create its own regional groupings in both the economic and security spheres (see chapters 2 and 7, this volume). In 2015, largely inspired by the European Union, the Eurasian Economic Union (EEU) was created to replace its predecessor, the Customs Union (International Crisis Group 2016a). The Kremlin's critics see these Russia-led regional groupings as an attempt to reconstruct the Soviet Union, while Vladimir Putin has described them as initiatives to promote economic integration and modernization toward a "Greater Europe" (International Crisis Group 2016a). In the case of the EEU, imitation, as Oscar Wilde noted over a century ago, may indeed be the sincerest form of flattery.

Still, Russia is no stranger to regionalism. After all, the Russian Empire as well as the Soviet Union served to maintain Russian hegemony in its peripheries by tying these regions closely to Moscow (Smith 1995; Sussex 2012). As such, these projects repeated a practice of building regional groupings (albeit coercive and centralized) for political purposes by many other (post)colonial powers of their time. Central and South American countries came together in the nineteenth and twentieth centuries to resist their overpowering and expansionist neighbor, a United States guided by the Monroe Doctrine that pursued regional hegemony (Mearsheimer 2014a). After the Second World War, Middle Eastern autocracies coalesced into regional groupings to coerce internal opposition and civil society groups (Barnett and Solingen 2007; Krause 2010). Regional organizations and various models of regionalism have been used to foster economic growth and development but have also been exploited to push back against a foe and an unwelcome regional intruder (Buzan and Wæver 2003). Regionalism has been known to empower small businesses and offer new outlets of regional diplomacy (Beeson 2010; Tsheola 2010; Wolff and Dursun-Ozkanca 2012; Ohanyan 2015), as has been the case with the EU. But it has also in certain circumstances split states internally by tying the loyalties of national political elites to external patrons that champion less-than-benevolent regional models, as, arguably, in the Russia-led EEU case.

With the advent of centrifugal world politics in the post–Cold War period, learning how to build regions that strengthen, develop, and democratize states while enhancing structures of global governance from the bottom up is the broad policy consideration driving this book. This, unfortunately, is particularly challenging in Russia's neighborhoods, where regional fabric among the states is threadbare and existing regional ties serve narrow and exclusive groups and stakeholders.

Indeed, Brexit has significantly unsettled advocates of regionalism. "Is regionalism dead?" is what my former student wrote to me after the Brexit referendum of 2016, having worked with me on a research project on comparative regionalism. One answer to this question is that regionalism predates the EU, with early experimentations with regionalism going back to nineteenth-century South America and twentieth-century southern Africa (Ohanyan 2015). Still, concerns for developmental and emancipatory regional models that enhance governance capacities of their members are justified. Moving forward, getting regions right is imperative if the current world systems of liberal order are to survive.

While we know much about the benefits of regional integration, our knowledge remains lacking when it comes to areas with weak or nonexistent regional fabric in political and economic life. The value of dense ties within and between states are firmly established in social science, but the costs of missing ones are underexplored. Furthermore, deliberate "unregioning," applied by actors external as well as internal to a region, also has gone unnoticed, despite its increasingly sophisticated modern application by Russia in its peripheries.

Such areas are not simply "unregionalized" and unintegrated. Described as "fractured regions" in this volume, the authors here highlight that they are far from being simply opposites of integrated regions. Fractured regions are distinct empirical realities that can be integrated political systems in some ways but completely fragmented in others. In fractured regions, immediate, strategic security considerations and market forces often pull in different directions. This mismatch is fueled by lack of democracy, with political elites pulling toward external political patrons as they resist bottom-up regional engagements from the public. Fractured regions are composed of states with deep political fissures between government and civil society. Fractured regions may be integrated in terms of regional, albeit illegal, flows of illicit drugs, for example, but may have only rudimentary capacities of regional governance. In other words, fractured regions are distinct systems where regional power applications from external players are common and where regionwide institutions may be proliferating; yet, despite regionally organized applications of power and institutions, key regional processes of governance fail to materialize. Fractured regions are institutionally thick. They are plural rather than state-centric: Many actors—state and nonstate—matter in producing and perpetuating regional fracture. Such regions challenge state-centric theories of international relations.

The costs of fractured regions for global security are significant, and the mechanisms of world disorder they consolidate are quite specific. The empirical chapters of this book offer nuanced analyses of regional fracture and delineate the concrete impact for world order that specific fractured regions produce. Viewed together, the empirical chapters tell a single story and share a single message: margins matter in the modern multiplex world of post-American hegemony (Acharya 2014a). Viewed individually, each chapter details the specific types of regional fracturing strategically applied by Russia in its peripheries and frontiers while also highlighting the costs of such policies in each particular region. As a whole, the edited volume advocates for a comprehensive and holistic analysis of Russia's foreign policies in its neighborhoods toward a more accurate and realistic understanding of the limits and opportunities of its global reengagement. At the same time, it argues that developing a Russia policy for the South Caucasus or for Georgia, for instance, without considering Russia's engagement in Central Asia or the Western Balkans is most likely to be ineffective. The theory of regional fracture developed in this volume illustrates the lowest common denominator of Russian engagement in its peripheries while also offering a granular understanding of the Russian role in specific conflicts and regions where such engagement unfolds.

Against this backdrop, this book has two goals. First, it introduces the theory of regional fracture and argues for its use as a fresh lens through which to examine the post-American world (dis)order. It explains regional fracture both as a phenomenon and as a significant analytical category in world politics, offering a framework to produce more nuanced understandings of how regional dynamics impact global security environments. The theory of regional fracture developed in this volume examines its significance for global security studies, and it explores the mechanisms by which fracture becomes a problem for regional and global security provision.

The second objective of this study is to apply the regional fracture theory to explain Russia's policies in its peripheries and explain their global significance relative to resurgent Russia in the post-American world. In this respect, the edited volume offers a bottom-up view on Russia, from its peripheries rather than from Western capitals. It explores Russia's post–Cold War foreign policies in the Eurasian context (Laruelle 2015a; Shevel 2011; Tsygankov 2013; Zimmerman 2002; Arbatov 1993) and then focuses on the string of regional conflicts in which Russia is a direct or indirect participant (Lynch 2001; Wood et al. 2016; de Waal 2002; Allison 2008a; Giles et al. 2015; Horowitz and Tyburski 2012; Pouliot 2007). The empirical cases include Ukraine, the South Caucasus, Armenia, Central Asia, the Western Balkans, and the Middle East.

To address both of these goals, the first part of the book introduces the theory of regional fracture (Ohanyan, chapter 1) followed by a Russia-specific discussion on regional fracture (Nalbandov, chapter 2). It further zooms in on a single state, Armenia, to demonstrate the external effects of regional fracture on a state, in this case explaining the way the fractured South Caucasus shapes Armenian statecraft (Giragosian, chapter 5). The chapter on Armenia also offers an illustrative case study on the way the internal sources within a state can produce or perpetuate fracture in a given region (in this case, the South Caucasus). The second part of the book includes post-Soviet cases of fractured regions and states in Russia's peripheries, highlighting Russian engagement in each of them. It is the third part of the book, with chapters on the Western Balkans (Bechev, chapter 7) and the Middle East (Katz, chapter 8), that examines how regional fracture as a phenomenon transcends Russia's immediate neighborhoods. Together with the conclusion (Ohanyan), this third part of the book assesses the extent to which regional fracture by default is a postcolonial legacy beyond Russia and how it can interact with its contemporary manifestations, fracture by design, carried out by hegemons external to the region.

Fractured Regions and Global Security

Three main themes emerge from the empirical section that illuminate how fractured regions become global security threats. First, fractured regions are levers as well as liabilities for neo-imperial and rising powers, requiring a closer analysis for the debate on rising power accommodation in an emergent multiplex world (Acharya 2014a, 2014b). As colonial legacies, they are levers because they are often redeployed by neo-imperial powers as foreign policy instruments to advance their strategic interests in the world system. But they are also a liability because they can constrain and challenge these very same neo-imperial powers, especially those seeking to adjust the world order as they aim to get a seat, or a better seat, at the geopolitical table. As a liability, fractured regions are neighborhoods with diminished societal engagement and limited trade flows into the region: these conditions undermine much-needed governance processes dealing with such regional problems as drug trafficking or environmental degradation. As a result, the rising power or neo-imperialist power, if lacking significant resources to devote to these margins for economic modernization and development, will be disadvantaged relative to its competitors. Brazil, being located in a highly regionalized environment, is in a much better diplomatic neighborhood with better links to regional governance than Russia, which has been solely reliant on energy resources in transacting with its neighbors, near and far. For these neighbors of Russia, regional institutions have thus far shown little value in organized problem-solving among states and societies (Jackson 2014). The inability to effectively respond to the crisis and riots in Kyrgyzstan in 2010 by the Collective Security Treaty Organization is a frequently cited example. Whether—and if yes, then how—Russia should be "accommodated" is a question that gains new currency when Russia's poor negotiating alternatives are considered in the contexts of its poor regional ties.

Fractured regions also constrain a rising or neo-imperialist power by nourishing state weakness and shallow governance around it. In addition to transborder flows of conflict and crime, fractured neighborhoods often further stress already weak states by pushing capital and possible foreign investment out of the region. States in fractured regions attempt to compensate by linking with far-removed capitals, which often entails higher trade and transaction costs. Inefficient uses of regional resources, such as infrastructure for health care, transportation, and tourism, further disadvantage individual nations' global competitiveness. While Australia and New Zealand moved toward "beyond-the-border regionalism" by integrating their public service delivery systems in many areas, the opposite is observed in most of Russia's fractured neighborhoods. Poor structures of cooperation in trade flows and water use in Central Asia are notorious for their dysfunctionality (Collins 2009; Bohr 2004), despite the existence of a range of putative regional organizations in this region.

The recurrent inability of great powers to shape the political behavior of their "allies" is a phenomenon that is the topic of much new research in political science (Cooley 2012; Jesse et al. 2012). The empirical cases in this book provide fresh insight and understanding of the mechanisms and factors that can greatly constrain great powers in their geopolitical spheres of interests. Chapter 3, on Ukraine and authored by Vsevolod Samokhvalov, explores the national agency of elites in manipulating their external patrons. The political crises of modern Ukraine are examined in this chapter through the lens of a loss of control by external powers. Concerns over regime survival by national elites, combined with gaps between informal and formal structures of political life, are two of the factors that have served to constrain greater powers in Ukraine's neighborhood. This tension between local powers and regional powers are also seen to be operative in the cases of the Western Balkans and the South Caucasus, covered by Dimitar Bechev (chapter 7) and Laurence Broers (chapter 4), respectively.

In short, regional fracture can be a liability for rising or neo-imperialist powers, and Russia in particular, as they seek to renegotiate their place in what appears to be a multipolar world order. At the same time, they can evolve to be tools in these powers' foreign policy arsenals. Regional fracturing can exact short-term and immediate security costs on the peripheries, thereby constraining their alternative policy choices and bargaining power relative to greater powers. The case of Russia's involvement in Ukraine and the South Caucasus is instructive to this end. The respective chapters by Samokhvalov and Broers demonstrate how the fractured fabric of regionalism in both neighborhoods has only strengthened Russia's hand by reducing foreign policy options of the regional states.

Second, fractured regions also condition great powers in smaller wars, so to speak. They consolidate ongoing armed conflicts in the regions and become sources of new ones. Lacking regionwide institutions that coalesce and integrate diverse segments of societies, peace processes around ongoing conflicts become challenging to cultivate and sustain (Ohanyan 2015; Crocker, Hampson, and Aall 2011b). Low levels of regional trade in such neighborhoods are perhaps the most visible outcome of regional fracture (World Economic Forum 2014). But the lack of broader ties and connections regionwide makes the ongoing conflicts difficult to resolve (Collier 2008; Brzezinski 1989; Toal 2017) and the conflicting parties unwilling to engage (Ohanyan 2015).

Indeed, the effects of fractured regions on low-intensity armed conflicts are specific and are different than the impact of regional fracture on great power rivalries. In addition to affecting the available room to maneuver for neo-imperialist and rising powers, fractured regions also impact lower-intensity conflicts. They do so by institutionalizing conflict lines and political divisions, and by instrumentalizing unresolved regional conflicts. For example, in chapter 8, studying the contemporary Middle East, Mark Katz traces the Israeli–Palestinian conflict and the Kurdish conflict in Turkey and the broader Middle East to the fractured regional contexts in each case. In addition, Katz also highlights that the fractured nature of the Middle East enabled Russia's entry into the Syrian civil war but that it also gave rise to serious constraints on Russia's room to maneuver. Similarly, the conflicts in Eastern Ukraine and the South Caucasus have also been arguably exploited by Russia for intervention as a "security provider": Fueling or building conflicts has become a way to cultivate demand for security cover that Russia has been eager to provide.

In exploring the effects of regional fracture on great power dynamics and smaller wars, the chapter by Bechev (chapter 7) on the Western Balkans asks a different question: Why is it that regional fracture in the Western Balkans stopped short of causing violence on a more significant, extraregional scale? Referring to the post-Dayton era, Bechev highlights that the institutional embeddedness of the Western Balkans within the broader European neighborhood served as a cushion absorbing the pressure from a politically manifested regional fracture.

The third theme relates to the distinction between regional fracture by default and by design. It captures the institutional legacies of debilitated regional neighborhoods in the post-Soviet years, reflecting decades of regional neglect in favor of an imposed Moscow-oriented alignment. With the collapse of the Soviet Union, countries found themselves in fractured regions by default as they struggled to build and exercise their young statecraft. These regions inherited poor regional infrastructure in terms of transportation and energy routes (Smith 1995), which translated into unfavorable context for resolution of ethnic conflicts that erupted in the twilight years of the Soviet Union. Inheriting regional fracture by default, these countries have now become targets of regional fracture by design, which is a strategic and deliberate foreign policy action currently practiced by Russia, from Donbass to Damascus.

The delineation between regional fracture by default and by design, while useful for analytical purposes, should not obscure the cyclical nature and the relationship between the two. The fracture by default, a condition of historical legacy, was mostly a fracture by design at some point. The chapters exploring the current state of the Middle East and the South Caucasus are particularly illuminating of how the contours of regional fracture were inherited from imperial progenitors, such as the Ottoman Empire and the British and French in the Middle East and Russia and the Soviet Union in the South Caucasus. These centuries-old regional fissures in such places are instrumentalized by today's local elites as well as regional powers; Laurence Broers in chapter 4, on the South Caucasus, fittingly refers to such elites as "entrepreneurs of fracture."

Regional Fracture as Geopolitics in 3D

The diversity among the forms of fractured regions emerges when considering the phenomenon in a comparative light. The cases covered in this volume reveal differences in the way regions can be fractured along political, institutional, and social dimensions. Regional fracture in the Western Balkans is quite different from that of the Middle East. The study of the cases as a whole enables us to understand how structural variance in fractured regions positions each region differently relative to geopolitical competitions, particularly relative to the confrontation between Russia and the West. With great power alliances currently shifting, the patterns of regional fracture will play a crucial role in the politics of realignments in the world system. The empirical chapters in this volume explore the different ways and patterns of regional fracture across regions as diverse as Damascus in the Middle East and Donbass in Ukraine. Taken together, these studies elucidate the different ways that Russia is embedded in its peripheries, and the specific ways in which these fractured regions propel as well as constrain Russia as it challenges a liberal world order. For instance, in the Balkans, Russia is limited to exploiting short-term political openings in various places without a genuine possibility of undoing the institutional ties of the European Union in the region. In Central Asia, by contrast, facing a shrinking political space given the rivalry between China and the US, Russia has proceeded to weave an institutional blanket over the region, although with mixed results.

The complexities of the "resurgent Russia" narrative that is popular today emerge only when all of the fractured regions in post-Communist Eurasia and the Middle East, and the political conflicts they host, are viewed in aggregate, as part of a single string of insecurity. Indeed, taken individually, each case of conflict or of a fractured region offers only one piece of the larger puzzle of Russian resurgence in world politics. The regional fabric of politics in post-Communist Eurasia and the Middle East is central to understanding the changing structures of world (dis)order in a post-American period and the specific role of Russia within such an order.

The extent to which regional fracturing is specific to post-Communist Eurasia, with Russia at its geopolitical core, is a question that is addressed head-on in the chapter on Russia by Robert Nalbandov. This chapter assesses the significance of geographic contiguity and the geographic location of fractured regions relative to Russia. It addresses the question of why the Baltics have avoided Russian engagement, despite geographic proximity to Russia, while the Middle East, which does not share a border with Russia, has become a target of Russian military intervention. Nalbandov examines the regional fracture theory in a comparative light with the theory of regional contiguity, as developed by Lewis F. Richardson (1961). While the former focuses on institutional, political, and social ties at a regional level, the latter elevates geographical location and proximity as factors that produce territorial frictions. Regional contiguity may explain Russian involvement in Central Asia, the South Caucasus, and Ukraine, but it fails to explain the role of the Kremlin in the Western Balkans and the Middle East and the absence of overt engagement in the Baltics despite geographic proximity. The fractured regional fabric in the Middle East and regional coherence in the Baltics partly explain Russia's foreign policy choices in both cases.

The comparative treatment of both theories in Nalbandov's chapter also exposes new frontiers in geopolitics (P. Kelly 2016). While geographic contiguity highlights the territorial and geographic dimension of geopolitics, regional fracture theory, with an emphasis on institutional and political boundaries within states, reveals the domestic frontlines where geopolitical rivalries are increasingly playing out. The regional fracture view underscores the institutional dimensions of geopolitical rivalry that often transcend geographic confines. As Nalbandov elucidates, the fractured nature of a region makes it inviting for Russian intrusions regardless of geographic proximity. The immediate policy implication that stems from this chapter is that regional cohesion and engagement between and among regional states is more promising as a strategy to contain Russia rather than as a bilateral state engagement with such a powerful neighbor one on one, as Georgia and Ukraine have tried in the recent past (Sussex 2012).

In addition to assessing the regional fracture theory, Nalbandov also examines the string of conflicts across the Russian underbelly and sets the stage for an in-depth examination of these conflicts from a regional fracture perspective. Laurence Broers's chapter on the South Caucasus, chapter 4, further highlights the coexistence of the theories of regional fracture and geographic contiguity. The case of the South Caucasus, as a region that has emerged as a site of great power competition in the post–Cold War period (Sussex 2012), illustrates well the new institutional and political complexity of regional fracture as a much older problem with deep colonial roots.

Broers also examines how regional fracture can occur both by default as well as by design, often instigated by extraregional powers such as Russia and the EU. He details how external powers acting in the region have instrumentalized the existing regional fracture by default and exploited it by design, toward advancing their own interests. The application of a regional fracture framework in the South Caucasus reveals how internal political conflicts between a "prerogative state" and a "constitutional state" are perpetuating ongoing processes of regional fracture and building new interstate rivalries. Broers details how political and oligarchic elites of various types in the South Caucasus have pursued bilateral or multilateral projects with extraregional powers, resulting in the pulling apart of the region in different directions.

Broers's answer to the question "How do the margins matter for world order?" is straightforward. He explores the ways that regional fracture has been a liability for Russia as well as a lever as it tries to reassert power in world politics. Broers illustrates the institutional dimension of regional fracture and explains how the proliferation of regional institutions has reflected vectors often pointing in different directions. Referring to this aptly as "entrepreneurial fracture," Broers highlights the capture of regional organizations by the "prerogative state," often for the purpose of regime survival or projection of hegemony for extraregional powers. Largely reflecting the transient and shallow nature of these institutions, Broers's chapter is in accord with recent scholarship on Russia's "constrained primacy" (Sussex 2012). The institutional proliferation that pulls the regional states in different directions amounts to "a multilateral gloss to bilateral asymmetries and creates bloc-based bargaining power vis-à-vis Western structures," Broers notes. He cautions that the regional fracture in the South Caucasus is heavily instrumentalized, resulting in its endless reproduction by the beneficiaries of such fracture. His attention to de facto states and the way they provide entry nodes for penetration into the region by its most recent hegemon, Russia, offers a fresh narrative on the systemic effects of fractured regions for world politics.

If both geographical contiguity and regional fracture theory offer explanations of the involvement and sustained engagement by Russia in the South Caucasus, the case for the Middle East is arguably more straightforward. Lacking any physical borders with Russia, the Syrian civil war rendered the broader Middle East institutionally and politically open and vulnerable to Russian intervention. Indeed, one of the many added values of the case on the Middle East in this volume of post-Communist regional fracture is the opportunity it offers for exploring the institutional and political dimensions of regional fracture as well as the great power balancing strategies such considerations have engendered in the Middle East, outside of the post-Communist space. It allows exploration of the question concerning whether regional fracture is a post-Soviet phenomenon or one with broader analytical mileage.

Perhaps the most obvious factor explaining the inclusion of the Middle East in this book is the Russian military intervention in 2014 in the Syrian civil war. However, chapter 8, by Mark Katz, offers a much deeper narrative, one focused on the imperial and colonial legacies of Middle Eastern regional fracture distinct from their contemporary manifestations. It parallels with the narrative of fracture by default and by design, as developed by Broers in the case of the South Caucasus. By describing the phenomenon of regional fracture in the Middle East, Katz traces the roots of this fracture to the Ottoman Empire and the subsequent European domination after the First World War. Implemented as a deliberate program of regional fracture at the time, the Ottoman and European actions represented fracture by design. However, over a century the situation has evolved into a case of regional fracture by default, creating a Middle East favorable to Russian entry and to Russian exploitation of regional cleavages. In short, the Middle East challenges the notion of regional fracture as a solely post-Communist phenomenon and demonstrates its broader imperial roots in world politics.

Katz also highlights three main dimensions of regional fracture and focuses on its internal consequences and evolution inside Syria. The evolutionary perspective that Katz develops in chapter 8 allows us to appreciate the historical trajectory of the phenomenon of regional fracture. It raises a rather specific question essential to understanding the other empirical cases: How different is regional fracture from "divide-and-conquer" policies routinely practiced throughout world history? The study of fracture in Syria and the Middle East exercised by external powers, whether the Ottomans, French, British, or Russians, reveals that regional fracture is indeed divide-and-conquer at its core. However, regional fracture as a phenomenon is politically and institutionally more complex because it evolves in the context of the rise of new postcolonial states that are internally divided and quite weak in terms of their administrative capacities. The multiplicity and institutional complexity of actors—state and nonstate—in such cases and their deeply networked character are some of the attributes that distinguish regional fracture from pure divide-and-conquer policies. The evolutionary and historical discussion of regional fracture, tracing from the Ottoman Empire to contemporary Russia, offers great nuance to this discussion.

Tackling the Syrian conflict, perhaps the most destructive conflict among the cases covered in the volume, Katz's chapter on the Middle East demonstrates the internal consequences of regional fracture. State weaknesses in a fractured Middle East have served to undermine institutional avenues for social change. They have invited external patrons to fuel radical and revolutionary changes inside the countries, Katz argues. External powers support their local allies to resist opposition to their power, and such legitimacy crises, also observed in the South Caucasus and elsewhere, undermine prospects of democratic development. In the specific context of the Arab Spring, Katz notes that the existing political and institutional fracture of the region was strong enough to uphold the authoritarian order in the aftermath of the Arab Spring but was insufficient to prevent its outbreak in the first place.

The fractured nature of the Middle East has clearly helped to strengthen Russia's position in the great power rivalry in world politics. It has also influenced the ongoing conflicts and the peace processes in the region. Katz explores how regional fracture formed and consolidated the Israeli–Palestinian conflict as well as the Kurdish conflict in Turkey and the broader Middle East. In the case of Russia's presence in the region and its deliberate efforts to build alliances with anti-American actors, the fractured nature of the Middle East appears to have provided fertile ground on which the Cold War has rematerialized.

In studying contemporary Russian involvement in the Middle East, Katz answers affirmatively the question of whether margins matter for politics. Katz argues that regional fracture, whether by design or default, strengthens great powers in some ways but undermines them in others. For example, the fractured landscape of the Middle East has rendered the region favorable for Russian involvement. Yet Katz also explores how Russia could not "have it all" and the ways in which it has faced significant constraints in its activities in the region: Russia was pushing into the region, but local elites in many of the countries were working to pull it in as well.

As with many geopolitical theories, the geographic contiguity framework explored by Nalbandov emphasizes territory and space as sources of friction, division, and conflict (Lobell 2016; P. Kelly 2016), a conclusion well supported by data on armed conflict (Goertz, Diehl, and Balas 2016; P. Kelly 2016). At the same time, societal closeness, the density of interactions, and opportunities of trade best supported by geographic proximity are said to promote cooperation and engagement between states and between societies (Potter 2016; Deutsch 1954). With deep and dense societal ties and intensive, albeit asymmetric, economic interdependencies between Ukraine and Russia (Dragneva and Wolczuk 2016), the Ukraine case can be used to argue for spatial proximity as a source of conflict as well as cooperation.

The theory of regional fracture applied in the case of Ukraine offers sets of answers concerning the timing, prior trajectory, and development of a crisis that is largely driven by multilayered processes of regional fracture inside the country.

Chapter 3, by Vsevolod Samokhvalov, describes the Ukraine as a theater for regional fracturing that has been under way since the collapse of the Soviet Union. The Maidan demonstrations in the winter of 2013–14, the subsequent civil war in Eastern Ukraine, and the annexation of Crimea by Russia are spectacular events shaped by regional fracture in the broader Eastern European space. Sandwiched between East and West, the narrative of "great power overlay" and superpower competition have been frequently invoked to describe Ukraine's political crisis (Götz 2016; Auer 2015). Europe, described as a "quiet superpower" (Moravcsik 2002), is often cast as clashing with an illiberal Russia, which is then identified as a source of political crisis in Ukraine. Relatedly, debate often centers on whether Russia is revisionist (Deudney and Ikenberry 2010), seeking to undo the liberal world order; a victim, unfairly treated by the North Atlantic Treaty Organization (NATO) (Mearsheimer 2014b); or a troublemaker, seeking to maintain regional influence by instigating conflict and security instabilities around its peripheries (Auer 2015). Across all of these perspectives, Ukraine is viewed as a passive subject, lacking agency, subject to external geopolitical groundswells.

Instead, Samokhvalov proposes that the internal fracture in Ukraine, while with deep regional dimensions, is hardly an ideological clash between East and West. Exploring the way regional fracture played out inside Ukraine, the author highlights the transitory nature of power resources and the fluid properties of elite networks that have oscillated between the two regional forces active in the country (i.e., Russia and the EU). The chapter reveals an internal dynamic similar to that of the Middle East and the South Caucasus, where internal regime survival concerns of the political elite have become a dominant determinant for the country's moving in one or another direction. In short, regional projects have often been captured by the elites to advance their narrow political and economic objectives. Similar to the regional dynamics in the South Caucasus, Samokhvalov highlights how a "democratic simulacra" of sorts is created, exemplified by sets of political parties that end up undermining independent opposition forces on both the left and the right. The gap between informal and formal political forces, also described by Broers in the context of the South Caucasus, is emerging as a key factor that is often exploited by external regional forces. The only constant inside Ukraine's political system since its post-Soviet independence has been the struggle for state-building discourse, waged between ad hoc coalitions and transient political groups that would often be caught up in external geopolitical rivalries. Similar to the argument by Katz on the Middle East, Ukraine, as a relatively "marginal" country in the world system, was rarely a passive follower of great powers. Instead, in addition to regional forces pushing in, local players have been as active in pulling in external patrons.

Samokhvalov's response to the question of whether margins matter is an unequivocal yes. By describing the political, institutional, and social dimensions of regional fracture manifest inside Ukraine, he explains the ways in which local actors can fuel and drive regional fracturing. While he reveals the corrosive side of regional fracturing for Ukraine's state-building project, he also portrays an unsettled discourse surrounding issues of identity and belonging. The regional fracture theory, applied in this case, has shown the simplicity of ideological-civilizational as well as spatial (i.e., East–West) narratives hitherto used to explain the internal dynamics in Ukraine. The fluid nature of the social dimension of regional fracturing, in a small way, seems rather progressive: Samokhvalov fittingly finds that "the social space [of Ukraine is] a complex amalgam of numerous . . . communities in which various social actors deploy necessary resources in order to promote their own identity projects and convert them into social and political capital." The chapter and its portrayal of the case of Ukraine raise an intriguing question of whether regional fracturing can, perversely, be constructive in some sense.

In contrast to Ukraine, regional fracturing has been less visible to the naked eye in the Western Balkans since the end of the wars of the 1990s. Indeed, this case study, developed by Dimitar Bechev in chapter 7 of this volume, reminds the reader that in contrast to the other neighborhoods in the peripheries of the EU and Russia, the Western Balkans is stable. It also asks the question of how this region avoided the violence that otherwise is associated with regional fracture. Bechev shows that the region, layered with dense institutional cover from the EU and NATO, has avoided becoming a theater for a full-blown geopolitical showdown, unlike Ukraine or Syria. At the same time, Bechev illustrates the nuance in Russia's reentry into the region as it tries to reassert its lost ground after the Soviet collapse.

Against this backdrop, and viewed comparatively with the other cases, the Western Balkans raises the issue of variation and degree of fracturing. Being heavily integrated into European regional institutions, this region, however, remains fractured in terms of the manner in which power resources are applied. Here, the gap between the rhetoric and the reality of regionalism has gained a life of its own: the local elite in the Western Balkans have developed the skill of playing the EU and Russia one against the other, a dynamic that is also observed in regions such as the South Caucasus or Central Asia. The chapter reveals that, while still oriented toward Europe, the national elites also have registered an inclination for hedging between the two patron-powers: the EU and Russia. This situation is also relevant for the question of whether margins matter. Bechev argues that the Kremlin has exploited the politically fractured nature of the Western Balkans in advancing its presence in the region. However, given the institutional anchoring of the Western Balkans within Europe, Russian success in the region has been rather limited.

Bechev also raises sets of questions regarding the impact of regional fracture on conditioning both great power rivalries as well as smaller-scale armed conflict of various intensities. Bechev provides a historical analysis of Russia's efforts to enter and consolidate its presence in the Western Balkans. The most recent stage dates to the Ukraine crisis, which strained the relations between the West and Russia. Regional energy projects linking Russia with the Balkans were shelved, but Russia continued engaging with the region, albeit in qualitatively new ways. From Bechev's analysis, it appears that it is in this stage that regional fracturing by design emerged as a foreign policy tool undertaken by Russia. Russia continued to provide diplomatic cover for Milorad Dodik's obstructionist policies in the Republika Srpska, which pushes the Bosniaks in Bosnia and Herzegovina to cultivate relations with Turkey. Instrumentalizing local cleavages in this way has become a useful tool for a resurgent Russia in its confrontation with the West.

Perhaps the largest political cost associated with regional fracturing in the Western Balkans is, as Bechev notes, that the region's "turn toward the EU has gone hand in hand with a reversal of democratization." The political elites have offered stability to their Western patrons in return for their indulgence of eroding standards of democratic governance. Referring to this situation as a "stabilocracy," Bechev illustrates the challenges of democratization in "gray" geopolitical areas and shared postcolonial backyards, of which the Western Balkans is an exemplary case.

In Central Asia, with perhaps unexpected likeness to the Western Balkans, there is a sharp disconnect between the rhetoric and reality of regional engagement. David Lewis, exploring Central Asia in chapter 6, contrasts the presence of large numbers of regional organizations, primarily promoted by extraregional powers, with the active regional fracturing in areas ranging from trade to tourism as practiced by the governments in each state. The institutional proliferation of regional organizations that add little value to regional governance and state development is indeed seen to be a key attribute of regionalism in the developing world.

However, Lewis clearly demonstrates that regional integration and regional fracture are not mirrors of one another. He argues that the multilayered nature of regional fracturing in Central Asia expresses itself in forms of regional cooperation at an elite level (albeit, sporadic, selective, and ad hoc) against a backdrop of persistent and multiple interstate conflicts and even border violence directed against civilians. His study explores how regional cooperation and neighborhood ties are further undermined by intrastate fractures between governments and the public. Governments in Central Asia portray their region as a source of instability and chaos rather than opportunities of growth and development (Collins 2009). The patrimonial, "prerogative" nature of states (also noted in Broers's chapter on the South Caucasus) actively discourages regional engagement by the public and is exacerbated by poor governance and high levels of centralization of power in capitals (Ohanyan 2007). The rise of illiberal regionalism, fostered by the shared understandings of regionalism as promoted by Russia and China (Jackson 2014), Lewis argues, has worked to shape a new regional "order" in Central Asia that rests on deep regional fractures and suppresses their political articulation.

The findings of the application of a regional fracture framework to Central Asia reflect the postcolonial condition of the region in the wake of the Soviet collapse. Fracture by default, as a Soviet legacy, and by design, as a mode of governance for the neo-patrimonial elites, has played out internally and externally in this region. Lewis portrays this as a dual crisis of sovereignty. Internally, poor institutional, social, and spatial connectivity (i.e., fracture by default, a legacy of the Soviet era) translates into fragile processes of state building, and nationalist policies directed against ethnic minorities produce interstate conflict and border disputes. Externally, fracture by design, deployed by the elites, is directed against Russia, the neo-imperialist power, as well as against the new neighbors. Both types of fracture are favored by the neo-patrimonial states for purposes of regime survival.

It appears from Lewis's chapter that past may be prologue in Central Asian regionalism, reflecting centuries of great power rivalry and geopolitical struggle. What is new, however, is the institutional dimension to the way extraregional powers engage this region. Lewis identifies specific institutional initiatives advocated by Russia, China, and the US, each attempting to reconstruct the region in accordance with their own national interests. The dynamic nature of this process plays out in terms of each extraregional power reacting to the others with counterprojects at a regional level. As a result, these actors end up diluting each other's power projections in the region and undermining each other's strategic roles. Importantly, they also end up challenging and undermining the coherence of a regional space in Central Asia. This has precipitated a vicious cycle of sorts: extraregional power competition in Central Asia contributes directly to regional fracture, which in turn weakens the strategic capabilities of all regional states attempting to claim a role in Central Asia.

The consequences of regional fracture on inter- and intrastate armed conflicts have been dramatic. Attempting to cross the Kyrgyz-Tajik border with potatoes and apricots to sell, twenty-two-year-old Mansur Makmudjon Uulu was shot dead by border guards, reports Lewis, stating that "everyday geopolitical tragedies are stark reminders of the fundamentally fractured nature of the region." By reporting on border killings of civilians by their governments, Lewis adds a new, intimate, and personal narrative of regional fracture, illuminating the high costs of fractured regions borne by citizens and often by those most marginalized.

Conclusion: Divide and No "Conquer"

Even with Brexit in the background, the value of regional engagement is not in question: it is the appropriate institutional form that regional engagement will take that is debatable. The more traditional understanding of regionalism points to it as an instrument of economic growth and democratic consolidation. But it should not obscure more diverse applications of regional forms of engagement. The regressive nature of regionalism in the form of drug trafficking, for instance, is broadly researched in social sciences. It is not the subject of this volume. Instead, understanding the specific deployment of unregioning, of regional fracturing, and of systemic and systematic disruption of regional ties by actors internal or external from the region has been the core objective in this volume. This volume offers a framework to distinguish between the rich kaleidoscope of regional models that are developing in the world, ranging from progressive and developmental to regressive, repressive, and corrosive.

Robert K. Kelly (2007) has famously called "to build better regional theory around the reality of weak-state dense environments" (224). Such a theory advocated for analytical connections between the internal weakness of states and their external regional foreign policy projections (Levitsky and Way 2006). The theory of regional fracture offers a framework to do just that. It gives us the tools to analyze the interdependence of internal and external dimensions of weak states. This volume describes fractured regions as systems that possess predictable patterns of engagement between their constituent elements, such as state and nonstate actors. Yet such engagements, occurring at different levels and among a variety of types of actors, produce structures that are fragmented and often pull in opposite directions. As "divide and conquer" creations at their core, fractured regions can also be referred to as systems with heavy overlay from extraregional powers (Katzenstein 2005; R. Kelly 2007; Buzan and Wæver 2003). Such descriptions, familiar from the realist and comparative regionalism scholarship, nevertheless omit the local agency in producing such fractures and the way local agency interacts with extraregional players. The study of the mechanisms of regional fracture, whether institutional, political, or social, yields a narrative that is significantly more complex than concepts of "hegemonic regionalism" or "extraregional overlay" tend to convey. Top-down understandings of regional fracturing may explain how divisions are created inside regions in the developing world, but they offer little when it comes to explaining the failure of external powers in consolidating their putative influence inside already weak and polarized regions. The theory of regional fracture developed and applied empirically in this volume is a modest effort to address that gap.

Note

1. There is a vibrant literature on defining regionalism, which I have reviewed elsewhere (Ohanyan 2015). Regionalism in this work refers to a process of greater economic integration between geographically contiguous states and their societies accompanied with mechanisms of policy coordination and cooperation of various depth and scope by governmental elites.

PART I

Theory of Regional Fracture

CHAPTER ONE

Theory of Regional Fracture in International Relations: Beyond Russia

Anna Ohanyan

In the summer of 2016, while on a tour in the remote Armenian village of Dsegh, I visited the house museum of Hovhannes Tumanyan, the eminent Armenian writer who lived and worked at the turn of the nineteenth century. The guide mentioned in passing that Tumanyan valued his role as a peacemaker in the Caucasus—even more so than his literary contribution, a legacy that has shaped Armenian culture for more than a century. The guide further explained that Tumanyan, who brokered peace agreements between various ethnic communities in the Caucasus and prevented interethnic violence in Russian Transcaucasia, was rewarded by being arrested twice for his public activism and eventually imprisoned by the Tsarist government. This rather stark fact jolted me from my poetic reverie back to my research—though I doubt that my guide fully appreciated the impact of this seemingly minor historical insight.

Tumanyan's imprisonment by the Russian Empire for his role as a peacemaker in the Caucasus is emblematic of the ways in which Russian imperial power has actively destabilized interethnic communities, in this case by punishing attempts at interethnic reconciliation. The incident foreshadows Russia's systematic efforts to block regional groupings on its peripheries throughout the twentieth century (Brzezinski 1989) and is an effective way of framing a larger discussion of how deliberate regional fracture has been used as a foreign policy tool by regional powers, though at a very high cost. By default or by design, regional fracture persists, flourishing at increasingly higher levels of institutionalization while undermining global security.

These "micro-moments" of the Russian Empire contrast sharply with a speech given by President Vladimir Putin of Russia on February 10, 2007, at the Munich Security Conference in Germany (Nalbandov 2016). The Russian president cautioned against "unipolarity" as a problematic model of global governance in the twenty-first century, admonishing the West to democratize world politics. He then quickly revealed the limits of his zeal to democratize international relations, calling for the *right* multipolar combination and the *right* web of alliances among a few great powers (including Russia but excluding the rest of the world) as a way toward an international peace and stability that, according to this perspective, would then percolate down to the rest of the states in the system. This "trickle-down" approach to politics, preached by mostly structural neorealists, including President Putin, represents a broadly shared perspective on world politics among policy elites on both sides of the Atlantic, from the marble halls of the White House to the red brick walls of the Kremlin.

Indeed, the search for the right combination of global power arrangements and the structure of polarity involving mostly larger states has been central to policy-shaping recommendations in global capitals. Traditionally, strategic restraint (Posen 2014) and accommodation of rising powers (Paul 2016) have been long-held assumptions for negotiating peaceful transition of power. Democratic peace theory, complex interdependence (Keohane and Nye 2012), and norm accommodation among states have been offered as additional mechanisms of peaceful change in the international system, as prescribed by neoliberal institutionalism and social constructivism over the years. Still, mechanisms and agents of peaceful power transition remain poorly understood within the discipline, with the existing knowledge scattered across subfields and theoretical traditions (Paul 2017).

The theory of regional fracture (TRF) developed in this volume suggests that it is essential for a nuanced perspective on peaceful power transitions and for strengthening of the rules-based liberal system of world order, in part because the global context has changed. In an age of hyperconnectivity (Ferguson 2017), heteropolarity (Der Derian, cited in Ohanyan 2015), and networked politics (Reinicke 1998; DeMars 2005; Ohanyan 2008, 2009, 2015; Slaughter 2017), the agency of states and regions, traditionally viewed as peripheral to the world "system," should be moved into the spotlight. TRF thus advocates for advancing the once "peripheral" agency of states and regions into the forefront of international relations (IR) theories. It does so by developing the concept of fractured regions and explaining its agency for understanding world politics and global security, zooming in on remote villages and borderland communities (rather than global capitals), and highlighting their centrality to the fabric of global security and the world order moving forward.

The Agency of Fractured Regions

Fractured regions, the subject of this volume, can be described as a group of states or societies that are interconnected both by geographic proximity and a degree of mutual interdependence (Nye 1968; Buzan and Wæver 2003).[1] They are institutional creatures that are recognizable as political systems within which constituent states and societies exhibit clear patterns of political behavior. They are identifiable by the mechanisms of their regionwide deployment of power resources and by the density and direction of their institutional ties and social connections. Fractured regions, while highly variable, share certain characteristics. At their core, they can be described as debilitated neighborhoods between states or societies; they possess regional ties and connections that are somewhat weak and that yield little value, whether in terms of economic development or problem solving and governance at the political level. Fractured regions are often postcolonial systems that mediate between the former empire's need to maintain influence over the region and the desire of the successor states to advance their newly found independent statecraft.

The value of regional connections between states is amply demonstrated by economists and political scientists alike (Collier 2008; Østby, Nordås, and Rød 2009; Schiff and Winters 2003; Fawcett 2004), whether for state-building processes, effective diplomacy and democratization, security provision, global governance, or trade and development. Interestingly, Brian Greenhill and Yonatan Lupu (2017) report on studies that document that "states are organizing themselves into more tightly-knit regional groupings than ever before" (183). Unfortunately, there has been less emphasis on the absence or weakness of such ties for economic development or political security and stability in regional neighborhoods. While the regional dimension of armed conflict and its global security implications are gaining momentum in security studies and in conflict analysis and resolution (Ohanyan 2015), the systemic effects and key markers of fractured regions remain underexplored and their agency, in the context of world politics, unrecognized.

Binary thinking has been an obstacle to recognizing the agency of fractured regions as diverse systems with significant implications for global security. Regions have been viewed in the IR scholarship as either fully or partially integrated or lacking in regional ties and therefore not part of a distinct category in world politics. The TRF challenges this binary narrative, focusing on Russia's assertive involvement in its neighborhoods, from the Donbass to Damascus. With a bit more nuance, TRF argues that fractured regions, like integrated regions, occupy a specific institutional geography and, as such, represent particular political and institutional systems. There is great variance in the way fractured regions are organized, and the study of such variance is essential for building better theories and policies on comparative regionalism in developing countries. Significantly, fractured regions can become highly disruptive to global security due to their particular patterns of organization. Some regional fractures can be more destabilizing than others, but discerning the sometimes subtle differences and variances among them is a necessary first step toward assessing their impact on world politics.

This book also differentiates between regional fracture by *default* and regional fracture by *design*. Fracture by design refers to deliberate policies by external hegemons and (post)imperial powers in preventing direct regionwide multilateral or bilateral ties between state entities under their sphere of influence. Examples range from the United States' policies in Latin America to Japan's and China's policies in Southeast Asia and, most notably, Russia's policies in its post-Communist neighborhoods (Nalbandov 2016; Roeder 1997). Fracture by default refers to poor transportation routes and administrative structures that make the development and maintenance of regionwide ties challenging, if not impossible (Ohanyan 2007).

Whether by default or by design, fractured regions can be highly disruptive to world politics. Diplomacy that fails to recognize the regional dimensions of ongoing conflicts is likely to be ineffective or miss the mark entirely. This chapter develops the concept of fractured regions, delineates its dimensions, and offers a framework in which to unpack the regional dynamics in selected security theaters impacted by direct or indirect Russian involvement. Developing a vocabulary and metrics to explain the phenomenon of regional fracture in its neighborhood helps in "getting post-Soviet Russia right" (Korolev 2015).

The interests of post-Soviet Russia and its leadership have been fluctuating over the past two decades but have always hit three key notes: territorial and national defense, economic prosperity, and regime and leadership survival (Horowitz and Tyburski 2012). In each of these areas, Russia has tried to translate its legacy effects in its immediate neighborhoods into influence (Horowitz and Tyburski 2012), and leveraging its regional ties with the political elite has been an important tool at its disposal. Placing these developments in a regional fracture framework will help to produce a more nuanced understanding of Russia's policies in the post-Communist space and the Middle East.

Regional fracture in neighborhoods surrounding Russia has strengthened its influence in some cases and weakened it in others. The specific characteristics of such fracture matter. Specifically, regional fracture by default creates an enabling environment for Russian intervention, and this, in fact, has been consistently practiced by Russia as a foreign policy. In this light, the TRF can explain the continuity of Russia's behavior as a colonial and postcolonial power in Eurasia. "Getting post-Soviet Russia right" requires unpacking fractured regions as an emerging category in IR. It requires an understanding of the way fractured regions are deployed in world politics and the way they shape institutional environments, enabling particular powers at the expense of others, impacting ongoing conflicts, and influencing the conditions of conflict and cooperation between states.

The remainder of this chapter situates the framework of regional fracture within the IR literature and discusses its theoretical value for the discipline. It then proceeds to examine its key dimensions, which will serve as a template for the empirical case studies that follow.

Regional Fracture and International Relations Theory

As I argue elsewhere in this book, fractured regions are not simply unintegrated regions; they exhibit institutional coherence and reflect logical patterns of formation and consolidation. Still, at their core they are spatial organizations around which particular regionwide political, institutional, and social patterns develop. As such, fractured regions compel a discussion about the regional dimension of world politics, a line of inquiry that has benefited from extensive scholarship to date. Comparative regionalism and colonialism are research areas with the most direct implications for the regional fabric of world politics. The following examines the TRF relative to both.

Fractured Regions and the Rise of Regions in IR

The rise of regions as an analytical concept and unit of analysis in IR has experienced ebbs and flows over the past few decades. Having been reenergized in the post–Cold War period (Lepgold 2003; Pouliot 2007), its emphasis on the pacifying and developmental effects for member states has carried over from earlier waves of scholarship. The emphasis on regionalism as integration has shaped the scholarly debates, which are currently moving into discussions on the institutional variations between regional forms around the world (Acharya and Johnston 2007; Lay Hwee Yeo 2010; Ohanyan 2015). By extension, the focus on institutions has directed the discourse toward regional organizations and multilateralism, leaving the contextual conversations that shape regional dynamics largely unattended.

The duality of regions both as a source of instability and a potential driver of development (Fawcett 2004) is a particularly important characteristic of regional politics in the developing world. The scholarship on regional security orders (Morgan 1997) and regional security complexes (RSC) (Barrinha 2014; Buzan and Wæver 2003) captures this sense of duality. Regional security orders that treat regionalism as potential sources of cooperation can best be described as following the dominant patterns and mechanisms of security management in a given area. This scholarship views states as the primary actors building and sustaining regional security orders of any kind, with varied degrees of power delegation to external regional organizations or supranational institutions.

In parallel, Barry Buzan (1991) defines regional security complexes as a "group of states whose primary security concerns link together sufficiently closely that their national securities cannot realistically be considered apart from one another" (190). Two attributes of regional security complexes are relevant for understanding regional fracture. First, reflecting on regional security dynamics in the post–Cold War period, the RSC theory emphasizes geographical proximity as a key characteristic in security projections in the context of both decolonization and the collapse of the Soviet Union. These developments gave rise to new states that emerged as players in the margins of world politics, with a limited capacity to project insecurities across a vast geographical terrain. Geographic proximity is also an important marker for fractured regions as political systems, and, as such, the framework of fractured regions resonates well with the RSC theory. Political geography has long relied on the concept of "shatterbelts" and "shatterzones" to highlight specific geographic areas that are especially prone to armed conflict and interstate warfare (P. Kelly 1986; Bartov and Weitz 2013).

RSC theory also views states as key constituent elements of regional security complexes, a position from which the TRF departs (Buzan and Wæver 2003) by rejecting the coherence of state structures as constituent elements in regional systems and subsystems. Pushing back against neorealist interpretations of regionalism, the TRF highlights the internally unstable nature of constituent states that also suffer from limited internal sovereignty (Risse 2013).

The TRF also highlights the ability of such regions, mostly located outside of Europe, to project insecurities globally. Smaller regions and seemingly isolated conflicts have already shown a propensity to project global insecurities, as has been painfully obvious with the Syrian civil war. This conflict, originally viewed as a self-contained problem in the Middle East, became heavily regionalized (Allison 2013); the flow of refugees into Europe and increased terrorist attacks in Europe demonstrate the capability of geographically contained fractured regions to project insecurity at the global level.

The TRF exposes the deep schisms inside societies with subnational groups and communities that have the capacity to develop their own regional security projects and visions for security provision. This has made it more difficult for external hegemons to control given regions than has been the case historically (Buzan and Wæver 2003; Fawcett 2004). For instance, while the Armenian government has aligned its security interests with Russia, the public backlash against Russian domination of the country, particularly among the younger generation, has been sustained and frequent. Indeed, in the summer of 2015 there was a peaceful protest movement in Yerevan organized in response to projected electricity price increases by a power company owned by the Russian government (Shahnazarian 2016). The government had to back down and transfer the ownership of the company to the Armenian Tashir group, which, along with the government, reversed the hike until July 31, 2016.

In terms of its specific characteristics, regional fracture can be conceptualized as a variable rather than a fixed condition. Regions vary in terms of the extent as well as the nature of their fracture. All regions, integrated or fractured, possess a certain fabric of regional action. In integrated regions, political spaces of regional actions are fully embedded in regional institutions and supported with regional values. Conversely, in fractured regions, regional fabrics of political action, and even regional institutions and values, can be rather patchy, uneven, and ad hoc, often pulling in different directions. As a result, deep and consistent collective action at a regional level tends to be shallow, making the region vulnerable to "great power overlay" (R. Kelly 2007; Morgan 1997).

Fractured Regions and Postcolonial Studies

Much of the IR scholarship, highly Eurocentric in nature, analyzes world politics from the perspective of great powers, hovering, for the most part, over grand geopolitical landscapes without zooming in for the granularity of "local politics" (Cooley 2012). Traditionally, the narrative of world politics has been told from the perspective of the geopolitical cores in the world system: systemic peace between a few great powers was believed to "trickle down" to the peripheries of the world system. Even when incorporating the developing world into IR, the tendency has been to downscale the dominant IR theories (R. Kelly 2007) rather than developing theories that are indigenous and organic to the political fabric of these regions. The TRF elevates these perceived backwaters of politics to the forefront of IR. It demonstrates their centrality to the fabric of world politics and spotlights their role in the discourse on the post-American world order.

In particular, the variously fractured regions in the developing world have become central in world politics, in part because of the persistence in these areas of armed conflict, either active or frozen. Perhaps less visible is their deep connection to the processes of decolonization that have been sweeping the world since the nineteenth century. While much of Africa and Southeast Asia seem to have completed the processes of formal decolonization, post-Communist Eurasia, by many accounts, is only in the beginning stages (Beissinger and Young 2002). While postcolonial Africa, with its unsettled borders and resultant interstate and intrastate violence, is perhaps a more recognizable example of a regional fracture, the application of a postcolonial framework to explain Russia's behavior in its neighborhood has been less straightforward (Smith 2016; Suny 1998). Still, the emerging consensus and historiography on the role of Russia in integrating its neighborhoods into the Soviet system describes it as imperial and colonial. Taras Kuzio (2002b) refers to Michael Doyle's definition of empire as "a relationship, formal or informal, in which one state controls the effective political sovereignty of another political society" (Doyle 1986). He then applies this definition to the case of the Soviet experience and describes the Soviet Union as a Russian Empire—a position shared by a growing number of researchers in postcolonial studies and Russian foreign policy (Beissinger 1993; Nalbandov 2016; Beissinger and Young 2002; Khalid 2007; Northrop 2004).

Fractured regions are products of unsettled borders, both physical and institutional; they are postcolonial spaces of renegotiations between "parent" and successor

Table 1.1 Russia's Interventions and Conflicts in Post-Communist Eurasia and the Middle East

	Violent	Nonviolent
Direct	Ukraine, Middle East / Syria, South Caucasus / Georgia	Central Asia, Western Balkans
Indirect	South Caucasus / de facto states	South Caucasus / Armenia / domestic

states. And postimperial legacies on regional fracture are quite specific. In a comparative analysis of postcolonial Africa and post-Soviet Eurasia, Mark Beissinger and Crawford Young (2002) highlight the dual objective of modernization and control as central to Soviet communism, which, in contrast to the Russian Empire, translated into deep intervention into the social structures of Soviet republics. Hypercentralization of governance resulted from this drive, which manifested itself in the shattering of the initiatives and attempts at regional engagement between states and communities. Attempts to remake social structures in an industrial image, requiring large-scale investments and a centralized and heavily bureaucratized state, undermined the existing but fragile capacities of regional engagement. Ethno-federalism with a Russian core further cemented regional divisions between Soviet republics and communities within them. The armed conflicts and wars in the wake of the "peaceful disintegration of Soviet Union" are a painful manifestation of these phenomena.

The nature of Russian foreign policy in its neighborhoods, from Donbass to Damascus, has been quite varied. The similarly varied regional fracture in its neighborhoods has largely conditioned Russian choices in each case. Even though the number of cases is still too small to make causal claims, the in-depth case studies presented in this volume illustrate that in deeply fractured regions Russian involvement is rather indirect and largely reliant on nonmilitary means, as is currently the case in the South Caucasus (table 1.1).

Fractured regions signal fragmented geopolitics, thereby reducing the costs of domination for Russia and removing the need for direct intervention. Fractured regions also translate into bilateralism pursued by successor states (see chapter 4, this volume), which also gives Russia significant room to maneuver without necessitating direct military intervention. Cases of geopolitical cohesion, when a region seems to be moving in one particular direction, seem to invite Russian intervention in a manner that is direct and often military, as was the case with Ukraine (see chapter 3, this volume). Unfortunately, none of the regions in Russia's neighborhood have pursued internal integration between neighboring states (as opposed to integration with distant metropolises), and one can only speculate as to the Russian response to such cases.

Fractured regions are also collections of newly independent and institutionally weak states (Ohanyan 2015). In their postcolonial formations, such states are trying to break free from their colonial masters, or at least attempting to carve out some space, however limited, for autonomous action (Contessi 2015; Cooley 2012; Horowitz and Tyburski 2012). Suffering from limited statehood (Risse 2013), they lack the capacity to forge regionwide multilateral ties with each other, which would be an effective way to contain their regional bullies (also the formerly imperial powers), as evidenced by experiences in Latin America and Southeast Asia.

In Russia's neighborhoods, the institutional weakness of successor states is exploited by Russia as it seeks to reintegrate and rewire its formerly imperial ties to them (Nalbandov 2016), despite their political goal to pursue autonomous foreign policy. Understanding the key features of fracture in a given region therefore illuminates the specific mechanisms of Russian involvement and helps to predict Russia's foreign policy in these neighborhoods. Moreover, without examining each fractured region in a comparative context, a coherent narrative of Russia's postcolonial foreign policy fails to fully emerge. Russian involvement in each region differs and vacillates, often to the chagrin of successor states, but understanding such regional differences is possible after a careful consideration of the fractured regional contexts in each case, which the empirical chapters that follow provide.

Viewing the fractured regions in Russia's neighborhoods as postcolonial systems exposes the processes and mechanisms of imperial deconstruction, which, Beissinger argues, is ongoing and potentially endless, determining the trajectory and nature of state building in successor entities (Beissinger 1993; Kuzio 2002b). Uncovering the main dimensions of regional fracture (discussed below) helps identify the specific mechanisms employed by post-Soviet Russia as it tries to maintain dominance and influence in post-Soviet spaces. Considering the emergent geopolitical marketplaces that are coming to define its formerly uncontested neighborhoods (Khanna 2008; Contessi 2015), maintaining hegemony is becoming increasingly difficult for Russia. While they are a legacy and a result of imperial deconstruction, fractured regions have also come to define Russia's policies and positions in world politics. With "local rulers" in Central Asia pitting Russia, the United States, and China against one another, and with Tbilisi pushing for North Atlantic Treaty Organization membership in Russia's backyard, fractured regions defy the geopolitical pathways charted in Moscow. Fractured regions as postcolonial systems also tend to orient toward faraway patrons at the expense of their immediate neighbors. It is this strategic weakness, intrinsic to fractured regions, that leaves the door open for Russian involvement. And Russian involvement may take many forms: direct (via the military) or indirect (by imposing unfavorable trade deals on its partners and/or obstructing energy routes that are unfavorable to Russian interests).

Regions, whether fractured or integrated, are best described in three dimensions: (1) the way *power* as a resource is deployed at a regional level; (2) the nature of *institutional structures* organized at a regional level; and (3) the extent to which *values* support agency at a regional level. Neorealism, neoliberal institutionalism, and constructivism, three dominant theories in IR, have a rich vocabulary for describing each dimension. While building on these theories, this study of regional fracture also pushes against theoretical boundaries that have been driving the largely Eurocentric field of international relations in the West (Tickner 2016; Acharya 2014b).

As the rest of this chapter argues, fractured regions are systems, often with a rather complex institutional geography. Fractured regions do enjoy a certain degree of institutionalization. The directions of those institutional and informal ties are more important for understanding the flow of power resources and the patterns of regional engagement than the ties themselves. The proliferation of institutions in the Middle East, Sub-Saharan Africa, and post-Communist Eurasia, all of which suffer from poor levels of regional integration, indicates that levels of institutionalization are poor predictors and markers of regional integration.

The emphasis on statehood as a key actor of regional security provision has been unhelpful in capturing the internal schisms between states and societies in many developing countries around the world. In the post-Communist context in particular, the end of the Cold War produced shallow markets that often operate in settings suffering from democratic deficits. High levels of corruption and oligarchic economies have empowered political elites and alienated the masses in society (Marat 2015; Vladisavljević 2014). Backlash against economic neoliberalism often turns into protest against democracy. In such polarized settings, national authorities have neither the capacity nor the political will to build regional institutions and structures that are deeply socially embedded and capable of delivering collective goods at a regional level.

In short, fractured regions possess loose webs of interaction rather than tight alliances, as has been the case in Russia's post-Soviet neighborhoods (Roeder 1997). And the few intergovernmental patterns in alliance structures that exist in such regions are closely linked to the regime survival of national authorities (Barnett and Solingen 2007; Ambrosio 2014; Roeder 1997). I now turn to describing regional fracture in terms of three specific dimensions: political, institutional, and social.

Political Dimension of Regional Fracture

Traditional understandings of power describe it as the ability of one actor to alter the behavior of the second actor (Dahl 1957). As such, power is viewed as a tool to alter political outcomes. More recent scholarship expanded this understanding of power by challenging its linearity. Martha Finnemore and Judith Goldstein (2013) maintain that material endowments and resources rarely translate power into policy success. As the empirical sections demonstrate, in this presumed linearity of power the direct, unmediated impact between two actors is particularly problematic. Instead, recent scholarship points to the larger environment of values and institutions supporting power relations between actors, which show an ability to condition power and the ways in which the two actors interact with one another (Finnemore and Goldstein 2013; Bachrach and Baratz 1962).

Especially relevant to this study is Michael Barnett and Raymond Duvall's (2005) typology of forms of power. These authors distinguish between cases in which power works directly between the two actors and cases in which it is mediated through social relations and institutions. Fractured regions are precisely those environments in which the impact of power resources—whether hard power, soft power, or economic power (Charap and Welt 2015)—is diluted and softened, with only marginal intended impact on the ground. Consequentially, in fractured regions, neither regional integration nor external hegemonic overlay materializes easily.

Lacking the regionwide institutions of governance and social connections between state and nonstate actors, fractured regions produce power vacuums that are typically filled by one or more external powers but that can also become destabilizing at a regional level. Comparative regional studies refer to great power influence in such regions as "overlay" (Buzan 1991; Fawcett 2004) and call into question whether fractured regions can even have an independent explanatory power in international relations, considering the predominance of external hegemons. However, the overlay argument obscures regional diversity and the variety of networked pathways (Ohanyan 2015) in which power resources are deployed in such regions by external actors. It also disregards the layered nature of the mechanisms of control that are at play by these actors. In cases where more than one external actor is attempting to shape the regional dynamics, the clash of competing hegemons in fractured regions produces effects of its own, which the narrative of external overlay fails to explain (Contessi 2015).

In fractured regions, power resources are typically leveraged by external hegemons through social connections and linkages at the elite level (Levitsky and Way 2006). These informal, uneven, and often transitory linkages give rise to the "islands of power syndrome" in fractured areas, which manifests in terms of the isolated nature of spaces within the state through which power resources are sporadically applied by political elites inside and outside of the region. Being temporary and transitory, these linkages reflect the "periodic power syndrome," which describes the weak and unsustainable hold of external hegemons on the fractured region. Importantly, this weak hold produces poor predictability of outcomes and limited chances in altering outcomes on the ground, creating the need by the external hegemon to constantly cultivate and sustain these links, often short of formal institutionalization. This periodic power syndrome shows that power resources are variable in nature and their application is subject to fluctuating coalitions between political elites inside and outside of the region.

Islands of Power Syndrome

Fractured regions, while lacking regionwide institutions of governance, often contain personal networks and social ties at the elite level through which power resources flow (Broers 2016a; Levitsky and Way 2006). Steven Levitsky and Lucan Way (2006) differentiate Western linkages and leverage over regimes in post-Soviet states, explaining their differing impact on regime change. Such uneven and varied institutional makeup of links with outside actors results in the power pathways in fractured regions being periodically contested, creating grounds for multivector diplomacies and patron shopping by the regional states (Contessi 2015; Jesse et al. 2012).

Indeed, power resources in fractured regions are deeply networked but confined to isolated spaces, formal and informal, rather than being comprehensive and inclusively regional. Such power ties in fractured regions evolve out of previously disrupted connections, which are quickly filled by new networks and reconstituted ties. Empirical studies of fractured regions in this volume indicate that severing ties between neighbors and their interethnic communities translates into the rerouting of connections to the external hegemon. The case of the Balkan states within the "Yugosphere" frantically building ties with the EU post-Balkan war in 1990s is only one example (Bechev 2011; Ohanyan 2015).

The islands of power syndrome highlights the reality that the Cold War practice of carving up regions and controlling the political and socioeconomic environment in "client" states is a geopolitical mirage. In fractured regions, the uniform application of power at the regional level by a single actor (whether government, organization, or group) is quite challenging, if not impossible. Developing a descriptive vocabulary and a conceptual and theoretical infrastructure to that end is overdue.

In fractured regions, power resources are usually deployed by outside actors through multiple networks and social ties between external hegemons and local political elites and often in competing and varied configurations. Postcolonial connections may or may not be the dominant network of linkage in fractured regions because such connections can coexist with fragmented and uneven pathways of power resources as applied by other geopolitical patrons. Jakob Tolstrup's (2014) argument about "gatekeeper elites" is appropriate here; it refers to political, economic, and civil society elites in target countries that can modify the influence of external actors (Korolev 2015).

In fractured regions, fragmented and ad hoc application of power resources prevent both the formation of a regionally functional system and a geopolitical overlay by an external hegemon. Moreover, regional social capital, captured by narrow political elites and the external hegemon, is institutionalized quite unevenly. Such ties are top-heavy, with little interface with the public. Bottom-up sources of social capital and networks for imposing a particular agenda on political elites are also sparse. As a result, the ability of networks (top-down or bottom-up) to produce regionally significant and consistent economic or political outcomes is quite limited. Importantly, postcolonial processes of state building become deeply embedded in regional fracture, becoming largely vulnerable to the structural forces of postcolonial deconstruction. The specific characteristics of regional social capital in fractured regions produce power resources that undermine state governance. They add to the problem of limited statehood (Risse 2013) by pulling state authority and legitimacy outward toward various hegemons, leaving domestic legitimacy heavily compromised.

The vicious cycle of limited statehood, regional fracture, and postcolonial deconstruction also undermines the power of the external hegemon. In fractured regions, the multiplicity of externally deployed ties and networks dilutes and compartmentalizes the power of the external hegemon itself and isolates the political elites in the target country. Fractured regions, endowed with diverse systems of social capital, can produce a push-and-pull dynamic between various external actors and the political elites. While such struggles prevent the growth of bottom-up regional connections, they also challenge the ability of the external hegemon to create institutional environments completely favorable to them. Afghanistan's condition as a rentier state throughout much of the twentieth century, and its eroded state capabilities, is a quintessential example of external powers having consistently struggled to advance their agendas in the country in spite of direct military and economic intervention (Rubin 2002).

Periodic Power Syndrome

A related problem in fractured regions relates to shifting coalitions of political elites, their ineffectiveness in applying power resources due to their temporary and transitory nature. Integrated regions, in contrast to fractured regions, have dense and durable social ties and connections that more effectively deliver political outcomes at a regional level (i.e., whether by influencing domestic politics through subnational and supranational structures or by exerting regional pressures on national actors). In such cases, applications of power resources are more predictable and functional at a regional level. In contrast, regional social networks in fractured regions are embedded in shallow institutional settings, with authorities in nation-states in the region often lacking public legitimacy. As a result, such networks are significantly more vulnerable to shifting geopolitical rivalries and external linkages as well as domestic political changes in each state.[2]

This periodic power syndrome is compounded by the dominance of top-heavy and highly politicized networks supporting fractured regions. Such networks are multiple yet shallow, failing to yield mechanisms of problem solving, governance, and cooperation. Regional social capital in fractured regions, inside and outside of the target countries, is an instrument of power deployed by the elites, and its deployment as a mechanism of power degrades the intermediary institutions that may be needed to nourish regionwide networks of social capital and associations. Power relations in the regional social networks of fractured regions tend to flow directly between two actors rather than through social relations or institutional intermediation (Barnett and Duvall 2005). Such arrangements produce political processes that are highly unpredictable, transient, unsteady, and often personalized.

In the context of Russia's fractured neighborhoods, Laurence Broers notes that when pro-Western elites acceded to power with varying degrees of Western support, Russian linkages in contested or vulnerable territorial peripheries were stimulated as a result. Georgia (2004), Moldova (2009), and Ukraine (2005, 2014) have all experienced accessions of pro-Western elites, after which, in each case, Russian linkages in Abkhazia, South Ossetia, Transnistria, Crimea, and Donetsk were reactivated (Broers 2016a). External hegemons' reactivation of linkages with elites reflects the uneven, sporadic, and transitory nature of these connections, connections that are nevertheless destructive enough to preclude the development of regionally encompassing social capital. The two syndromes of political fracture at a regional level therefore constitute mechanisms of postcolonial control as well as weakness for external hegemons. In the case of Russia, both syndromes reflect its attempts to recapture lost ground or to reclaim and renegotiate neo-imperial relationships with old "clients."

The Institutional Dimension of Regional Fracture

Institutions are effective markers of regional social capital but only to a certain extent. In the context of this research, institutions are networks and formal organizations that operate at a regional level. Access to these networks allows participants to scale up their operations (Ohanyan 2009), whether by expanding their business to neighboring countries or by enhancing the regional recruitment of terrorist organizations. Whether perverse or benign, institutional resources constitute a key component of regional social capital because access to these resources creates regional mechanisms of collective action. In this way the institutionalization of regional social capital strengthens its long-term durability. Regional networks that are institutionalized have deeper connections to target communities and a better chance of survival.

However, the degree of institutionalization and institutional thickness are insufficient to explain either regional integration or fracture, particularly outside of the European Union. Both integrated and fractured regions can have highly institutionalized environments. Therefore, in addition to institutional density, a wide range of other institutional factors need to be considered as descriptors and indicators of regional integration or regional fracture: the quality and institutional geography of regional institutions (i.e., whether or not midrange or intermediary institutions exist and the direction of institutional ties); the extent to which existing institutions are developmental (defined by their ability to mobilize and deploy resources for improved regional engagement); whether the institutions are active or static, networked or hierarchic; whether they operate above or below the state; and how much steering from the government they require.

The comparative regional studies scholarship has a clear institutional bias: regions that are more institutionalized are erroneously associated with higher levels of regional maturity and regional independence (Prieto 2012; Hettne and Söderbaum 1998; van Langenhove 2003). It would follow from such an analysis that fractured regions lack an institutional fabric. While the maturity of a region is often measured by the breadth and depth of its institutional ties at a regional level, a current trend in post-Communist Eurasia, particularly in Russia, is one of institution building to maintain regional hegemony, freeze asymmetries, and shape the parameters of regional politics to its benefit (Barnett and Duvall 2005). Regions with unresolved conflicts become vulnerable to great power rivalries, a situation that is increasingly unfolding through institutional models. Russia's increasingly defensive posture in its neighborhoods has resulted in directly coercive measures, as in the case of Eastern Ukraine and the annexation of Crimea. Its institutional mechanisms for maintaining influence are also dominant, as evidenced by the Eurasian Economic Union or the Collective Security Treaty Organization (CSTO).

Levels of institutionalization are examined extensively within the IR literature, with the first few waves of neoliberal institutionalism positing that the thickening of international institutions creates a rules-based environment in international politics (Drezner 2013), thereby challenging power-based settings and driving a "wedge between power and outcomes" (Snidal 1996). More recent scholarship maintains that, at the global level, the growing institutional thickening forms regimes as well as regime complexes that create opportunities for forum-shopping by states; as a result, the costs of monitoring state compliance in an increasingly complex legal environment are higher. The debates about international institutions and global governance now concern the ability of global institutions to maintain order and a predictable institutional environment in the context of institutional proliferation.

In fractured regions, institutional proliferation is hardly the problem. These are predominantly power-based environments, as opposed to rules-based or value-driven environments, even if institutions are present. The challenge in fractured regions is "getting the institutions right," referring to the need to build broad-based and inclusive institutions that can withstand power pressures from stronger states. Institutional density is definitely an important part of this conversation. Indeed, institutional density and institutional functionality, as opposed to territorial proximity and geography, have emerged as central to "new regionalism" theories. In this approach, some measure of interaction density, supported by regional institutions, is necessary for "regions" to make sense as a unit of analysis in world politics (R. Kelly 2007). Many institutional dimensions resonate with functionalism, a rich scholarship and an established theoretical tradition in IR that sees institutional connections and interactions as essential building blocks for regional formation (Deutsch 1953; Obydenkova 2006). Institutional dimensions of regional integration in this context include nonstate-actor involvement at a regional level, the role of regional bureaucracies (Montecinos 1996), and the existence of intermediary institutions between the government and the civil society that cultivate regional ties (Ohanyan 2015).

Institutional density, which traditionally is viewed as a progressive factor in IR literature, must be examined closely and critically in the case of fractured regions. Fractured regions are nested in an institutionally thick global environment, which often undercuts their institutional evolution. Growing institutional thickening at the global level creates pressures for fractured regions by pulling states in the regions into larger and more global regional forums, often at the expense of investing in more immediate regional neighborhoods. The plethora of forums and spaces for political activity offers opportunities for forum shopping to states of differing political and economic might. States in fractured regions are generally active institutional citizens in global forums, but their regional citizenship is definitely lacking. At the regional level, the fabric of engagement is institutionally sparse and vulnerable to capture by regional hegemons.

In sum, the institutional dimension of regional fracture can be described in two broad strokes. First, institutional spaces of regional engagement in fractured regions are organized in clusters, somewhat similar to the ways in which power mechanisms are applied. Even if such institutional clusters exhibit institutional density, their impact and regional reach remains limited. Second, in many cases fractured regions are postimperial systems, collections of new states seeking political autonomy in an increasingly integrated global environment.

Islands of Institutions Syndrome

Fractured regions mostly have institutions that are patchy and uneven in terms of their geography within the region. Being organized as clusters, they tend to be exclusive in nature (Rozman 2010), heavily captured or cultivated by an external hegemon (Barnett and Duvall 2005). As a result, regional institutions often lack the administrative capacities and the political will to reach down to the public level. Regional diplomacy remains politicized, limited to summits and infrequent meetings between higher ranking officials.[3] Latin America, with its rich history of regional experimentation, has been through periods of regional fractures in which regional institutions failed to deliver concrete and sustainable outcomes to the public (Montecinos 1996). Similarly, the Chinese post–Cold War experience with regionalism failed to generate genuine engagement in deep regional diplomacy even though China joined several regional groupings in Southeast Asia (Rozman 2010). Ultimately, regionalism is a political process; failing to get the institutions right can create waves of disillusionment with regionalism, as has been the case in Latin America (Montecinos 1996). The selective engagement of states with regional institutions also contributes to the cluster-like organization of regional institutions in fractured regions that in turn challenges the governance capacities of nation-states in the region. Institutional islands of regional action rarely add up to regionwide spaces of governance, which is problematic considering that the regional dimension of statecraft is emerging as a necessity in an era of such transnational problems as trafficking in drugs and humans, environmental degradation, and cybersecurity, to name only a few. The example of Central Asian states pulling into regional clusters but lacking meaningful capacities for regional multilateral governance is a case in point.

Imperial Fingerprints or Institutional Legacies

As discussed earlier, fractured regions are often postcolonial systems. The institutional dimension of regional fracture reflects the "imperial biases" that translate into the hegemonic dominance of external powers. Smith has asserted that integrationist tendencies "can be seen as outcomes of imperial consciousness and power" (Smith 2016, 174). Existing research documents how, in cases of imperial collapse, "soft imperialism" usually defines new relationships between the "parent" and the successor state. Integration schemes and favorable trade deals are some of the instruments to that end. This seems to be the case in fractured regions as well, where institutions work to cement power imbalances in relationships between states and their formerly colonial patrons, whether the EU or Russia. The fractured nature of regions in settings of the geopolitical marketplace requires postcolonial powers to continuously defend their turf, often necessitating high levels of institutionalization of relationships in order to maintain their durability in the region. In some respects, regional institution building by the former empire becomes an instrument of postcolonial power and control when seen against a backdrop of "clients" that do not always follow their patrons, colonial or otherwise (Jesse et al. 2012).

In contrast to other formerly colonial states, Russia maintains territorial borders with most of its former colonies, which is one of the reasons why it has been unable to "let go" (Nalbandov 2016) in contrast to most other former colonizing powers. Seeking and pursuing institutionalized forms of multilateralism since the collapse of the USSR has been a clear trend, as evidenced by the formation of the Commonwealth of Independent States, the Customs Union / Eurasian Economic Union, and CSTO, among others.

Similar to Soviet institutions, this new wave of institution-building produces highly centralized structures with top-down authority structures. While some respondents in governmental research centers in Moscow have insisted that the Eurasian Economic Union (EEU) is a qualitatively new integration project inspired by the EU,[4] others have been skeptical that the EEU (as opposed to bilateral diplomacy) has been effective in serving Russia's national interests well.[5] The academic scholarship and evaluation on the EEU as a transnational organization oriented toward regional development has been rather mixed. While the role of the EEU in trade reversion from many post-Soviet states toward the EU and back to Russia connections is widely supported (Podadera and Garashchuk 2016), its developmental impact on member states has been debatable. Many analysts have argued that regional institution building is emerging as a mechanism by which Moscow tries to reassert control over much of the post-Soviet space that it lost with the end of the Cold War (Nalbandov 2016; Sussex 2012). Others claim that such an organization is a natural way of conducting regional diplomacy and development broadly pursued by many powers and states around the world. Still, there is sufficient research to indicate that the power imbalance between states, and Russia's hegemonic interests in post-Communist Eurasia, are major factors in shaping the operation and future prospects of this organization. Imperial pathways shaping contemporary processes of region building are clearly manifest in the case of Russia and the EEU. Russia's impact on specific fractured regions in the post-Soviet space are examined further in the empirical chapters in this volume (see the chapters by Samokhvalov, Broers, Lewis, Nalbandov, and Giragosian). In sum, the institutional dimension of regional fracture is manifest in the consolidation of preexisting power imbalances by powerful actors rather than in incentives for enhanced problem solving at a regional level. Regional institutions are thin, uneven, centralized, and highly politicized, which is exemplified by the experience of fractured regions around Russia's peripheries in post-Communist Eurasia.

Social Dimensions of Regional Fracture

The third dimension of regional fracture refers to values and identities and the extent to which they are able to influence regional dynamics, whether in terms of integration or fracture. Value resources, as a marker of regional social capital, have proven to be essential for deeper regional engagement. Values, along with identities and ideas, are credited by constructivist theories of international relations for shaping agents' thinking and therefore constructing their understanding of their own material interests (Wendt 1992; Barnett and Finnemore 2004). The application of constructivism to regional studies maintains that region building and regional integration is largely driven by the collective identity of the actors involved (Prieto 2012). The idea of "regionness" or "regionhood" (Söderbaum and Shaw 2003; Söderbaum 2004; van Langenhove 2003) points to the process of "becoming" a region in which the formation of regional identity is a key component. Importantly, regional identity is usually viewed as a necessary component for regional institutionalization (Paasi 1986). Overall, higher levels of regional identities (i.e., individual and collective identification with the region) are considered to be, in varying degrees, an essential building block for strong and cohesive regions (Fawcett 2004; Semian and Chromy 2014; Prieto 2012).

Values, ideas, and identities at a regional level can have a powerful causal impact on region-building processes partly because they shape the more concrete goals, principles of actions, and expectations of each actor relative to regional integration (Kirchner and Domínguez 2011). Shared values and norms as markers of regional social capital can animate regionally coordinated actions by governments and non-state groups alike. On the other end of the spectrum, and more commonly observed in the developing world, are values for safeguarding state sovereignty (Kirchner and Domínguez 2011). Developing countries often join regional forums to enhance their ability to suppress internal dissent rather than to strengthen the governance capacities of the state (Barnett and Solingen 2007).

The perspective of regions as socially constructed systems is consistent with the comparative regionalism literature (Ohanyan 2015). Some view identities as constituent (as opposed to causal) factors for the development of strong regional institutions (Hettne and Söderbaum 1998; Bechev 2011),[6] while others argue for the direct role of identities in producing developmental regionalism (Semian and Chromy 2014). This research points to regional development through tourism and regional flows of migration, which are described as forms of regional identification (Kneafsey 2000). One question permeates the interdisciplinary scholarship on regionalism: the extent to which regional identity is developed organically, bottom up, through community connections, or whether it is an imposed project from the top (Semian and Chromy 2014). The latter is significant in policy terms because the success of a particular regional project depends on the extent to which it is a development vision of the authorities but lacking community support as opposed to growing organically out of local ties and connections (Semian and Chromy 2014) and enjoying public support.

In fractured regions, the links between regionalism and identity formation are multifaceted. In such settings, stronger regional identities are not directly associated with regional institutions, and regional fracturing as a process can unfold under conditions of shared regional identities. This is partly explained by the divisive nature of social capital, a key dimension of collective identification existing within fractured regions. In such settings, social capital at a regional level (often within the same ethnic group), while territorially cross-cutting, can develop between countries with varied levels of political enmity/comity. Kurdish communities distributed across Iraq, Syria, and Turkey, or Russian communities in Ukraine, Belorussia, and the Baltics, are some examples. In such settings, the contours of social capital are dictated by the distribution of power resources within the region, as discussed earlier in this chapter. Such territorially cross-cutting social connections can become sources of regional integration or fracture. The regional fracture theory identifies mechanisms that may determine the political pathways in which such connections develop.

Social fracturing of a region can also develop via institutional mechanisms that directly target and disrupt social connections. For example, in conflict zones, institutional mechanisms are often deployed by authorities to undo social ties that are ethnically cross-cutting. Conflict regions are described as "zones of social capital deficiency" (Goodhand, Hulme, and Lewer 2000). While there is a shared understanding that conflict erodes trust and cooperation within both formal and informal organizations (Vervisch et al. 2013), other scholars suggest that conflict areas simply reroute social ties, thereby creating new lines of inclusion and exclusion. This process produces further institutional erosion at the regional level because the new, rerouted regional ties are simply adjustments for collapsed or nonexistent structures of regional governance and are too sporadic and fragmented to translate into regional institutions.[7]

The disjuncture between the institutional and social dimensions of regionalism is characteristic of fractured regions. Russian tourists flocking to Tbilisi just a couple of years after the Russo-Georgian War in 2008 illustrates this trend. Moreover, much of the Latin American experience with regionalism, starting in the early nineteenth century, reflects shared regional identities, yet the continent struggled for another century to produce regionwide institutions. The opposite is also true: stronger institutions may or may not produce shared regional identities and values, at least in the short term. Much of the experience with regionalism within the Soviet Union supports this scenario. Despite a nearly century-long experience with deep, regionwide institutions within the Soviet Union, cohesive regional Soviet values failed to transpire, and the "nationalities issues" produced several ethnic conflicts in and between post-Soviet states soon after Mikhail Gorbachev's reforms in glasnost, or political openness, were introduced in the 1980s.

Conclusion: Building Borders in Shifting Lands

The theory of regional fracture maintains that the direction, density, and diversity as well as depth of regional ties determine the patterns of regional integration and fracture. It pushes the comparative regionalism scholarship into new terrains, arguing that fractured regions are not merely mirror images of integrated ones. We know more about the processes and mechanisms of regional integration, whether in economic or political terms. However, we know less about regions that are held together only by loose ties rather than strong coalitions. The study of fractured regions requires delineating its various dimensions and uncovering the rich diversity and variance in forms of regional fracture. This study argues that some forms of regional fracture are more destabilizing in terms of security than others.

The study of fractured regions also helps to explain why the retreat of great powers from their spheres of influence has been insufficiently compensated by the rise of regions as actors in world politics. The comparative regionalism scholarship has shown that regions vary in terms of their institutional attributes, which determine their strength as independent players in world politics. This theory of regional fracture makes an alternative argument: fractured regions are multidimensional systems that can be partially integrated in certain areas, such as institutions, yet somewhat collapsed in other areas, such as values. The multilayered nature of regional fracture is further perpetuated by the internal fissures between states and their societies. Such institutional fragmentation pulls the states in different directions in terms of regional integration or fracture. The theory of regional fracture challenges the bias in contemporary regional studies toward institutional density and statehood as constituent elements shaping these processes.

The theory of regional fracture offers a fresh lens for explaining Russian foreign policies and aspirations in its neighborhoods. Drawing from the Russian case, the theory of regional fracture illustrates the challenges faced by the smaller states in the post-American world but also sheds light on the more limited choices of regional hegemons. As postcolonial systems, fractured regions have emerged as institutionally and politically contested areas, a development that has prompted a new set of responses by the regional hegemons. In the Russian neighborhoods, erecting borders, both institutional as well as physical, has been a clear response to the fractured regions it is struggling to control.

In terms of physical boundaries, fractured regions signify the unfinished boundary delimitation projects that were subsumed and sealed in the Soviet Union only to erupt with its collapse. A decade after independence, in Central Asia (between Uzbekistan and Kyrgyzstan alone), 60–140 boundary points are still disputed (Farrant 2006). Unsettled physical boundaries, wrapped up with more complicated claims of human rights and state's rights, have produced the present-day cleavages between successor states in fractured regions, which Russia has been eager to exploit.

Applied in various empirical contexts, the chapters in this volume profile fractured regions in Russia's neighborhoods that are varied, diverse, and qualitatively distinct, thereby allowing for a more theoretically nuanced understanding of regional politics in general and Russia's foreign policies in its neighboring regions in particular. Russia's foreign policy behavior has been explained by regional security complex theory, its imperial habits, the individual attributes of President Putin, and Russia's internal politics. None of these offers a complete set of factors that are driving Russia's behavior in post-Communist Eurasia and the Middle East; they all place the emphasis on Russia, leaving little room to explain the context in which Russia operates. In this respect, regional fracture theory offers a bottom-up approach to theorizing in comparative regional studies—a perspective from Russia's peripheral, disorderly, and shattered neighborhoods.

The regional fracture approach pushes back against the dominant IR theories of "overlay" and "power rivalry," which obscure layers of politics and make effective or useful explanations to policy makers difficult or impossible. With the discovery of a more diverse typology of regional fracture, policymakers can produce more responsive approaches to ongoing security problems. Some forms of regional fracture are harder to overcome than others, but even more benign forms of fracture still require tailored responses.

Notes

I am grateful to Laurence Broers for the invaluable feedback and insight that he generously shared when reviewing early drafts of this chapter.

1. In terms of their territorial dimensions, fractured regions are distinct from "shatterbelts" or "shatterzones," which are described as spatial distribution of interstate conflict and geographic regions "plagued both by local conflicts within or between states in the region, and by the involvement of competing major powers from outside the region" (Hensel and Diehl n.d.). Philip Kelly (1986) defines a shatterbelt as a geographic region over whose control great powers seriously compete. Fractured regions, in contrast, are defined by historical legacies—strategies of local elites and great power alliance structures that elevate local rivalries from such regions into the global system. The distinction between fractured regions and shatterbelts is clarified as a result of several conversations with Laurence Broers, for which I am thankful.

2. The sudden U-turn of the Armenian government in 2014 in joining the Russian-led Eurasian Economic Union and moving away from EU's Eastern Partnership Agreement, after negotiating with the latter for several years, is a good example of this phenomenon (Ohanyan 2015).

3. Gerard Libaridian, interview with the author, April 25, 2017, Cambridge, Massachusetts; and Vartan Oskanian, interview with the author, July 14, 2017, Yerevan, Armenia.

4. Anonymous, interview with the author, August 7, 2017, Moscow, Russia.

5. Alexander Krilov, interview with the author, August 11, 2017, Moscow, Russia.

6. Alexander Iskandaryan, interview with the author, October 13, 2012, Yerevan, Armenia.

7. In contrast to more optimistic assessments of the value of social capital for economic development, a growing chorus of voices suggests that social capital can support and reproduce patterns of exclusion as well as inclusion (Bebbington 2002). In fractured regions, bonding (as opposed to bridging) social capital within specific ethnic groups and between groups with geopolitically coherent interests is more commonplace.

CHAPTER TWO

From Donbass to Damascus: Russia on the Move

Robert Nalbandov

Back in the 1990s Gennady Zyuganov, the Communist Party Chair of Russia, laid down the prospective grounds for the Russian geopolitical reasoning: "The main task of Russia in the immediate future is 'gathering the lands' and reviving a new Soyuz state. There is no other way. Either we, one step at a time, peacefully and voluntarily are able to integrate the 'post-Soviet space' and reinstate control over the geopolitical heart of the world, or we are facing degradation and a colonial future" (qtd. in Isingarin 1998). A decade later, in his article in the newspaper *Zavtra* (Tomorrow), Alexander Prokhanov, the voice of neo-imperialist Russia, explained the basics of the new Russian outlook on its foreign policy:

> On the territory of the shattered Soviet empire, among the imperial debris, on the orphaned scraps of the disappeared Red kingdom, Putin promises to build a new imperial community. . . . But even if it proves to be a bluff, this bluff is associated with a yearning for Empire. The desecrated spaces, oppressed peoples, plundered developmental potentials, [and] wailing sacred stones of the Empire speak up through Putin's voice. . . . The ideology of justice as the main resource of the upcoming Empire will become attractive to all peoples inhabiting Eurasia. . . . Put your ear to the cobblestones of the Red Square. And you hear the roar of the Fifth Empire. (Prokhanov 2011)

The first thing to notice in this program statement is the synergy between the regional dimensions and functional modus operandi. It presents the clientele of the Russian foreign policy as not only the former Soviet Union but also the whole of Eurasia and possibly beyond, stretching Russia's conflict beltway all the way from

Moldova, Ukraine, Georgia, and the Nagorno-Karabakh to Syria. Each of these conflicts has experienced Russia's role in diverse forms but with the same primary rationale. The ongoing active and frozen conflicts are considered part of a dual Russian narrative of a combination of its geolocation, that is, the place on the Eurasian continent (which is analyzed here from the standpoint of the theory of geographic contiguity) with the regional fractures, as practiced by Russia in its surrounding neighborhoods, near and far.

The chapter starts with the review of the symbiosis between the regional and functional areas of Russian foreign policy by juxtaposing the theory of regional fracture with the theory of geographic contiguity. It proceeds with the application of the regional fractures while ultimately taking an attempt at explaining the potential long-term replacement of the geographic contiguity theory. It also hypothesizes the possible future military involvements of Russia outside of its borders based on its current role in the conflicts.

Geographic Contiguity versus Regional Fractures

The explanations of the symbiosis between various dimensions of the Russian foreign policy start by juxtaposing the theory of regional fracture with the theory of geographic contiguity. Pioneered by Lewis F. Richardson (1961), the latter outlook on international relations posits that the countries tend to structure their foreign affairs by the lengths of shared borders, which "are institutions that directly contribute to state formation and state authority" (Gavrilis 2008, 5–6). Stuart Bremer argues, "Shared access to a physical area can lead directly to inter-state friction, even if the states involved agree as to where the border lies between them" (Bremer 2014, 7). State frontiers are important to interstate conflict not only because they define who they separate from each other but also because they represent the major media of interactions between the bordering societal groups (Nalbandov 2009). That is why, as Colin Flint and Peter Taylor (2014) suggest, "simple contiguity as an empirical fact must be integrated with a more sophisticated understanding of the processes of conflict, especially the operation of power" (11). Such a view opposes the social constructivist outlook, which places the identity of the actors on the top of the variable pyramid.

Borders, as magnets, attract interstate insecurities. Paul Hensel (2000) finds that "contiguous adversaries are more conflict prone than more distant states, accounting for more than half of all armed conflicts since 1816 and more than two-thirds of more serious forms of conflicts" (21). Hence, the question "With whom are the states fighting?" is directly related to which states they border by influencing the ways the states frame their foreign policy preferences. The duration of the boundaries between the states is ultimately linked with the foreign policy alignment: the bigger the portion of country A's border shared with country B, the higher the latter's interests in the domestic policy of the former.

Post-Soviet Geographic Contiguity

The disintegration of the USSR opened the Pandora's box of civil wars, which ignited geographic contiguity reasoning in the earlier versions of Russian foreign policy. This thinking dictated to Moscow that it could not afford to ignore the over-the-fence domestic conflicts in the formerly "brotherly" republics. It openly intervened in some of them (first Georgia and later Ukraine) but kept a minimal presence in others (Moldova, Central Asia, and Nagorno-Karabakh). In the following years Russia became preoccupied with its own painful transition to a market economy and internal conflict in Chechnya, dropping the territorial conflicts in its neighborhoods from the radar. Putin's ascent to power in 2000 marked a normalization of the domestic situation and the renewal of the regional dimensions of its foreign policy. This time also coincided with a slow but consistent increase in oil prices on the global markets, which allowed Russia to bank on playing a more important role in the region.

The shift from a geographic contiguity outlook to regional frictions was fostered by a negative reaction of the international community to the Russian annexation of the Crimean Peninsula and its hybrid war in Eastern Ukraine in 2014. As a backlash to the less than lukewarm reception to his speech at the 70th UN General Assembly in September 2015, in which he blamed the West for the upsurge of terrorist activities in the Middle East and proposed that the West should partner with Russia, Putin embarked on the Machiavellian journey to Syria in support of the long-term Western rival and Russia's major arms importer, Syrian president Bashar al-Assad.[1] While geographic contiguity explains Russian interventions in the former Soviet republics, it fails to accurately predict its military actions in Syria, which are aligned with the theory of regional fractures. Application of the theory of regional fractures will help in understanding why Russia decided to expand its geopolitical interests beyond its nominal borderlands.

Russia and the Former Soviet Union Republics

In explaining the key variables driving Russia in the new millennium toward the former Soviet Union (FSU), the rich past of interactions occupies a central theme. Bilateral relations have been the priority direction of Russian foreign policy ever since its independence, placing the geographic contiguity among the primary factors affecting its relationships with the former republics. The total length of the Russian border is 38,692 miles, making it the largest country in the world. The following segments of its land borders are shared: Estonia (290 mi), Latvia (168 mi), Belarus (770 mi), Ukraine (1,395 mi plus 217 mi of the maritime borders along the Azov Sea), Georgia (547 mi), Azerbaijan (217 mi), and Kazakhstan (4,722 mi). The duration of the maritime borders in the Black Sea with Ukraine and Georgia is 242 miles, and 360 miles along the Caspian Sea with Azerbaijan and Kazakhstan.[2] Thus, the aggregate length of the FSU borders is 8,940 miles, or 23 percent of the overall borders of the Russian Federation. The only two other countries it shares borders with are China (2,616 mi) and Mongolia (2,165 mi), which makes an additional 12 percent. Insignificant maritime borders stretch with Japan (121 mi) and the United States (31 mi).

In addition to the shared borders, modern Russia keeps the memory of seventy years of living together with the FSU nations, and several centuries more with some of them within or under the protectorate of the Russian Empire. In its attempt to build relations with these nations, the very crux of Russian identity is revealed. On the one hand, Russia is guided by the purest type of primordialism, which espouses "the idea that the nations are an ancient, necessary, and perhaps natural part of the social organization, an organic presence whose origins go back to the mists . . . of time" (Spencer and Wollman 2002, 27). On the other hand, Russia is trying to build bridges into its modernist future but, in doing so, is guided by the grip of its "past imperfect" (Wegner 2012) that it is neither willing nor ready to give up. The Russian political mainstream views the Western parts of the former Soviet Union as buffer zones between itself and the rest of Europe.

The Ukrainian Anschluss

The causes of the 2014 crisis in Ukraine and Russia's participation in its civil war in 2014 go back to the interactions between these nations over centuries. The first part of Russia's multifaceted policy in Ukraine is framed by the historically developed patterns of denying the raison d'être of the Ukrainians' nation and presenting them as a non-nation. With its historical core of the Kyivan Rus', Ukraine represented the basis for and the cradle of the common Eastern Slavic identity (Subtelny 2009) and was the center where the future Russian Empire spawned. The period of Ukrainian history under Russian and, later, Soviet rule was marked by large-scale russification (making it Russian), which was replaced by sovietization (making it Soviet). According to Anna Reid, "Russians deny their [Ukrainians'] existence. Ukrainians are a 'non-historical nation,' the Ukrainian language is a joke dialect. . . . The very closeness of Ukrainian and Russian culture, the very subtlety of the differences between them, is an irritation" (qtd. in Subtelny 2009, 64). The rebuttal of the ethnic uniqueness of Ukrainians became an integral part of the systematic nationalism policy toward Ukraine in the Soviet Union. Ukraine is also important for Russia politically: it is part and parcel of its neo-imperialist outlook. As Zbigniew Brzezinski rightly observes, "Without Ukraine, Russia ceases to be an empire, but with Ukraine suborned and then subordinated, Russia automatically becomes an empire" (Brzezinski 1994, 80). Systematic identity denial by the Russian imperial and then Soviet authorities created long-lasting stigmatization in Ukraine and had its part in the current regional divide in Ukraine, inviting Russian intervention in 2014.

The Orange Revolution of 2004–5 marked a new era for the country, which was all too eager to switch gears from former president Leonid Kuchma's corrupt regime (Wilson 2005, 53–54) to a European-style democracy.[3] Sadly, the promises of political change and economic revival made by incoming president Viktor Yushchenko appear to be short-lived. Viktor Yanukovych, the leader of pro-Russian eastern provinces, was appointed as prime minister in 2006 and later won the presidential elections in 2010 (D'Anieri 2010), marking an almost 180-degree reversal from volatile democracy to a possibly stable but stagnant rule. Yanukovych's regime, as Oxana Shevel and colleagues (2015) note, was similar to Kuchma's: its inability to provide effective governance domestically and to choose firmly either way for the country's international orientation led to the second revolution in 2014, the Euromaidan. This time the protesters and the government supporters clashed with firearms, "water cannons, stun grenades and rubber bullets" as well as Molotov cocktails and boulders.[4] Russia quickly accused the West of provoking the conflict and supporting the Ukrainian neo-Nazis and right-wing paramilitaries (Byshok, Kochetkov, and Semenov 2014, 11), who, in all honesty, were a minuscule minority.[5]

In retrospect, the Euromaidan did more harm than good for the Ukrainian statehood. In a way, it was a prelude for the Russian intervention in Crimea in February–March 2014. Shortly after the success of the Euromaidan, groups of similarly uniformed and armed people, whom the popular Russian narratives call "Green People" and "Polite People," occupied the main administrative buildings in the capital of Crimea, Simferopol, hoisting the Russian flags. According to Igor Girkin, a former KGB officer and the minister of defense of the Donetsk People's Republic, "Members of parliament were all gathered by the militia who brought them all into the rooms so that they could vote" (Neiromir-TV 2015) in the referendum on joining Russia. On March 17 Crimea officially became a new federal district of Russia. In parallel, two Eastern Ukrainian cities—Luhansk and Donetsk—declared independence from Ukraine and announced the creation of their corresponding People's Republics, provoking the start of the Anti-Terrorist Operation by Kyiv. After the initial military actions, the conflict slowed down to a latent phase by September 2014, only to resume in January 2015.

Currently, Russia says it continues to abstain from any participation on the side of the "volunteers" (Ministry of Foreign Affairs of Russia 2014), declaring that it sends only humanitarian cargo, and Ukrainian authorities continue to blame Russia for supporting the insurgency. Total casualties by November 2014, according to a UN report (Evans 2014), had reached 4,300 military and civilian deaths, with an additional half-million refugees and internally displaced persons. The annexation of Crimea brought several tangible and emotional benefits for Russia. Russia feared that the new pro-Western (i.e., pro-European and pro-American and, therefore, by definition anti-Russian) government in Kyiv would deny Russia its only military foothold on the Black Sea: Sevastopol. According to some sources, "by the end of May [2014] Crimea should have become the central base of [North Atlantic Treaty Organization] NATO in the region or . . . the stationary unsinkable aircraft carrier near the Russian fence" (Vanin and Zhilin 2014). The base in Crimea, as Paul Schwartz (2014) notes, "provides Russia with the ability to project power in and around the Black Sea, while also serving as a potent symbol of Russian power," an intangible goal that Moscow values equally with the territorial gains.

The takeover of Crimea bears grave consequences for European energy security: Russia could expand its energy carriers' cache and distribution networks. According to Frank Umbach, "It is . . . expected that Russia will claim large parts not just of Crimea's, but also of Ukraine's continental shelf and Exclusive Economic Zone (EEZ), which may seriously complicate the division of the Black Sea continental shelf and EEZs with Romania and Turkey" (Umbach 2016). The occupation thus allowed Russia to boost its great power status domestically and project its status abroad as a full-fledged naval power. The ongoing hybrid war in Eastern Ukraine provides further foothold for Russia in Eastern Europe; allows Russia to keep the control over the energy transit routes through Ukraine to Europe; offers a useful distraction for its actions in other parts of the world; and, simultaneously, prevents further human development in Ukraine by pulling it further away from its European orientation.

Lasting Standoff in Moldova

Like many of the former Soviet republics, Moldova became a part of the tsarist empire as a result of its expansionist war against the Ottoman Empire in 1815, after which annexation was approved by the Congress of Vienna. The influence of its eastern neighbor on political and, most importantly, cultural life in the newly gained land, as the pro-Russian view explains, was framed by "conducting advanced European thought, especially educational concepts, under the banners of which the irreconcilable struggle with medieval obscurantism took place" (Stati 2012, 132). After the October Revolution, the portion of Moldova called Bessarabia proclaimed itself a republic and aspired to join Romania. In 1939 the Molotov-Ribbentrop Pact placed Moldova under Soviet control, which continued after the World War II victory (Batalden and Batalden 1997, 65). Moldova also experienced the influence of russification, only in this case it meant turning its script from Latin into Cyrillic and changing the name of the language from Romanian into "Moldovan." This process entailed the creation of "a new mythology . . . in which Soviet scholars spoke of a distinctive Moldovan language, that was a foundation of distinctive non-Romanian Moldovan national identity" (Roper 2002, 103). These steps followed the general Soviet stance to invent the new *Homo Sovieticus* on the shambles of previously existing national identities destroyed by the Soviets in the first place.

The end of the Soviet rule aggravated previously dormant interethnic tensions within Moldovan society, which subdivided people of different ethnic backgrounds, according to Nikolay Bibilunga, into the caste groups of "locals," "title nations," "immigrants," "newcomers," and the "occupants" (Bibilunga 2010, 116). In August 1989 Moldova adopted the language law reinstating the "Romanian" language and its Latin script (Casey-Maslen 2014, 68). In June 1990 the government in the capital of Chişinău declared independence, soon followed by the Transnistria autonomous region, which sparked ethnic tensions (Nechayeva-Yuriychuk 2010, 136).[6] To aggravate the fragile peace even more, the leadership of Transnistria signed a petition to join the Soviet Union, which ended up in a large-scale military confrontation in March–July 1992 between the Moldovan military (Pavkovic and Radan 2011, 532) and the separatists, allegedly supported by the Russian 14th Army deployed in Transnistria (Lieven 1998, 247). The Joint Control Commission (JCC), composed of the Moldovan, Russian, and Transnistrian representatives, was soon set to provide for the deployment of a joint peacekeeping force. Consisting of six Russian battalions, three battalions from Transnistria, and only three from Moldova (Dailey 1993, 7), the JCC outnumbered the latter and put Chişinău in a disadvantageous position. In 2005 US and EU troops joined the JCC (Eriksson 2011, 72) to provide for the impartial monitoring of the situation.

The official role that Russia claims to have is that of an unprejudiced and neutral mediator, although with its support to the Transnistrian regime, traditional sympathies toward Russian-speaking "compatriots" as well as its imbalanced presence in the peacekeeping forces,[7] it was hard to hold up a veil of transparency and impartiality in the conflict with largely a zero-sum game. According to the Organization for Security and Co-operation in Europe (OSCE), the Russian presence in Moldova amounts to five thousand troops: "extremely well-armed . . . and the only armored force in Moldova capable of offensive action" (OSCE 1994, 4). During the 1999 OSCE summit, Moscow pledged to remove its military base from Transnistria by 2002, a decision received unfavorably by its pro-Russian population. As a result, the Russian Duma blocked this move under the pretext that "the unresolved conflict and NATO expansion demanded preservation of the Russian military presence. Transnistria, which, unlike the Republic of Moldova, sides with Russia and the Commonwealth of Independent States (CIS), needs firm guarantees of its future special status within the single Moldovan state" (Tsukanova 2010, 295).

In April 2014 the Transnistrian foreign minister and vice–prime minister, Nina Shtanki, declared, "The fact that Transnistria wants to be a part of Russia is not a decision after a Maidan, but solves the problems after the Maidan and is the will of the people expressed in the referendum of 2006. Besides, it is no secret that we are a part of the 'Russian world.' We insist on it: historically, mentally, and legally" (*Komsomol'skaya Pravda* 2008). Her Russian colleague Sergey Lavrov added more fuel to the Moldovan fire, "The Chişinău authorities are clearly trying to move in an undemocratic direction. . . . Transnistria has the right to decide about their future on their own, if Moldova does not retain nonaligned status. And we will defend this basis" (Vesti TV Channel 2014a). The message sent to the government in Chişinău and the European and American side was clear: in the case of the closeness of Moldova with the EU or NATO, it would meet the same fate as Ukraine.

The geographic contiguity reasoning in Moscow views the task of preventing Moldova's closeness with the alliance as one of the strategic objectives of Russia's foreign policy toward the country in question. Russia needs a non-allied Moldova as a buffer zone between itself and NATO. Russia also has a soft-power tool of energy harassment due to Moldova's energy dependence on gas and oil from Russia. As of today, only 3 percent of Moldova's energy use comes from local sources, with gas consumption being 65 percent of total energy supplies (Sobják 2013, 1). The Russian company Gazprom is both the gas supplier and the owner of 50 percent of Moldovagaz, the national gas company. As V. V. Ogneva and L. A. Brysyakina explain, "As a proper response to attempts to diversify supply routes of fuel in the EU bypassing Russia and the policy of double standards against Russian energy correction, it could act asymmetrically [in Moldova] in favor of the eastern and southern directions" (Ogneva and Brysyakina 2011, 2). Moldova could well become another target of Russian energy politics in the case of Europe's continuous efforts to look for alternative sources of energy. Even the new Iasi-Ungheni pipeline from Romania would not eliminate its dependence on Russian gas since it would provide only 5 percent of the total needs of Moldova, but it is a step in the direction of its energy independence, which could be potentially punishable by Moscow.[8]

Perpetual Blood Romance in the Caucasus

The Caucasus has traditionally occupied a unique place in Russia's geographic contiguity reasoning due to its strategic location. During its territorial expansionism in the eighteenth century, Russia fought twelve wars against the Ottoman Empire for the access to the Black Sea. With the collapse of the Soviet Union, Russia lost most Soviet ports, along with their connections to Europe and beyond. Russian marine trade became costly and somewhat limited due to the nature of its own seaports, located mainly in the cold north and the far east of the country. Besides, the Black Sea, in its current geopolitical context of Ukraine and Georgia looking steadily toward the West and NATO, threatens to turn it into the soft underbelly of Russia. An ideal condition of the region for Russia, thus, would be having loyal, at best, or non-pro-Western governments in the Caucasus, at least.

Repeated Impromptus in Georgia

The first Russian interventions in the conflicts in Georgia took the form of unrecognized noncombatants and under the aegis of peacekeeping missions with conflict-resolution mechanisms after the military clashes between the titular Georgian nation and the Abkhazian and South Ossetian minorities. The "War of Language Laws" in the early 1990s stemmed from the openly discriminatory rhetoric of its first president, Zviad Gamsakhurdia.[9] At that time, according to Andrey Zdravomislov, "imperial components of the Georgian politics toward Abkhazians stimulated Abkhazian nationalism, which gave an impetus to the Georgian nationalism" (Zdravomislov 1997, 21). Each subsequent step taken by Abkhazians and Ossetians to advocate for more linguistic freedoms and cultural rights was considered as lessening the rights of the title Georgian nation. The open hostilities in South Ossetia erupted in December 1990 and lasted for a year and a half, resulting in complete economic devastation of the region, severance of transport routes connecting Georgia with Russia through South Ossetia, and its de facto separation from Georgia.

In June 1992 the second president of Georgia, Eduard Shevardnadze, signed a cease-fire agreement with Russia as a guarantor of peace and security, which established a peacekeeping organ in the form of the JCC, composed of representatives from Georgia, South Ossetia, North Ossetia, and Russia. The JCC, just as its analog in Moldova, left Georgia in a disadvantageous position facing three "unneighborly" counterparts—Russia, South Ossetia, and North Ossetia. The war in Abkhazia started in 1992 soon after the end of hostilities in South Ossetia. In retaliation to the Georgian troops, which had entered Abkhazia in August 1992 and occupied its capital, Sokhumi, the Abkhazian forces with help from the paramilitaries from Russia eventually overran the Georgians. Under the terms of the July 1993 agreement with Russia, the CIS peacekeeper troops, formed exclusively by the Russian military, arrived in Abkhazia and became the guarantors of de facto peace.

The relationship with Russia and the two breakaway regions further deteriorated after the Rose Revolution in November 2003, when the Georgian government was replaced by a group of progressive pro-American politicians led by Mikheil Saakashvili. In the summer of 2008 the frozen conflict erupted in South Ossetia, now with Russia's official and full-scale military intervention in support of the South Ossetian military (Fawn and Nalbandov 2013). Russia entered the scene with a peacekeeping agenda: then Russian president Dmitry Medvedev called for "enforcing peace upon Georgia" (*Komsomol'skaya Pravda* 2008). De facto peace was reinstated on August 12 after a six-point peace agreement was signed between

Medvedev and Saakashvili with the mediation of French president Nicolas Sarkozy. The conflict almost simultaneously "unfroze" in Abkhazia. Inspired by the victorious advancement of Russian troops in South Ossetia, Abkhazian forces seized the momentum and launched a successful attack on the Georgian troops in the Upper Kodori region, the only part of Abkhazia they controlled. Not long after the cessation of hostilities in South Ossetia, Russia legally institutionalized the results of its intervention by officially recognizing South Ossetia and Abkhazia as newly independent states and members of the international community. Today South Ossetia and Abkhazia are strengthening their political gains by seeking further military assistance from and political alliance with Russia via the military bases on their territories and aspiring to join the commonwealth of Russia and Belarus.

There are several reasons for Russia's military involvements in Georgia, all born out of the geographic contiguity. Changes next door, especially with Georgia's increased interest in it on the part of the United States and European countries, raised several red flags for Moscow. In Jim Nichol's interpretation, Russia aspires to "coerc[e] Georgia to accept [its] conditions on the status of the separatist regions, to relinquish its aspirations to join NATO, and to depose Saakashvili as president. In addition, Russia may have wanted to 'punish' the West for recognizing Kosovo's independence, for seeking to integrate Soviet successor states . . . into Western institutions such as the EU and NATO, and for developing oil and gas pipeline routes that bypass Russia" (Nichol 2009, 12). The last point fits well with the "Heartland" theory. The Baku–Tbilisi–Supsa and Baku–Tbilisi–Ceyhan oil pipelines and the Baku–Tbilisi–Erzerum gas pipeline connect the Caspian Sea with Europe via Georgia and Turkey, bypassing Russia. As a result of the war in South Ossetia and having been gravely concerned with the fate of its own oil revenues, Azerbaijan started negotiations with Russia to double the volume of oil transit from the Caspian via its northern route. According to some estimates, complete transfer of the oil to the Baku–Novorossiysk region would bring Russia $1.3 million per month (Hanson 2008). Worth rather a small amount, this rerouting coupled with the transit of other energy carriers would leave the control over oil flows in the hands of Moscow and almost entirely out of the reach of the West.

From a political standpoint, the Russian side did not hide their highly negative assessment of possible moves of Georgia toward closer integration with NATO. Medvedev was quoted telling Saakashvili at the CIS summit in St. Petersburg that "Georgia's accession to NATO would increase bloodshed in South Ossetia and Abkhazia" (Zhungzhi and Huirong 2012, 201). By this statement, Russia warned Georgia far ahead of the conflict of its potential reaction to Georgia's Western drift. From domestic perspectives, the anticorruption-inspired Georgia was an eyesore for Russia since it contained a dangerous precedent for civil mobilization, something that the Russian government seeks to avoid. Finally, the geographic contiguity drove Russia close to South Ossetia with its brethren in their "external homeland"

(Brubaker 1994) in North Ossetia, a part of Russia, which also acted as a "surrogate lobby state" (Jenne 2004, 748) for Abkhazia.

Strange Inputs in Nagorno-Karabakh

Russia's involvement in the conflict in Nagorno-Karabakh is intimately connected with its relationship with Armenia and Azerbaijan. Current Russian foreign policy in Armenia is multifaceted and multidimensional. In the energy sector, Russia has undertaken the role of provider for energy security in Armenia starting from the Nagorno-Karabakh war (Merabyan 2014, 94).[10] The economic components of Russian foreign policy in Armenia include retaining leverage in most of its industrial sectors, including railroads, banking, cellular companies, and other smaller enterprises. Russia also has substantial business interests in Azerbaijan, especially its oil, which cannot go unnoticed in Armenia and which Moscow uses as its sway. One of the forms of such leverage is through the institutions: Armenia is an active member of the CIS and the Collective Security Treaty Organization (CSTO), and in 2015 it joined the Customs Union with Russia, with which it has no common borders.

Geographic contiguity played its role in the CSTO defense treaty, which was set as a viable deterrent since "a Turkish attack on Armenia would have been treated as an attack on Russia, and since Turkey is bound to the United States and Western Europe by similar terms under the North Atlantic Treaty, the stage would have been set theoretically for a conflict between NATO and Russia" (Croissant 1998, 82). As a consequence of Armenia's joining the CSTO in 1992, a much worse regional, and quite possibly global, confrontation was prevented, with the accession of Azerbaijan a year later. The CSTO agreement bound the hands of the states in their aggressive intents, but it did not cover intrastate conflicts, of which Nagorno-Karabakh is an example. Thus, having Russia bound to defend Armenia had positive and negative aspects, especially when it came to further economic integration with the former.

The Russian participation in the Nagorno-Karabakh conflict was bifurcated from the very start. According to Michael Mandelbaum, "The disarray in the Soviet armed forces led soldiers from units in the south Caucasus . . . to sell arms to the warring parties and to join the fighting on both sides—out of conviction or as mercenaries" (qtd. in Menon 1998, 129). It was a strange form of participation in which the Russian troops stationed in the former Soviet republics supported both sides. Fariz Ismailzade and Kevin Rosner corroborated: "Russia actively supplied weapons, military and technical assistance to both Armenia and Azerbaijan in order to deepen each state's dependence on Russia" (Ismailzade and Rosner 2006, 7)—an adaptation of an old Roman "divide and conquer" policy. Further, Robert Donaldson and colleagues believe that Russia "exert[ed] influence over both countries. Moscow played little role in sparking the initial dispute, but it has sought to monopolize the mediation and peacekeeping efforts to settle the conflict" in its Caucasian backyard

(Donaldson, Nogee, and Nadkarni 2014, 200). According to Alla Yaz'kova, Russia's role in the Nagorno-Karabakh war was connected with "Russian attempts to cement its military presence in Armenia, and preventing interventions of Turkey and Iran" from geopolitical perspectives (Yaz'kova 2009, 27).

From the standpoint of geographic contiguity, the conflict in Nagorno-Karabakh in the early 1990s was a grave concern to Russia. It also wanted to keep the historical linkages between the two Christian nations of the Caucasus, apparently seeing the advantages of this political cohabitation in the face of the NATO threat coming from Turkey. Moscow was deeply concerned with Georgia's slow drift toward the West and wanted to ensure its widespread political, economic, and military presence in the region through its military base in the Armenian border city of Gyumri. At the same time, Russia had to approach the interethnic tensions between Armenia and Azerbaijan very carefully and not upset the latter, with which it also has strong economic ties.

In a more recent resumption of hostilities between Azerbaijan and Nagorno-Karabakh in 2016, Russia was all too eager to use this situation to its benefit and to exert pressure on Armenia and Azerbaijan alike through its brokered agreement. The war lasted for only four days and cost an estimated one-hundred-plus lives from both sides. Russia quickly proposed to act as a mediator, a role that was not heartily welcomed by Yerevan, Stepanakert (Nagorno-Karabakh), or Baku. As Jack Farchy (2016) notes, "Moscow's move to act as peace broker could allow it to increase its already substantial influence in an energy-rich region that is a key focus of EU plans to diversify gas supplies from Russia." Nagorno-Karabakh; its patron-state, Armenia; and Azerbaijan alike shun the prospects of having another JCC established in the bordering regions, allowing Russia to further augment its military presence in the region. Such an outlook is based on the fact that "Russia is likely to increase pressure on Armenia to surrender some of the occupied districts to Azerbaijan. If the Armenian government refuses, Azerbaijan would probably be less constrained by Russia from launching another military campaign to change the status quo by military means" (Kokcharov, Melikishvili, and Gevorgyan 2016). As it is evident from the reactions across the board of the belligerents in Nagorno-Karabakh, Russia's self-imposed "help" is not quite welcome in the region.

Energy Weapons in Syria

The Soviet Union had been a loyal ally to Syria since Syrian independence from France in 1946. In 1971 the USSR established its military foothold in the port of Tartus, which it abandoned soon after its collapse (Özdal et al. 2013, 29). New Russia also offered Syria a steady supply of military equipment (Cordesman 2004; Cordesman, Nerguizian, and Popescu 2008, 163; Brookes 2005, 223).[11] As a response to the negative reaction of the Western powers to the use of chemical weapons by the regime of Syrian president Bashar al-Assad in the city of Aleppo in 2013, Russia took the mediation role and assisted the handover of Syrian chemical weapons (TASS News Agency 2015). This was hailed in Moscow as a major point scored for Russian diplomacy. Soon after, Russia started negotiations with Syria about selling them long-range surface-to-air missiles—specifically, S-300 PMU-1, aka SA-10 Grumble—to assist it in defending itself from possible air strikes.[12]

The starting point for the 2015 intervention in Syria in support of Assad's regime took place on September 28, 2015, after Putin spoke at the UN General Assembly anniversary session. He accused the US-led antiterrorist coalition of contributing to the instability in the Middle East by spawning the Islamic State in Iraq and Syria (ISIS) and indirectly supplying it with arms via the Syrian antigovernmental forces. He also proposed a new counterterrorist coalition, including Russia, Syria, and other states as equal partners, a plan that went directly contrary to anti-Assad policies of the Western countries. The ethos of Putin's speech enveloped the idea of Russia reentering the global arena not as another player but as one of its primary decision makers.

Without getting the due appreciation from the global community for his proposals, two days later Putin ordered a direct intervention into Syria on behalf of its government. There are several explanations for Russia's actions, both of which are contrary to the geographic contiguity outlook and reinforce the regional fractures logic: the wish to bring Russia back to the world's decision-making table and to put Europe on the oil needle of the Middle East. Russia's principal long-term aim is to gain leverage over the US-led international democratization efforts and to sustain Assad's regime. Apart from the regional geopolitics, Putin may be seeking to have the Western-imposed sanctions lifted since it is in the process of self-rehabilitation to being a peacemaker. As an intermediary goal, the continuous presence of the Russian troops in Syria places the West in a political crux since they may serve the same purpose as its "peacekeepers" did in Georgia (2008)—as living shields, which, if attacked, would trigger even larger and deeper engagements, probably beyond Syria. Even if the Russians will, eventually, become bogged down in Syria, they would have accomplished the short-term objective: to block any further ground deployment of the US troops in Syria.

This last point anchors to an even more compelling explanation of the Russian intervention. When in the early twentieth century Halford Mackinder presented his "heartland" theory of regional politics at the meeting of the British Royal Geographical Society, little did he know that a century later Russia would master his vision in its foreign policy in the Middle East. The Heartland theory exposed the worst fears of Europe by stating, "Who rules East Europe commands the Heartland: Who rules the Heartland commands the World-Island: Who rules the World-Island commands the World" (Mackinder 1981, 106). The reality in Syria in 2015 reflects the response to the downfall of the world's oil priced fostered by the Western sanctions on Russia for its intervention in Ukraine. Putin strives to cut down most of the alternative oil and gas supplies to Europe by fully covering the Heartland's need in oil. Russia also wants to get back to the region where the USSR had been successfully competing with the United States during the Cold War.

In December 2014 the EU officially closed the South Stream pipeline project, which was planned to bring Russian gas to Europe across the Black Sea. The estimated capacity of the offshore part of the pipeline was some 63 billion cubic meters of natural gas annually. The EU blocked it for being "a political project, not based on economics, but on the wish of the Putin government to circumvent Ukraine vis-à-vis gas supplies to Europe" (Karins 2014). Also, the EU's antimonopoly "Third Energy Package" laws do not allow a gas supplier to be both an exclusive owner of the pipeline capacities as well as the controller of such an infrastructure. Russia then started exploring alternative means to put Europe back on the South Stream track, and Syria proved quite handy in this endeavor. Its projected rival, the Iran–Iraq–Syria "natural gas pipeline [was] to be built by 2016 from Iran's giant South Pars field, traversing Iraq and Syria, with a possible extension to Lebanon" (Escobar 2012), to eventually reach Europe, its target export market.

With Iran poised to reenter the European gas market, this pipeline will take over the substantial share of the EU gas imports. Here is where Assad becomes useful for Putin: he refused to sign a proposed agreement with Qatar that would run a pipeline from the latter's North field, contiguous with Iran's South Pars field, through Saudi Arabia, Jordan, Syria, and on to Turkey, with a view to supplying European markets—albeit crucially bypassing Russia. According to Agence France-Presse, Assad's rationale was "to protect the interests of [his] Russian ally, which is Europe's top supplier of natural gas" (qtd. in Ahmed 2013). In sum, by assisting Assad militarily and solving his main problems at home (the Western-backed opposition and the ISIS), Putin aims to keep Syria under a pliable ruler preoccupied with regime survival and to make concessions to an exogenous power (here: Russia) in return for its security support.

What's Next?

The future of the Russian foreign policy would run along the crossroads of geographic contiguity and regional fractures. There is, however, a peculiar symbiosis between these two outlooks: while geographic contiguity included regional fractures as a part of its factor variables, the latter contradicts the former. In other words, there can well be regional fractures within the immediate geographic proximity to Russia or even along its borders—the ongoing war in the eastern parts of Ukraine is an excellent example of such a symbiosis. On the other hand, there are many regional fractures located well beyond the Russian borders. Thus, it would be an expression of an unfounded naïveté to suppose that Russian would go checking its borders for any sign of instability or go around the globe checking the potential hot spots. The principles for its foreign involvement are founded on two considerations: rationality and identity.

Simply put, Russia's future involvement in the domestic affairs or interstate disputes along its borders or far away would be based on how much money it has at its disposal to spare for military action. The Russian gross domestic product took a severe hit in the past several years due to the sanctions and drops in oil prices: from positive 2.1 percent of annual growth rate in January 2015 to the stunning 4.5 percent decline a year later. Although it managed to regain most of this decline by January 2016, its growth rate is still negative 0.6 percent.[13] According to *IHS Jane's* analysis, the Russian air strikes in Syria cost it $4 million per day, with the monthly expenditures fluctuating between $80 and $115 million (Hobson 2015). While currently not a severe burden to the Russian budget, the protracted conflict can have quite an adverse impact on the Russian domestic economics.

The rational reasoning in the Russian foreign policy closely coexists with its question for (re)building its identity. In 2014 Putin talked about the Russian bear as the embodiment of his foreign policy, "The Bear won't ask anyone's permission . . . it is not going to . . . move to other climatic zones, where it is uncomfortable. But it will not give up its Taiga to anyone" (Vesti TV Channel 2014b). By bringing in the metaphor of Russia as a bear pulled from its taiga lair in the midst of winter hibernation by reckless intruders, Russia consciously put itself on the outskirts of the Western civilization and is proud to oppose everything of value to the West. The bear metaphor has dual connotations. First, similar to the term "Lebensraum," or "living space," coined by nineteenth-century German geographer Friedrich Ratzel, Russia is only "cleaning" its living space from the shambles of the Soviet Union. Following the geographic contiguity logic, the Russian bear thus needs the fortified buffer zones to truly feel safe.

The second part of the bear metaphor is rooted in the depth of the superpower construct of the Russian identity and has found its reflection in the regional fractures logic. As the old Latin saying goes, *aquila non captat muscas* (an eagle does not chase flies); Russia would appropriately choose its battles to showcase its superpower status. Russia's future battlefields would thus crisscross those of the United States, the world-acknowledged superpower. A fundamental quality of a superpower—to hinder the policies of another superpower, which was mostly lost with the demise of the Soviet Union—had found new life in the bear metaphor. Following this logic, and wherever its economy permits, Russia would try to intervene in those regional friction areas where there is already a US presence or its vital national interests in one form or another: the Middle East, Latin America (most probably Venezuela and Cuba), and Europe. The Russian bear needs the American eagle to truly feel great.

Notes

1. "Read Putin's U.N. General Assembly Speech," *Washington Post*, September 28, 2015. https://www.washingtonpost.com/news/worldviews/wp/2015/09/28/read-putins-u-n-general-assembly-speech/.

2. Granici Rossii [Russian borders], Geography of Russia, February 12, 2017. https://geographyofrussia.com/granicy-rossii/.

3. Kuchma was accused by some in Ukraine of allegedly ordering the kidnapping and assassination of local journalist Georgiy Gongadze (coincidentally an ethnic Georgian), who was famous for his anticorruption articles.

4. "Ukraine President, Protest Leaders Agree on Truce," *Gainesville Sun*, February 19, 2014. http://www.gainesville.com/article/20140219/WIRE/140219514.

5. "Vibory Prezidenta Ukraini 25 Maya 2014," Ukraine Elections, September 16, 2016. http://ukraine-elections.com.ua/election_data/vybory_result/prezident/2014-05-25. As shown by the results of the presidential elections held in May 2014, shortly after the emotions and the grief of the Euromaidan had calmed down, Dmytro Yarosh managed to gain the support of only 0.7 percent of the electorate and not 37 percent as presented for domestic viewers by the Russian state propaganda distributor, Channel 1.

6. The ethnic composition of the region is of interest: Nataliya Nechayeva-Yuriychuk brings up the figures of 33.5 percent ethnic Moldovans, 30 percent Ukrainians, and 30 percent Russians.

7. The term was designed by the Russian government to define people who, after the dissolution of the Soviet Union, ended up outside of Russia but who identified themselves ethnically, linguistically, or culturally with the Russian nation.

8. "Moldova Inaugurates New Gas Pipeline, Will Get Gas from Romania to Lessen Dependence on Russia," *Fox Business News*, August 27, 2014. http://www.foxbusiness.com/markets/2014/08/27/moldova-inaugurates-new-gas-pipeline-will-get-gas-from-romania-to-lessen/.

9. Zviad Gamsakhurdia, "We Have Chatted Too Long with the Separatists: A Conversation with the Chairman of the Georgian Supreme Soviet," *Moscow News*, December 2, 1990, 11. The following quote from the Gamsakhurdia interview gives a glimpse of the situation with ethnic minorities in early independent Georgia: "We wanted to persuade the Ossetians to give in. They took flight, which is quite logical since they are criminals. The Ossetians are an uncultured, wild people—clever people can handle them easily."

10. Eighty percent of shares of the national company ArmRosGazprom belong to Gazprom, which since 2006 owns an Armenian heat power plant. The Russian Inter RAO EES manages the Metsamor nuclear plant, the only one in the Caucasus, and also owns the electricity distribution networks in Armenia.

11. There are multiple examples of such deals. Among others, between 1992 and 1994 Syria spent $1.2 billion on modernization of its equipment from Russia. In 1989–99 Russia sold Syria Kornet-E ($65 million) and Metis-M ($73 million) antitank guided-missile systems. Russia also sold Syria SA-18 surface-to-air missiles in violation of its commitment under the Helsinki Agreement not to support terrorist regimes.

12. "SA-10 to Syria," Global Security Analysis, https://www.globalsecurity.org/military/world/syria/sa-10.htm.

13. "Russia GDP Annual Growth Rate," Trading Economics, http://www.tradingeconomics.com/russia/gdp-growth-annual.

PART II

Lenin's Revenge: Regional Fracture in the Post-Soviet Space

CHAPTER THREE

Fractured Eurasian Borderlands: The Case of Ukraine

Vsevolod Samokhvalov

In this chapter I use the case of Ukraine to analyze three dimensions of regional fracture. In particular, I argue that the conventional interpretation of Ukraine as a country split by the "East or West" dilemma tends to reduce the complexity of the reality in this Euro-Eurasian borderland. I demonstrate that regional fracture in Ukraine is a more multilayered phenomenon that invokes numerous links between internal players, the broader population, and external hegemons. I argue that regionally relevant political developments in Ukraine are outcomes of interplay between several factors situated inside and outside the country, such as interests of and struggle within local and imperial elites, structural dependence of the Ukrainian economy on Russia, long-standing societal links, and changing interests of external hegemons. The concept of regional fracture, which allows the inclusion into analysis of the interplay between the above-mentioned factors, can explain Ukraine's long-standing oscillation between democracy and authoritarianism and between Euro-Atlantic and pro-Russian foreign policy, which is often simplistically described as "Ukraine's geopolitical conundrum" between East and West. I show how the concept of regional fracture allows a more nuanced understanding of the Ukrainian and regional politics, which cannot be accounted for by the East-versus-West dichotomy. In the framework of this analysis, I show how regional fracture theory can explain—what East–West dichotomy fails to do—the complex dynamics of the Ukrainian revolution and the ensuing crisis in the Crimea and Eastern Ukraine.

Islands of Power: Political Dimension of Regional Fracture in Ukraine

The concept of regional fracture allows the significant variance in the Ukrainian political trajectory, which combines both democratic and authoritarian trends in the post–Cold war era, to be accounted for. The common narrative describes this duality as an oscillation from democracy to authoritarianism and was often framed as a geopolitical conundrum or Ukraine's or an inability to make a Huntingtonian choice between Western democratic civilization versus Soviet past / Eastern authoritarianism and Asian barbarity (Huntington 2011, 342, 420–30). The western part of Ukraine—the historical region of Galicia—which was long part of the Austro-Hungarian Empire with its parliamentary tradition, has often been described as the stronghold of Ukrainian national democracy, while the east of Ukraine was labeled the epicenter of pro-Russian paternalist and authoritarian policies. There are, indeed, symbolic elements that make Western Ukraine look similar to its Central European or Baltic neighbors, such as widely spread religious traditions, a Uniate Church affiliated with the Holy See, and limited use of the Russian language. Some of these identity markers are analyzed in more detail in the section on the social dimension of regional fracture.

The thesis of this section holds that such a "cultural" interpretation, however, often disregards a complex interplay between a significant portion of nonideological political elites, charismatic personalities from Western, Eastern, and Central Ukraine as well as with changing interest of external hegemons. This section shows how an interplay and sometimes coincidental combination of factors and personalities shaped Ukraine's uneasy relationship with both the post-Soviet space and the European project. It shows that the transient nature of power resources in Ukraine resulted in a permanent state of ideological and political flux, unfixed rules, and a permanent process of bargaining and negotiating between the European, pro-Russian, and neo- and paleo-Soviet political projects. It also shows how little interest shown by the EU and the US in Ukraine created the feeling that Ukraine was a gray zone, which then mobilized Russia to pursue more active policies in Ukraine, effectively leading to the Ukrainian crisis of 2013–17.

The above-mentioned cultural interpretation omits the fact that—in addition to the major Ukrainian nationalist movement Rukh—several other actors played an important role in Ukraine gaining its independence in 1991. In fact, in addition to West Ukrainian ethnonationalists, the independence agenda for Ukraine was driven by the significant constituency of the Communist nomenclature and industrialists from Central and Eastern Ukraine (Wilson 1994, 3–4, 103). One of the most telling examples is represented by the head of the Supreme Council of the Ukrainian Soviet Socialist Republic and the first president of a newly independent Ukraine, Leonid

Kravchuk, who had earlier served as secretary of the Central Committee of the Communist Part of the Ukrainian Soviet Socialist Republic. Importantly, Kravchuk initiated a Ukrainian referendum on independence, which he used as an argument against any reincarnation of the Soviet Union in any (con)federal form until the last days of the USSR. Additionally, after the collapse of the USSR, and despite significant economic costs, Kravchuk refused to participate in any substantive work on transforming the USSR into a viable post-Soviet confederate arrangement. Under this ex-Communist leader, Ukraine refused to ratify the charter of the Commonwealth of Independent States (CIS). In addition to the Communist nomenclature, a significant number of the Ukraine-based economic elite—heavyweights of the mining and metal industry—were frustrated by the inability of Moscow to manage economic and political change. As a result, they also supported the drive for independence generated by Western Ukraine. This evidence allows us to conclude that, despite the conventional narrative, Ukrainian independence has been an outcome of the interplay between local actors, that is, an alliance of the ethnonationalists of Western Ukraine and the imperial elite (directors of heavy industries in the East) and defecting Communist administrators in Kyiv, who formalized the divorce. This trend was enabled by the split within the pro-Soviet elite (Mikhail Gorbachev versus conservatives) and the rise of the Russian elite (Boris Yeltsin), which—at least initially—weakened control of the Soviet power structures over Ukraine and thus empowered supporters of Ukrainian independence.

Such a coincidental combination of local and external factors, which resulted in Ukraine's independence, conditioned the nature of the power and politics of Ukraine. After Kravchuk resigned as president, Ukrainian politics featured several fractures, including the speedy fragmentation of the political space, networks, and personalized politics; short-term coalitions; and a lack of links between communities and elites. As a result of such fragmentation, the political power itself—the ability to shape socially and regionally significant outcomes—has been a sporadic phenomenon that repeats the contours of the above-mentioned concept of the islands of power, referred to in chapter 1. Such a transitory nature of power conditioned the country away from one ideological and geopolitical orientation to another. Effectively, all five Ukrainian presidents, either pro-Western or pro-Russian—pursued similarly contradictory internal and political policies, a phenomenon that can be better explained by constellations of various factors rather than by the concept of "great power overlay." The role of external hegemons was often quite controversial in this regard. Sometimes support of authoritarian projects by Russia was met by local resistance and a push for democratization. In parallel, the mismatch between the EU technocratic and moderate approach and value-based pro-Ukrainian discourse resulted in growing Euro-skepticism and growing passivity of the local population, and led to a rise of authoritarian regimes in the country.

The second president of Ukraine, Leonid Kuchma, made his career as part of the Soviet economic elite in its high-tech space/military industry in Eastern Ukraine. Despite all expectations and his electoral promises, this director of the major Soviet military industry in Ukraine adopted a far less friendly line toward the CIS (D'Anieri 1999). He initially pursued a strategy for European integration. However, after the West exerted serious pressure against his authoritarian practices and corruption, Kuchma switched to a multivector foreign policy and, after severe isolation and internal unrest in 2001–2, seriously considered joining the Common Economic Space with Russia. However, this oscillation can hardly be explained by strategic calculations or international structural factors. The primary factor was Kuchma's precarious political position, that is, his balancing between Western Ukrainian nationalists, Central Ukrainian urban liberals, and East Ukrainian oligarchs. As it was put by a prominent analyst of Ukraine, Taras Kuzio (2002a), "Kuchma's foreign policy is neither pro-Russian nor pro-Western. It is pro-Kuchma."

Similarly, Kuchma's internal policy was defined less by ideology than by an attempt to accumulate power resources. In addition to co-opting state institutions into corruption deals and authoritarian practices, Kuchma sought to create several major financial-industrial groups in major industrial centers and play one against another. Kuchma also sought to undermine the existing political landscape by creating democratic simulacra—political parties that would undermine independent opposition forces on the Right and Left extremes of the political spectrum. The suspicious death of Viacheslav Chornovil—a charismatic leader of the right-wing movement Rukh (Movement for National Independence)—led to a split in this major Center-Right opposition bloc. Similarly, several leftist projects launched by President Kuchma, such as the Progressive Socialist Party, undermined major left-wing opposition forces. As a result of these policies, several attempts by pro-European forces to mobilize the broader society to oust Kuchma from office failed due to the lack of institutional resources. Kuchma's attempt to rig the election and bring to power the even more controversial governor of the Donetsk region, Viktor Yanukovych, resulted in the "electoral" Orange Revolution in 2004 (Lane 2009).

One more reason for the electoral revolution was the attempt by Kuchma and Yanukovych to draw on external resources. In 2004 the popularity of the Russian president, Vladimir Putin, in Ukraine was higher than that of any politician in Ukraine. During the electoral campaign Putin visited Ukraine several times and met President Kuchma and Prime Minister Yanukovych. Such a strong presence, however, was counterproductive and reveals the controversial nature of external power resources. On the one hand, it allowed Yanukovych to gain popularity in some regions. On the other hand, Yanukovych's reliance on an external hegemon allowed the opposition to reverse the situation and mobilize supporters by contraposing a native Ukrainian choice to foreign intervention. As Zbigniew Brzezinski put it, despite the high visibility of some Western Ukrainian nationalists with their links to the diaspora in Canada and the US, the Orange Revolution was driven by the broad alliance of West Ukrainian nationalism and Central Ukrainian liberalism (qtd. in Samokhvalov 2006).

Despite its strong pro-European rhetoric, the foreign policy of the "Orange" elite in 2004–10 featured numerous contradictory moves. These moves, once again concerning the primary nature of power resources, prompted pro-European Ukrainian politicians to betray their commitments to principles of European integration and maneuver between different political programs. For example, pro-European president Viktor Yushchenko, while pursuing the politics of the nationalist historical and ideological narrative, signed long-standing gas contracts with Moscow in 2005. While negotiating these contracts with Moscow, President Yushchenko relied on the mediation of a Russian–Ukrainian oligarch with close connections in the Kremlin and a dubious past, Dmytro Firtash, who was born in Western Ukraine (Balmaceda 2008, 128). Other refined nationalist political leaders from Western Ukraine, including Taras Chornovil and Hanna German (former editor of Radio Free Europe in Ukraine), joined and became main speakers of the "pro-Russian" Party of Regions. These and several other examples demonstrate that politicians from allegedly anti-Russian and ethnonationalist Western Ukraine did exclude working closely or even acceding to Russophile projects.

The opposite is also true. Prominent leading politicians from Eastern Ukraine have never been dogmatically committed to a pro-Russian course. One of the leaders of the Ukrainian Orange Revolution, Yulia Tymoshenko, played an even more prominent role in the regional fracture. Coming from Eastern Ukraine, Tymoshenko pursued an even more anti-Russian rhetoric in her public speeches (Tymoshenko 2007). However, a year later—while renegotiating a Russian–Ukrainian gas contract—Tymoshenko made significant concessions and signed an even more profitable contract for Gazprom. This decision created an even higher degree of Ukrainian dependence on Russian gas. Such behavior by and conflicts within the allegedly pro-European elite were disappointing even for the Ukrainian pro-democratic constituency. As a result of such controversial policies of the Ukrainian democratic elites, Ukrainians elected an overtly authoritarian and highly controversial leader, Yanukovych. Symptomatically, even the European elites found Yanukovych a more reassuring choice after the anarchic and corrupt Orange elites in Ukraine (Wilson 2014, 38).

That lack of institutionalized political structures revealed itself through the striking absence of any solidarity between various democratic constituencies during the electoral campaign and the authoritarian reign of President Yanukovych. Pro-European and pro-democratic outgoing president Yushchenko effectively campaigned for pro-Russian and authoritarian candidate Yanukovych. Public intellectuals called for a vote against everyone, thus paving the way for Yanukovych's victory. The lack of links between various communities and political actors revealed itself in 2010–12, when Yanukovych effectively dismantled all the democratic elements in Ukrainian politics. Political parties could not mobilize public support to mount resistance to the effective usurpation of the state institution and repressions against leaders of the opposition by Yanukovych. Ukrainian judiciary and expert communities were unable to speak with authority against the excesses of the regime. Public intellectuals either failed to articulate alternative state-building programs or did not realize they had an important social role to play at that crucial juncture. Even the most skillful political animals—Ukrainian oligarchs—were helpless against Yanukovych's gradual takeover of the lucrative industrial assets of Ukraine (Romanenko 2012).

Finally, like his authoritarian predecessor, Leonid Kuchma, Yanukovych managed to bring to the forefront several artificial opposition projects. In 2010–12, the ultra-Right Svoboda (Freedom) received privileged access to major media outlets, controlled by the government or affiliated oligarchs, and thus gained a higher degree of popularity (Wilson 2014, 62). As a result of the populist rhetoric, even the center of the Ukrainian political spectrum was fragmented. Two new centrist opposition projects were supported by the leading Ukrainian oligarch Firtash with good connections in Moscow. Arseniy Yatsenyuk, the founder of the Front for Change party, along with the Ukrainian Democratic Alliance for Reform, led by the Ukrainian boxing champion Vitali Klitschko, relied on this support (Leschenko 2016). The presidential administration also took over part of the leftist agenda, thus pushing the Socialist and Communist parties to the margins even further left (Wilson 2014, 63). Such a high number of political elites with questionable legitimacy resulted in further erosion of the link between political parties and society. This gap between the ruling class and broader society led to the next step of regional fracture, when one simple political maneuver by President Yanukovych resulted in the Revolution of Dignity and the war with Russia.

Even though Yanukovych formally replaced the nascent democratic institutions with a regime of personalized governance, regional fracture played an important role in the redemocratization of Ukraine. Despite Yanukovych's crackdown on the formal democratic institutions, the number of public protests organized by politically underrepresented societal players was growing. In 2011–12 two major waves of protests were organized by small traders and retired army officers. This suggests that, despite the degrading formal democracy, Ukrainian substantive democracy was maturing.

The regional dimension of the political events was also pronounced in the Ukrainian Revolution of Dignity, or Euromaidan.[1] The power of the attraction of the EU was the initial driving force in organizing protests in November–December

2013. These protests, however, became violent and eventually led to Yanukovych's flight from Ukraine when he tried to adopt the highly controversial dictatorial laws of January 19, 2014. Replicated from Russian legislation, the newly adopted laws allowed protest leaders to frame their movement as a civilizational choice, escape from "the regime of bandits and dictators," and further legitimize violent action against the police (Wilson 2014, 127).

The outcome of the Euromaidan highlights once again the controversial nature of external hegemons. Contrary to the widespread narrative, the European Union did not seek to oust the allegedly pro-Russian Yanukovych. Quite the contrary, the EU mediators—concerned about potential collapse of the state and ensuing chaos—pushed protesters to seal a deal with Yanukovych. The deal envisaged an extension of Yanukovych's power for almost a year, which would eventually lead to the conservation of his regime. Ironically, the person who Russian politicians consider the most "anti-Russia and pro-American" politician of Europe, Polish foreign minister Radoslaw Sikorski, exerted the most pressure on the revolutionaries. The role of Europe's contender in the region—Russia—is at least as controversial. In the situation of political deadlock—when Yanukovych still had full control over the internal troops and riot police—it was Russia's decision to organize a rescue mission and the evacuation of Yanukovych that allowed the opposition to take over power. In this regard, regional fracture theory can explain Ukraine's several waves of democratization and authoritarian return, which structuralist theories could only discard as a contingency (Levitsky and Way 2010, 24).

Regional fracture theory can also explain the phenomenon of the lack of democratization under the famous pro-European president, Petro Poroshenko. On the one hand, Poroshenko is famous for his pro-European activism. On the other hand, he served as minister of foreign trade under Yanukovych, had significant business interests in Russia, and conducted numerous negotiations in Moscow. His high visibility (backed by his own TV channel)—his political networks, media resources, and social capital (a pro-European image)—combined with the surge of patriotism in the face of the Russian threat created the island of power that allowed Poroshenko, whose popularity had been about 4 percent several months before the Euromaidain, to take over power.

President Poroshenko resorted to various informal practices and deals. He put the judiciary and prosecution office under his personal control (Romaniyuk 2016). As a result of his controversial policies, a pro-European parliamentary coalition has effectively ceased to exist. Instead he engaged in situational coalitions with the leftovers of the pro-Russian Party of Regions, rebranded as Opposition Bloc, and other political parties and independent members of Parliament, such as the Radical Party of Oleh Lyashko and centrist Yatsenyuk's Front of Change. All the players prefer to engage in informal bargaining and dealing with the presidential administration, thus perpetuating the power-based nature of Ukrainian politics. The presidential administration has effectively become an informal decision-making body shaping government politics. The culture of informality seems to prevail over the Western project in Ukraine. Younger and Western-educated reformers, foreign journalists, and independent (even if oligarchic) TV channels are being gradually squeezed out from the government and public sphere. The president's effective control over the prosecutor's office creates a space for abuse of power, which leads to the persecution of journalists and pressure on business.

Overall, Ukrainian independence was driven by a broad coalition of forces whose interests coincided but were not identical. Western Ukrainian nationalists were driven by the pursuit of an ethnocultural renaissance and escape from Russia. Eastern Ukrainian elites saw no reason to continue relations with the dysfunctional Soviet bureaucracy. Former imperialists seized the opportunity of strengthening their positions. This coincidence of interests, combined with broader socio-economic and post-Chernobyl grievances, reflected the island of power syndrome that paved the way to Ukraine's independence. However, the constellation of interests of diverse groups was not fixed on one goal.

As a result, interests started to diverge, which led to further fracturing of the Ukrainian political space, and conditioned further the geopolitical conundrum of Ukraine. A permanent fight for control of the state-building discourse, ad hoc coalitions, and geopolitical maneuvers and compromises conditioned Ukraine's oscillation from Europe to Russia and back. This prevented Ukrainian elites from incorporating the country into any of the regional projects—European, Eurasian, or post-Soviet. Despite the pro-European policies of President Poroshenko, several informal links and informal practices tend to reconstitute Ukraine as a part of the post-Soviet political space. Given the fight between various regional elites within Ukraine with specific links either to Russia or to Europe, it looks as though it will be increasingly difficult for Ukraine to be fully integrated into one of the regional projects (either European or Eurasian). Given Russian aggression, the Ukrainian public seems to be failing to create the necessary bottom-up pressure for preventing elite corruption and some authoritarian practices in the political dimension. This power dynamic has revealed itself in the institutional dimension of the regional fracture, which is discussed in the next section.

Institutional Dimension: Regionalism and Regionalization

In terms of institutional dimensions of regional fracture in Ukraine's neighborhood, the patterns of regional fracture seem to hold. As is typical for fractured regions, institutional proliferation at a regional level is evident, but so is the lack of the ability on the part of these institutions to mobilize collective action at a regional level. Ukraine's regional citizenship in its neighborhood has been uneven and shallow, particularly relative to Ukraine's institutional support to Russia-led groupings. It has consistently pursued policies of opting out from deeper forms of post-Soviet and hegemonic regionalism. While joining the newly created CIS in the aftermath of the Soviet collapse, Ukraine refused to sign the charter that sought to transform the fuzzy post-Soviet grouping into a proper international organization. In terms of trade, Ukraine's participation featured numerous oscillations that reveal the power of the internal political dimension. For example, Ukraine signed some agreements establishing free economic zones in CIS in the early 1990s. However, later, it introduced hundreds of exemptions to the nomenclature of goods for free movement, which were subject to the vested interests of Ukrainian financial and industrial groups. Effectively, Ukraine remained part of the post-Soviet economic space, but this partnership was conditioned by a "spaghetti bowl" of bilateral agreements, as it was put by specialists in the political economy of Eurasian regionalism (Vinokurov and Libman 2012, 65–75). Even when allegedly pro-Russian Kuchma announced his intention to join the Single Economic Space with Russia, Kazakhstan, and Belarus, his privatization policies effectively promoted national capitalism, which sought integration into the global trade system.

The mismatch between regional institutions and effective regionalization has also been striking under the pro-European president Yushchenko (2005–10). On the one hand, Yushchenko spoke about Ukraine regaining its independence and returning to Europe. Namely, he sought a deeper EU-Ukraine Neighborhood Policy Action Plan and pushed for a Ukraine–NATO membership action plan. On the other hand, Yushchenko paid his first international visit to Moscow and sought to develop trade relations with Russia. Notably, he relied on informal networks with the Kremlin in order to maintain the same level of energy relations, and Russian–Ukrainian trade turnover increased significantly under him. Russian companies, especially banks, increased their presence in Ukraine under the Yushchenko presidency. One could be tempted to describe these mixed policies as purely multivector diplomacy, which implies dispassionate balancing between different several external hegemons. In the case of Yushchenko, multivector rhetoric should not be taken at face value. In his cultural and "memory policies," Yushchenko consistently sought to escape from the Soviet past.[2] He enhanced the nationalist historical narrative, vilified the Soviet past, and promoted Ukrainian as the only state language. So even though Yushchenko tried to present Ukrainian foreign policy as a pragmatist approach, his internal policies led to further regional fracture. His close personal connections with the highly nationalist Ukrainian diaspora in North America gave extra evidence for this. This disconnect revealed itself during the Russian–Georgian war of 2008—when Kyiv tried to prevent the Russian navy based in Ukraine from leaving its stations and heading for the Georgian coast—which showed the limitation of the "multivectorist" explanation.

These two trends, however, were not the only ones shaping the institutional landscape in the region. Several other projects sought to appropriate certain geographic signifiers for discursive region construction. For example, Ukraine sought to become a member of the regional organizations, such as the Black Sea Economic Cooperation, which sought to dilute the post-Soviet space in a broader regional project—stretching from the Balkans to Central Asia and Africa. However, one of the most interesting regional projects launched by Yushchenko highlighted the fractural line running across space and time. Ukraine has been instrumental in setting up the Community of Democratic Choice, founded by the countries that had concerns about Russia's domination in the post-Soviet space—Georgia, Ukraine, Azerbaijan, Moldova, and swing member Uzbekistan (GUAMU). The Community of Democratic Choice has been supported by several other countries in Eastern Europe who have always been wary of Russian expansion into Eastern Europe, that is, the Baltic States, Romania, and Poland. The presence of nondemocratic states in this new group suggests that it was not a value-driven community but rather a Poland-driven Intermarium project of the early twentieth century or cordon sanitaire against Russia.

The example of the GUAMU and Intermarium highlight one more feature of regional fracture—its temporal character. In addition to the fracture between a premodern (Russian/Soviet) empire and the postmodern (European) empire, identified by Robert Cooper (2004), the post-Soviet space is living also as a temporal fracture—between the modern time of nation-states and premodern time of empire. Modern time space is Central Europe (countries pursuing their own nation- and state-building projects and forging alliances against the former metropole) and the premodern Russian imperial project for the post-Soviet space. This temporal fracture is even more pronounced in the social dimension.

Contradictory policies of the allegedly pro-Russian Yanukovych reveal a similar ambiguity in Ukraine's regional citizenship. Despite the general narrative, Yanukovych spent three years of his presidency pursuing a course for European integration and avoiding a closer bond with Eurasian integration. On the one hand, Ukraine agreed to join a new multilateral free trade zone of the CIS. On the other hand, Yanukovych was adamant in his rejection of a closer integration project—the Russia-led Customs Union and, later on, the Eurasian Economic Union. Even though the Customs Union helped to increase the aggregate gross domestic product growth of the three countries of the union, even most pro-Russian politicians in Ukraine realized that, in the existing political architecture of the Kremlin, Russian companies would have much stronger lobbying capacities, which would inevitably place Ukrainian businesses in an underprivileged position and eventually lead to these businesses being taken over by their stronger and more aggressive Russian counterparts (Zarembo 2012).

Another reason for skepticism was a great disappointment about the deals reached between Kyiv and Moscow on gas discounts and basing rights for the Russian fleet in Crimea. In particular, after the Party of Regions secured the prolongation of Russia's basing rights in Sevastopol, the discount on gas prices that Ukraine received from Moscow was considered less than symbolic. Additionally, a growing number of gas pipelines constructed by Russia in order to bypass Ukraine became strong evidence that Russia did not want to share part of its gas rent with Ukraine, thus reducing Ukraine's transit potential and, consequently, its revenues from transit and export of Russian gas. In this context, Moscow's offer to collect export tax on all gas pumped through Ukraine seemed too good to be true. The foregoing reasons were serious enough to outweigh all the potential benefits of remaining in the post-Soviet space and to opt for integration with the Deep and Comprehensive Free Trade Area (DCFTA) with the EU.

Under Yanukovych, Ukraine continued to maximize its commitments, selecting for adoption as many EU technical norms as possible (Langhbein and Wolczuk 2012, 867). The fact that Yanukovych appointed two of his closest associates, head of the National Security Council Serhiy Klyuyev and Vice-Premier Serhiy Arbuzov, to negotiate DCFTA and upgraded the status of the Ukrainian ambassador to the EU to the level of state representative demonstrates the importance of the European dimension for Yanukovych in 2010–13. Certainly, Ukraine's decision to sign the DCFTA was sold to Russia and other international players as a pragmatic move aimed at linking Ukraine to the international market of 600 million comparatively rich Europeans. To save both Russia's and its own face when rejecting Russia's offer, Ukrainian prime minister Mykola Azarov (with the silent support of President Yanukovych) offered an alternative "3+1" formula that would allow Ukraine to maintain its special status in relations with the Customs Union of Russia, Belarus, and Kazakhstan, given its special commitments to EU–Ukraine DCFTA. Similarly, Ukraine has not been keen to develop a strong formal link with regional security institutions. Even though Ukraine extended the rights to bases for the Russian navy in the symbolically important harbor of Sevastopol and several dozen other locations in Crimea, Kyiv refused to join the Collective Security Treaty Organization—the main post-Soviet security organization. This also reveals tension between formal regionalism and effective regionalization in the post-Soviet space.

Symptomatically, Yanukovych appointed the then-highly respected centrist businessman and politician Petro Poroshenko to the position of minister of economic development and dispatched him to Moscow to handle the issues of trade wars in March 2012. It was only Russia's unprecedented trade war against major Ukrainian importers that pushed Yanukovych to make a choice. With the growing budget deficit, looming gas crisis, and complaints from major industries, Yanukovych made his signing of DCFTA conditional on the allocation by the EU of significant financial support of €160 billion and invited Brussels and Moscow to start trilateral negotiations. These two proposals were rejected by the EU and resulted in Yanukovych's decision to pause EU–Ukraine negotiations. This decision stirred the first wave of protests of pro-European activists between November 21 and 30, 2013—called Euromaidan.

Overall the cautious EU policies toward Ukraine somehow contributed to further regional fragmentation. The fact that the EU had not offered Ukraine any prospect of membership allowed Russia to consider it part of its own sphere of influence. The events of Euromaidan have also shown the reluctance of the European Union to make a stronger effort to include Ukraine into the European regional project. In the most critical days of Euromaidan in late February—when more than a hundred people were killed in the center of the Ukrainian capital—the European mediators, led by the foreign ministers Radoslaw Sikorski of Poland and Frank-Walter Steinmeier of Germany, forced the Ukrainian opposition to seal a deal that would extend Yanukovych's regime until the end of 2013. Apparently, civil war and imminent chaos in Ukraine pushed the EU not to insist on Yanukovych's resignation. The episode demonstrates that—unlike the generally accepted version about the West supporting the pro-European revolution in Ukraine—Europe in fact sought to mediate a conflict and was prepared to support the reign of the pro-Russian president in order to prevent collapse of the state. Even though this decision falls into the peacekeeping and conflict-resolution paradigm, it demonstrates that Europe is not prepared to engage in some practices of redrawing the geographic map, which again prevents further structuration of geographic space and sustains regional fractures.

Similarly, policies of the allegedly pro-European Poroshenko and the pro-European coalition reveal serious tensions between ever-denser institutionalization of EU–Ukraine relations and Ukraine's effort to maintain numerous channels for Russian–Ukrainian economic exchange. On the one hand, President Poroshenko signed the EU–Ukraine Association Agreement soon after taking office. On the other hand, Kyiv refrained from disrupting any multilateral negotiations with Russia on potential repercussions of the EU–Ukraine DCFTA for Russia. There continues to be consensus between the Ukrainian government, businesses, and society over the view that the free trade area with Russia is compatible with the EU–Ukraine DCFTA. The major Ukrainian energy company, Naftogaz of Ukraine, maintains working relations with the Russian energy champion Gazprom and makes strong efforts to continue this collaboration to remain the key energy transit country (Kobolev 2016). Some of the major Ukrainian industries continue their collaboration with their Russian counterparts, and even the government up until recently carried on business with the breakaway republics. Only after the mass blockade organized by veterans of the war and radical political forces did the government reluctantly stop trade with the Donetsk and Luhansk People's Republics.

The fractured nature of Ukrainian politics conditioned sporadic institutional proliferation at the regional level and "Ukraine's geopolitical conundrum." On the one hand, elite groups pursue pro-European or pro-Russian integration. However, this integration remains declarative. The Ukrainian government and major business players are interested in maintaining a shallow level of institutionalization while trying to manage interdependence with Russia or Europe. As a result, pro-European presidents, such as Kravchuk and Yushchenko, failed to move closer to European integration because of a plethora of corrupt practices that allowed them to maintain their power. Current president Petro Poroshenko, the most "pro-European" president, also faces similar accusations of not being willing to fight against corruption and introduce transparent political culture in Ukraine. Similarly, pro-Russian president Yanukovych preferred to adhere to the shallow free trade zone agreement with the CIS but refused to join the Customs Union with Russia, Belarus, and Kazakhstan as it would limit his room to maneuver inside the country and on a regional level.

Finally, by actively promoting a new set of institutions that includes countries of Central Europe and the Black Sea region, one more fracture line, which runs across time, is revealed. For example, the long-standing attempts to create some sort of new cordon sanitaire, comprising countries of Central Europe and the Black Sea region, highlight tension between premodern space of multinational empires and the modern age of nation-states. Despite politically neutral labels, such integration schemes as GUAM (Georgia-Ukraine-Azerbaijan-Moldova) or the Community for Democratic Choice include countries of Central Europe and the Baltic region, which have strong reasons to be concerned with and to balance against the Russian regional hegemony. This project, however, undermines both European and Eurasian regional projects. Intermarium, a new geopolitical project that has recently been actively promoted by the countries of the region, echoes the geopolitical logic of the late nineteenth and early twentieth century. This means the tension between formal or declarative acts and everyday practices becomes even more obvious in the social dimension.

Social Dimension of Regional Fracture: Values and Identities

The third dimension of regional fracture refers to values and identities, and the extent to which they influence regional dynamics, whether in terms of integration or fracture. In the framework of Huntington's theory, Ukrainian identity has often been described as fractured and torn apart between Russian and European civilizational choice (Fesenko 2015). Language and religion were markers of civilization and implied that Ukrainian-speakers would be supporters of independence and European choice, while Russophones would support a common regional identity with Russia and post-Soviet space. The main fallacy of this approach was the fact that it treated civilization as mostly a culture-based entity and, within this logic, considered social dimension a fixed and clearly defined entity. This conceptualization of the divide within Ukraine did not take into account a complex and evolving nature of social dimension. The case of Ukraine shows that its social space can be better described as a complex amalgam of numerous (certainly more than two) communities in which various social actors deploy necessary resources in order to promote their own identity projects and convert them into social and political capital. This observation suggests that one has to disaggregate the social dimension into several elements in order to identify how various actors fight for social capital and create their own communities. So, in some terms the regional fracture of social dimension can also bear a positive potential. When the vague concept of identity is disaggregated into several markers—even such important ones as language, memory, behavioral codes, and practices—it creates space and the need for negotiation and bargaining over meanings, thus weakening the totalizing discourses of Self–Other and enhancing instead the culture of dialogue and tolerance of difference.

Before tackling specific issues of social dimension and the role of specific actors or communities, it is important to clarify the difference between two conceptualizations of identity. The first posits national identity as an epiphenomenon of the Andersonian imagined community, created through education, mass media, and propaganda. The major markers of such a community have always been a common language, imaginary shared history, values, and vision for the future. The second, a more anthropological approach, conceptualizes identity as a plethora of shared everyday experiences and behavioral codes that generate specific representations and the way people act (Bourdieu 1990, 52–53). One of the simplistic East–West dichotomies for Ukraine has long argued that the main clash in the social dimension in Ukraine is taking place between two identity projects defined in Andersonian terms. The first identity project envisages a return to Europe as a flight from "Russia's deadly embrace." The new pro-Ukrainian identity implies what Richard Sakwa described as a monist project—speedy Ukrainization—actively promoting the Ukrainian language as the only state language, unmaking the Soviet past, and squeezing out the Russian language and culture from the Ukrainian public space (Sakwa 2015). Moreover, this pro-European identity seeks to exclude Russia from Europe (White and Feklyunina 2014). On the other hand, the "post-Soviet identity" suggests celebrating some successful elements of Soviet history and challenges the exclusivity of the Ukrainian language in the public space in Ukraine. This identity project effectively constitutes Ukraine as part of the post-Soviet region with a special role of the shared past and the common Russian language.

However, the above concepts significantly reduce the current state of art in identity projects in Ukraine. The point of this chapter is to show that the Ukrainian identity project is in fact a more fractured amalgam of various groups of populations that feature sometimes the most grotesque combinations of identity, thereby allowing various identity entrepreneurs to offer numerous imagined micro, meso, and macro communities to various audiences. Such an excess of supply of identity/community projects results in a permanent process of negotiations, contestation, and bargaining, which prevents further structuration of social space and deepens regional fracture. As a result, any fixed imagined geography becomes an impossibility. I explain this point in some detail below.

If one applies the Andersonian concept of national identity, it becomes obvious that, even in the democratic pro-European movement in Ukraine, there are at least several political programs that profess different attitudes to the major markers of national identity, language, and memory. Ukrainian liberals have very different opinions about the status of the Ukrainian and Russian languages and, thus, constitute Ukrainian social space as a fragmented amalgam. The major tension has been generated by the conflict between those who support Ukrainian as the only state language (with Russian being ignored as a local dialect or even banned as the language of the aggressor) and those who believe that the Russian language should be granted special rights at the national or, at least, local levels (in the areas with a significant Russian-speaking population). This variance in the attitude toward the Russian language revealed itself in the first days of success of the Euromaidan revolution in February 2014.

After pro-Russian president Yanukovych fled the country, the ethnonationalist party Svoboda pushed a vote to abolish special status for the Russian language. However, the acting president of Ukraine, representing the centrist party Front for Change, Oleksandr Turchynov vetoed this decision because it might provoke resentment within the Russophone communities. Eventually, despite Turchynov's veto, this controversial vote resulted in an antigovernment mobilization in the Crimea and the east of Ukraine. Currently, this question has been downplayed by the elites, given the Russian intervention into Ukraine. However, the very fact that even a pro-European democratic coalition and democratic parties themselves could not shape a consensus on the question of the state language and its relation to a major minority language reveals a significant level of fragmentation of social space. Additionally, a significant number of Russian speakers consistently support parties or political leaders who advocate the idea of granting Russian special regional or "state language" status. The line of fragmentation, however, does not coincide with party ideologies or East–West rift lines. For example, even in some parts of Western

Ukraine, especially areas populated by Hungarian and Romanian minorities, Russian has been a lingua franca and has been treated as a marker of multiethnic civic projects of Ukrainian statehood. At the same time, the south and east of Ukraine have a significant percentage of the Ukrainian-speaking or bilingual population, which demonstrates a high degree of loyalty to the Ukrainian language. One could argue that in the Ukrainian social space, national identity, at least in terms of language, is still highly fragmented and that the striped profile of the Ukrainian linguistic map can hardly be reduced to an East–West binary.

The question of shared history has often been described as another important element of national identity. And it also reveals that there are many tensions between numerous constituencies even within the pro-European camp. One of the conventional recipes advanced by the supporters of swift Ukrainian nation-building has been to "re-invent Ukrainian history" as a story of the fight for independence against Russian/Soviet domination. Within this framework the Russian/Soviet period was to be framed in terms of Ukraine's victimhood. Victory in World War II and industrialization are now to be described with references to the enormous sacrifice that the Ukrainian nation was forced to make. The artificial famine in 1932–33 is construed as genocide against Ukrainians. And even the transfer of Crimea to Ukraine in 1954 under Khrushchev is often depicted as a challenge for postwar Ukraine, which had to mobilize its depleted resources to build water channels, energy infrastructure, and roads and to cultivate lands in the peninsula. Numerous bans and repression against Ukrainian culture are commemorated as an execution of the national cultural revival. The conclusion is obvious—escape from the Russian prison of nations is a matter of survival for the Ukrainians. The opposite story, often promoted by Russian and pro-Russian intellectuals and media, claimed exactly the opposite, that is, that Ukraine was always a subject of exploitation and occupation by Western great powers and Poland and that it was only when under the Russian Empire and the USSR that the Ukrainian territories were reunited into one land, the country was industrialized, and the Ukrainian culture flourished. After the victory of the Euromaidan / Revolution of Dignity in Ukraine, it seemed that the pro-independence "Ukraine victim" discourse would prevail.[3] However, despite the fact that hundreds of Lenin's monuments were toppled and the parliament adopted a highly controversial legislation on decommunization, which included changing Soviet-style names of the cities and streets, it would be too early to claim that the pro-independence "Ukraine victim" paradigm has triumphed in Ukraine.

There are at least two factors that drive even most pro-European Ukrainian political actors to halfheartedly embrace the pro-independence story and to cautiously balance between the two programs. The first is the extremely controversial nature of the pantheon of fighters for Ukrainian independence. Numerous studies highlight elements of anti-Semitism, ethnonationalism, and dictatorship in the political programs and practices of the main hero of Ukrainian independence—the Organization of Ukrainian Nationalists. Collaboration of some Ukrainian nationalists with the Nazi administration and their participation in the mass executions of the Jewish and Polish population of Ukraine makes them dubious candidates for the pantheon of national heroes of a modern European country. Leading pro-European politicians in Ukraine opposed or distanced themselves from this paradigm. For example, the mayor of the Ukrainian capital and one of the leaders of the Ukrainian pro-European movement, Vitali Klitschko, when asked about his attitude to the Ukrainian Nationalist Assembly, openly rejected this discourse by saying "They are not my heroes" (Klitschko 2013). This negative response to the heroization of the Ukrainian Nationalist Movement and criminalization of the Communist Party in the social dimension had a specific negative response from the most ardent advocate of Ukraine in Europe, Poland. Additionally, criminalization of the Communist past, promoted by the pro-European coalition in Ukraine, provoked protests from many Western scholars, who raised concerns about the quality of academic freedom in Ukraine (Marples 2015).

Similarly, the breakaway regions in the east of Ukraine demonstrate the same fragmentation of the social space and regional fracture. One can discern at least three separate successful identity projects deployed in these areas. The first identity project, launched by local opinion makers and spin doctors, NovoRossia (New Russia), drew on Russian imperial history of the nineteenth century. The self-proclaimed Donetsk People's Republic features elements of this discourse on its banner. The second identity project is "people of Donbass," which is linked to the economic uniqueness of the region—that is, its long history of coal mining and heavy industry. This project helps to constitute the east of Ukraine as an independent entity, a value in itself that merits full independence or at least the broadest possible autonomy in Ukraine. Finally, the state symbols of the self-proclaimed Luhansk People's Republic feature a third identity project based on the shared Soviet past with the strenuous effort of industrialization. In addition to the three above-mentioned competing identity projects, one could add several other efforts to constitute the east of Ukraine as a unique community. Some efforts were made when small Russian warlords organized in a local Russian-speaking Cossack militia from Southern Russia with their strong mythology. The list can go on.

This demonstrates that, similar to the above-mentioned institutional dimension, the fragmentation line in the social dimension also runs across time. The pro-independence historical paradigm in today's Ukraine is a product of the Andersonian era of nationalism or—as Robert Cooper put it (2004)—transition from the premodern era of multinational empires to the modern world of nation-states, which deified the nation and its heroes, who gave their blood in the fight for the nation-state. Its implementation can be realized only in serious tension with contemporary postmodern European values embodied by the EU's professing tolerance and respect for national minorities. And again, similar to his pro-Russian and pro-European predecessors, Poroshenko seeks to find solutions that appeal to all constituencies. For example, responding to appeals by the nationalists, Poroshenko announced October 14 as the Defender of Ukraine Day. On the one hand, he appealed to ethnonationalists in Western Ukraine because the decision had a direct allusion to the date when the Ukrainian Insurgent Army was established. On the other, the official presidential decree mentioned that the date of October 14 was chosen for religious reasons and referred to the date of the Intercession of the Theotokos, which has been celebrated by Ukrainians since the sixteenth century (Interfax-Ukraina 2014). This decision shows that even Ukrainian ideology represents a patchwork of long-term and recent history elements stitched together with equivocal symbols and silent allusions.

This is not to say, however, that this pro-independence, ethnonationalist paradigm has been articulated exclusively by Western Ukrainians.[4] First, it should be stressed that significant areas in the east and south of Ukraine have been loci of Ukrainian nationalist history. For example, three major industrial regions in the east centered on Kherson, Zaporizhia, and Dnipropetrovsk (renamed "Dnipro" after the law on decommunization was adopted) are tightly linked to the long-term tradition of the Ukrainian Cossack republics (semiformal military democracies). Significant territories in the south have been territory of the Ukrainian anarchic-communist movement led by Nestor Makhno, who competed with Bolshevik ideology and even created an anarchic protostate in these areas in 1917–21. In contemporary Ukraine, several intellectuals who promoted the "pro-independence paradigm" were born and raised in Central and Eastern Ukraine. One of the leading Ukrainian-speaking mythmakers is the controversial writer and scholar Oksana Zabuzhko, who was born and raised in the east of the country.

Going beyond the East–West dichotomy, one can identify significant Russophone minorities in the south of the country, which present quite a mixed picture in terms of loyalty and identity. While analyzing Crimea, some authors point to its long-term historical connections with Russian imperial history (Kent 2016). On the one hand, Crimea's historical connection is a strong emotional phenomenon related to regional consciousness, thus entailing a sense of belonging to the Russian world (Zimmerbauer and Paasi 2013). On the other hand, the striking example of Odessa, another mostly Russophone South Ukrainian city on the Black Sea coast with strong emotional bonds to Russian imperial glory but that did not generate significant support for pro-Russian separatism, demonstrates that shared history and language is often insufficient to explain significant social phenomena. For a number of years, the local community refused to remove a monument to Russian empress Catherine the Great, who, according to the Ukrainian nationalist history, was one of the murderers of the Ukrainian nation. At the same time, while preserving some symbols of the Russian imperial past, most Odessans did not support the separatist movement in April 2014. The example of Odessa—where commitment to supranational shared history with Russia goes hand in hand with political loyalty to the contemporary Ukrainian state project and European values—further highlights fractures in the Russophone social space of Ukraine. If described in Cooper's terms, some regions of Ukraine represent an example of a postmodern logic: they reject any type of spatially bound ideology (East versus West, Europe versus Russia), refuse to politicize history and language, and stick to consumerism and the ideology of economic liberalism (Cooper 2004).

This is not to say that there is no certain identity consensus subscribed to by a critical mass of Ukrainians. By depicting Russia as a threatening Other, Ukrainians managed to create a certain sentiment of national unity (cutting across ethnic and religious identifications). It remains to be seen how stable such a national unity will be if Russian threats become less imminent. However, even this shallow consensus often faces serious challenges presented by everyday practices that often constitute the very basic and intimate anthropological identity conceptualized by Bourdieu (1990, 52). The tension between the pro-European identity of Ukraine promoted by the current government, on the one hand, and a plethora of everyday practices that often rely on and reproduce a regional post-Soviet identity, on the other, reveal additional fractures inside Ukraine. There are ample examples of the tension between Eurocentric nation-building identity programs promoted by the Ukrainian elite and practices that reconstitute post-Soviet space as a single social entity.[5] For example, even though most of the population agrees with the statement that the country has been invaded by Russia, about half of the Ukrainians consider Russia a fraternal nation (Pravda.com.ua 2016). About a third of the churchgoers of this traditional society still attend Russian Orthodox churches even though the patriarch of Moscow has repeatedly expressed his support of Putin's geopolitical ambitions in Ukraine.

The elite program for new Ukrainian identity faces challenges even in the process of its implementation. For example, the pro-independence discourse invokes several policy measures to protect Ukrainian social space against the "Russian information war." Ukrainian regulatory bodies governing television and radio broadcasts banned a number of Russian TV channels, specific soap operas, and Russian books promoting Russian imperialism. The Ukrainian Ministry of Culture imposed a quota for Ukrainian-language songs obligatory for broadcast by Ukrainian FM stations. At the same time, most of the Ukrainian TV channels and FM radio stations use Russian language heavily in their broadcasts and communications. Many of the Ukrainian media outlets still have to purchase and broadcast a number of Russian or Soviet TV products because the Ukrainian TV industry has not been able to develop the necessary capacity to satisfy the demand for Ukrainian media products. A number of Russian journalists and media managers work in the Ukrainian media. On the other hand, even the most ardent Ukrainian ideologues often have to rely on Soviet themes in nation-building TV projects.[6]

Another striking example of the tension between the regional identity (shared with Russia) and pro-independence drive can be exemplified by two extremely mutually exclusive policy choices. On the one hand, the government of Ukraine adopts a number of measures to prevent further separatist movements or Russian intervention in the east. The government sought to impose constraints on the traffic of goods to and from the occupied territories. On the other hand, it faces moral choices as to how to deal with significant trade and human flows across the demarcation line between the occupied territories in Crimea and the east of Ukraine. Similarly, in the situation in Georgia, a significant number of Ukrainian tourists keep visiting Crimea during their summer holidays, and work migrants from the ethnonationalist region of Western Ukraine keep shuttling between Moscow and Kyiv. This demonstrates that there are a number of fracture lines running across the Ukrainian social space both in terms of representations and practices. Some of these fractures occasionally coincide with certain long history traits but are not identical to them. There are more examples, and they mostly represent a legacy of recent history rather than an essentially culture-based East–West dichotomy.

Overall, a more detailed analysis and conceptualization of identity in the case of Ukraine reveals that the theory of regional fracture can better explain the multitude of political programs, identity projects, and grassroots societal practices. A number of various political programs pursued by various parties and societal players demonstrate that Ukraine is a complex amalgam of various communities that profess different attitudes toward the Russian and Ukrainian languages, shared Soviet past, and European values even within the same region in the south and east of Ukraine. It also reveals significant tensions between the elitists' largely Eurocentric identity project and a plethora of societal practices that constitute Ukraine as a part of the post-Soviet space. The process of permanent negotiations and bargaining between various symbols and markers of European and Soviet identity projects suggests that Ukraine has gone through the difficult process of bridging some regional gaps and fractures, but the process is far from complete and will raise new problems in the immediate future.

Conclusions

The case of Ukraine highlights additional explanatory power of the regional fracture theory. This chapter has shown that it is regional fracture theory—which combines various levels of analysis and focuses on the interplay between various internal actors and external hegemonic forces—that can explain Ukraine's geopolitical dilemma better than Huntingtonian and East–West dichotomies. Drawing on the regional fracture theory, this chapter has shown that Ukraine represents a complex amalgam of several (certainly more than two) communities, elite groups linked to various external hegemonic forces. These links and leverages between different actors are uneven and sporadic (Levitsky and Way 2006), which makes power a sporadic and fluid phenomenon. As a result, regionally relevant outcomes are often defined by contingencies and coincidental combinations of internal and external factors. This "islandness" and fluid nature of power can explain a number of turning moments in contemporary Ukrainian history. For example, regional fracture theory can better explain how Ukrainian independence was gained by the coalition of Ukrainian ethnonationalist and imperial administrative elites as well as by a stronger Russia and weaker Soviet center. Each of the above actors supported the Ukrainian state project, but their later interests did not remain identical.

This fractured nature of Ukraine's independence shaped its political spectrum accordingly and resulted in serious oscillations in internal and foreign policy as well as in the overproduction of formal regional institutions. And these oscillations do not fit into the East–West dichotomy. Some economic elites of Eastern Ukraine supported deeper cooperation with Europe, where their markets were, while others with closer contacts in Russia insisted on a pro-Eurasian trajectory. An informal elite networks and a loose system of nonideological allegiances resulted in unpredictable policies, U-turns, and contradictory signals coming from Ukrainian presidents. On the one hand, Russian elites were dealing mostly through highly corrupt kinship networks and eventually helped Ukrainian elites to mobilize the broader society for mass protests against President Yanukovych. On the other hand, the West also relied on elite networks and could not cope with the mass mobilization taking place in 2013–14. These weak linkages resulted in violent political fragmentation—violent protests that were not controlled by the leaders of the institutional opposition. This obvious unpredictability of outcomes can explain the behavior of the European Union during the Ukraine crisis. Initially, the EU supported Ukraine's right to sign DCFTA, and when Yanukovych decided to freeze the talks, Brussels and Washington acted with great sympathy toward the protesters. However, once it became clear that mass mobilization of Ukrainians could result in Europe's biggest nightmare—state collapse—European negotiators tried to force opposition leaders into signing the deal with Yanukovych. In the current military conflict, both Russia and Europe seek to find their own "islands of power." Moscow still relies on industrialists and pragmatists of the East; Europe seeks support from the liberal politicians and civil society organizations of Central, Western, and Eastern Ukraine.

In the social dimension, the fracture best exemplifies the complexity of the Russian–Ukrainian crisis, which cannot be reduced to an ethnolinguistic conflict or civilizational clash. However, numerous examples of Russophone communities in the east or south of Ukraine fighting against (pro)Russian forces challenge the concept of ethnolinguistic explanation. The same applies to Huntington's concept of the clash of civilizations in Ukraine. According to Huntington, the rift line between Western civilization and Orthodox civilization should run between Western Ukraine and the rest of the country. However, tense relations between Western Ukrainian ethnonationalist activists and their nearest neighbor, Poland, show that currently some of the "pro-European" forces in Ukraine effectively seek to align Ukraine with the nineteenth-century Europe of nation-states and ethnonationalist ideologies. This fact shows that the regional fracture is not an outcome of the East–West dichotomy but rather represents a complex amalgam of long-term and short-term history exercised on a local, national, and regional level.

Notes

1. Even though the two terms are used interchangeably, they are far from identical. For more detail, see Samokhvalov 2015.

2. A "memory policy" is "everything that the state encourages you to remember through textbooks, state-sponsored celebrations, and monuments." See Guixé i Coromines 2016, 12–30.

3. It is worth mentioning that even this fundamental event in contemporary Ukrainian history is an object of discursive contestation here. Some people mark it as "Euromaidan" and construct Ukrainians as a part of the European community. Some others term it "Revolution of Dignity," depicting Ukrainians as a superior and unique nation that has to negotiate with Europe on its own terms.

4. For such an argument and its critique, see, e.g., Molchanov 2015 and Samokhvalov 2016.

5. The Eurocentric nation-building program in Ukraine promoted by elites implies that Ukraine has made its choice in favor of European integration. It admits the normative superiority of European education and living standards, and it aspires to adopt European values and standards in governance, education, and other public spheres.

6. Even in the discursive construction of the new pantheon of heroes, the Ukrainian government heavily relies on Soviet resources. For example, the new video promotion of the Ukrainian Armed Forces relies on intertextual dialogues with Soviet movies about Red Army victories in World War I. See, e.g., "Ukraina: Den Pobedy: Ded," available on YouTube: https://www.youtube.com/watch?v=eQk6UupEJuA; and "Ukraina: Den Pobedy: Babushka," available on YouTube: https://www.youtube.com/watch?v=c3EgHMTDtng.

CHAPTER FOUR

The South Caucasus: Fracture without End?

Laurence Broers

The South Caucasus is the most notoriously fractured of the post-Soviet regions. In the 1990s the region was defined by its exceptionality to what was otherwise a surprisingly peaceful Soviet collapse; in the 2000s it emerged as the epicenter of new collisions between the West and a revived Russia. In 2014 the South Caucasus ceded that dubious honor to Ukraine but remained crosshatched by multiple axes of seemingly indelible fracture. These include multilayered inter- and intrastate conflicts over borders and the contested sovereignty of secessionist territories; intrastate fractures between regimes and societies; geopolitical tensions between the West, Russia, Turkey, and Iran; and transnational spillover from insurgencies in the North Caucasus and Middle East.[1] Ubiquitously framed as a crossroads, major infrastructural linkages built across the region since independence in fact work around, and thereby further embed, significant political fault lines. In the context of many highly asymmetrical power relationships between the region's actors, a complex web-like structure has consistently fed balancing strategies upscaling local fracture to the geopolitical plane. By the same token, opportunities for external powers to insert themselves into local struggles have been plentiful. Discourses of danger, to borrow a term from an academic critique of exaggerated security threats in Central Asia (Heathershaw and Megoran 2011), have too often been vindicated in the South Caucasus by recurrent relapses into violent crisis in 1998, 2004, 2006, 2008, and 2016. At the same time, relentless geopolitical framing of the region's problems obscures the extent to which South Caucasians have regarded their own governments, rather than external threats, as sources of insecurity. In this quintessential fractured region, geopolitical patron-clientelism, the viability of secessionism, and instrumental bilateralism have emerged as alternatives to regionalism.

Whether the South Caucasus can or should be considered a region, and on what basis, is a perennial question in academic and policy literature that has no unequivocal answer. In quest of coherence, several scholars and policymakers have proposed alternative, multiscalar definitions of the Caucasus (see the discussion in German 2012, 23–26). Yet none have taken sufficient hold to exclude an alternative reading of the South Caucasus as a region only by default, a vacuum between other regional complexes, a "negative region" in which interdependence is based on enmity rather than amity (German 2012, 24–25; see also de Waal 2012; Oskanian 2013).

The term "South Caucasus" emerged in the 1990s as a politically correct alternative to "Transcaucasia," a term burdened by being a translation of the Russian Zakavkaz'e ("on the other side of the Caucasus"). Nevertheless, this linguistic reframing cannot escape the fact that it is only in imperial geographies that the regional boundedness of the South Caucasus is self-evident. The European conquest of a Middle Eastern frontier (Swietochowski 1995, vii), and Russia's penetration of areas to the south of the Caucasus mountain range supplanted a prior, highly durable division of the area into contiguous peripheries of the Ottoman Empire and Persia dating back to the sixteenth century. To the southwest, territories would continue to change hands as Russian and Ottoman armies fought repeatedly up to World War I. To the southeast, Persia was more permanently removed: a stable new frontier along the Araz River established in the treaties of Gulistan (1813) and Turkmenchay (1828) delineates the southern borders of Azerbaijan and Armenia to this day. These borders do not, however, encompass historical understandings of either nation. "Western Armenia" and "Southern Azerbaijan," respectively, remain resonant conceptualizations of territory beyond a bounded South Caucasian space or identity. To the north, the great natural barrier of the Caucasus Mountains divides the restive Russian North Caucasus from Georgia, a short-lived local hegemon in the Middle Ages whose capital, Tbilisi, was later the regional center under Russian imperial rule. North and south of the Caucasus Mountains the region's proverbial ethnolinguistic diversity lives on, testament to the historical fragility of political incorporation by either imperial or indigenous states.

In the twentieth century, the South Caucasus experienced two moments of unity in the contexts of imperial collapse and regeneration. In April 1918 the Transcaucasian Democratic Federative Republic was cast adrift from revolutionary Russia and lasted only a month before separate Georgian, Azerbaijani, and Armenian republics were declared. Delimiting national homelands resulted in a succession of violent territorial conflicts. Annexed two years later by the nascent Soviet state, the three republics were reconstituted according to the templates of Soviet ethnofederalism; conflicts in Georgia and Azerbaijan were resolved through the establishment of autonomous republics or regions. All were collected into the Transcaucasian Socialist Federative Soviet Republic (usually known by its Russian acronym, ZSFSR) for fourteen years before being definitively divided into separate Armenian, Azerbaijani, and Georgian republics, the latter two featuring five autonomous units between them.[2] Hence, when the Soviet Union collapsed in 1991, there was no indigenous regional tradition for the South Caucasus to go back to. There were only imperial geographies and the historically ephemeral, violently contested, and ideologically problematic traditions (all were socialist in outlook) of the 1918–21 era of national republics.

In the light of this history, two planes of fracture—by no means mutually exclusive—have dominated contemporary scholarly and policy analysis of the South Caucasus. One is the legacy of Soviet institutionalization of national-territorial units, which, in accordance with wider Soviet practice, established national homelands for territorialized "titular" nationalities. Unlike in most other areas, however, by annexing the short-lived republics of Armenia, Azerbaijan, and Georgia in 1920–21, the Soviet Union inherited societies that were both ethnically diverse and ethnonationally mobilized after the violent contestation of borders during their brief independence. The Soviet solution to this issue was to deploy autonomous institutions as a means to resolve prior conflict between majority and minority groups (Saparov 2015). The correlation of these autonomies with ethnoterritorial conflict in the 1990s has led to considerable analytical emphasis on territorial autonomy as a source of post-Soviet conflict (the classic argument on this is Cornell 2002). While this correlation appears to hold true for the conflicts in Abkhazia, South Ossetia, and Nagorny Karabakh, other scholars have questioned the causal primacy of autonomy relative to other variables such as prior histories of violence, demographic fear, the nature of majority nationalisms, and the modalities of elite incorporation (e.g., Saparov 2015; Welt 2004; Broers 2009). Nevertheless, the Soviet delimitation established Georgia and Azerbaijan as internally fractured spaces with institutionalized minority identities and elites in Abkhazia and South Ossetia (in Georgia) and in Nagorny Karabakh (in Azerbaijan), strongly oriented toward neighboring republics (Russia and Armenia, respectively). These mobilized in the late 1980s to mount militarily successful challenges resulting in the horizontal fractures of Georgia and Azerbaijan in 1992–94 that have persisted to this day, often gathered under the unsatisfactory rubric of "frozen conflicts."

A second plane of fracture on which contemporary readings of the South Caucasus turn is the competition among extraregional actors for hegemony. As a multifacing periphery sandwiched between a former colonial metropole (Russia), two regional powers (Turkey and Iran, both also historical metropoles), and the less geographically immediate but normatively influential West, the South Caucasus has been exposed to a proliferation of externally generated regional initiatives.

The August war in South Ossetia in 2008 crystallized the collision between the post–Cold War expansion of Western-led regionalism and Russian aspirations to hegemony in an area (its "near abroad") construed as a zone of privileged Russian interest (for diverse readings of geopolitical competition in the South Caucasus, see, e.g., Cornell and Starr 2009; Asmus 2009; Suny 2010; Toal 2017; Kamrava 2017; Hunter 2017). For many observers, including many in the region, the geopolitical plane of fracture is preeminent and has been powerfully reinforced by the outbreak of Russian–Ukrainian conflict in 2014 and the emergence of a new "frozen conflict" in Eastern Ukraine. In this view, we have been witnessing what is in some ways a return to Cold War patterns in which "smaller states became victims of the larger conflict" (Sakwa 2012, 77). There is nevertheless through these debates the risk of a reductive and circular argument attributing regional fracture to external forces. Tabloid tropes of "Russia's/Putin's frozen conflicts" streamline contextually varied situations into an easily recognized unicausal storyline with undue reifications of Russia's motives and capacities through time and space. In the South Caucasus this monotonic interpretation of geopolitics homogenizes the past as Caucasian events of the 1990s are rescripted according to the templates of 2010s Ukraine.

The experience of other world regions shows that ethnoterritorial conflict can be overcome and is neither necessary nor sufficient to sustain regional fracture. Balkan fracture has outlasted ethnoterritorial violence. While Central Asia has generally to date defied (exaggerated) expectations of large-scale violence, fracture remains deep (see chapters 6 and 7, this volume). Ethnoterritorial conflict thus has a contingent, rather than predetermined, relationship with regional fracture. The much-used conceit of "geopolitical pawns," a post–Cold War iteration of the "captive nation" trope, imposes a hegemon's gaze upon flattened terrains divested of local detail or purposeful agents. As Kirsten Williams, Steven Lobell, and Neal Jesse (2012) remind us, small states do not always bend before hegemons. Georgia has consistently opted to balance against the external power that could most obviously support it to restore its territorial integrity—Russia (Oskanian 2016). Armenia's bandwagoning with Russia has been halfhearted at best (Delcour 2014), while Azerbaijan has sought to avoid bandwagoning when doing so could arguably have strengthened its hand in the conflict with Armenia. There are implicit questions here regarding what I refer to as the "multilateralist calculus" of South Caucasian elites, that is, how they assess the value of regionalism and how, as small states usually in asymmetrical relationships, they shape and use the wiggle room available to them.

While all of the South Caucasian states are small, they are typically also qualified as weak. The weak-state literature offers a different perspective on regional fracture, stressing informal structures and actors, on the one hand, and the performance of power over implementation of policy, on the other (Koehler and Zürcher

2003; Zürcher 2007; Ohanyan 2015; Heathershaw and Schatz 2017). Armenian, Azerbaijani, and Georgian elites were all factionalized by informal networks, generating syndromes of state weakness during the chaos and conflict of the 1990s (see Wheatley and Zürcher 2008 for an overview). Regional gross domestic products per capita (Armenia, $3,500; Azerbaijan, $5,496; and Georgia, $3,796 in current 2016 USD) remain comparatively low by post-Soviet standards.[3] Moreover, respective resource endowments are not reflected in correspondingly differentiated human development indices. In the UN Development Programme's Human Development Index, in 2015 the three countries ranked close together within a score range of 0.769–0.743, with Georgia attaining the highest and Armenia the lowest position.[4] These rankings put the South Caucasian republics among the lower performers in postsocialist Eurasia. Ethnoterritorial and geopolitical fractures explain neither the leveling in performance among the three South Caucasian states nor their poor overall governance relative to other post-Soviet and postsocialist peers. These outcomes point instead to the impacts of further layers of intrastate fracture, to which the next section turns.

The Elusive Singularity of the State

Although typically framed as a product of external influence, contemporary South Caucasian resistance to regional cohesion is equally rooted in domestic practices of power. Jarring with the presumed weakness of South Caucasian states is the apparent resilience of the informal networks underpinning their regimes, which in both Azerbaijan and Armenia have held power continuously since the 1990s. Variously rooted in Soviet, regional, kinship, transnational, and wartime networks (or combinations thereof), these informal solidarity groups form alternative grids of power cutting vertically across the formal institutions of government. Numerous concepts have been devised to understand the interactions between formal and informal structures. Comparative analysis has drawn parallels with the African "shadow state" to discuss manifestations of post-Soviet state weakness, including the Caucasus (Beissinger and Young 2002; see also Schlichte 2017). Other scholars have drawn on the concept of the "dual state," that is, informal, networked "prerogative states" (see Fraenkel [1941] 2017) or "state spaces" (cf. Lefebvre 2009) that are nested within and circumvent, colonize, or simply override the formal constitutional order constructed around Western liberal-democratic templates (Sakwa 2010, 2012, 2013; Lewis 2017). The concept of neopatrimonialism, signifying a traditional mode of patrimonial authority coupled with the scale, institutions, and capacities of the modern state, has been applied to the South Caucasus, especially Azerbaijan (e.g., Safiyev 2016). A less normatively connoted concept of informality rejecting linear expectations of modernization has also sought to salvage informal politics from an exclusive association with corruption, nepotism, and dysfunction (e.g., Rekhviashvili and Polese 2017).

The contours of the "dual state" differ across South Caucasian states. Armenia's informal regime maps onto broader physical and discursive conceptualizations of Armenian statehood, embracing the secessionist entity in Nagorny Karabakh, the adjacent occupied territories, Armenian business interests in Russia, offshore holdings, and sources of funding and advocacy in the diaspora (Lewis 2017; Panossian 2001). This structure is a source of constant fracture since the Armenian political elite is networked across a framework that is not territorially or institutionally coextensive with the de jure Armenian state. Armenia's fractured spaces, and the legitimacy of the elite that binds them, are predicated on a wartime spatial imaginary challenging the formal borders of the state (Broers and Toal 2013). Azerbaijan's dual state emerged at the nexus of Soviet-era informal regional "clans" and the country's post-Soviet oil and gas wealth. Azerbaijan developed along the lines of a post-Soviet rentier state, entailing a highly centralized decision-making structure, operating informally as what some have called a "sultanistic" regime clustered around a small number of networked factions (Guliyev 2005, 2012). Azerbaijan's informal regime worked through an elaborate offshore architecture and secured societal compliance through rent-based public expenditure programs and showcase development projects (Franke, Gawrich, and Alakbarov 2009; Kendall-Taylor 2012; Altstadt 2017, 113–26). Georgia's trajectory differs from its neighbors through the tenuous, reversible yet tangible capacity of the constitutional order to impose itself on the neopatrimonial system inherited from the 1990s. Under President Eduard Shevardnadze, the Georgian government was unable to contain alliances between disaffected elite factions and a Western-trained civil society. This alliance came to power in the 2003–4 Rose Revolution by leveraging divergence from Western normative expectations of good governance (Wheatley 2005; Mitchell 2009; Welt 2010a). Yet these expectations were hardly met by the reinforcement of presidential powers, weakening of the judiciary, and human rights violations that followed the Rose Revolution (Wheatley and Zürcher 2008, 24–27). Informal governance subsequently crept back into Georgian politics because the revolutionary government's liberal agenda was unable to cope with the social costs of marketization and political-economic crisis (Rekhviashvili and Polese 2017; Slade 2017).

The resilience of informal regimes in the South Caucasus has resulted in an enduring source of fracture in two cross-cutting realms of contested politics: the visible, formal realm of government/opposition contestation through political parties, civil societies, and elections, and the invisible, informal realm of intra-elite factional struggles. All South Caucasian states have seen intense contested politics, with outcomes reflecting the nature and means of the informal regime in each case. With occasional but serious bursts of political violence (for example, in 1996, 2003–4, and 2008, when ten protesters were killed as postelectoral demonstrations were put down), the Armenian elite has been able to contain advocates of the constitutional order—civil society, nongovernmental organizations (NGOs), and "self-determined citizens" (Ishkanian 2015). Debilitating migration has also eased domestic tensions while deepening the long-standing fracture between territory and people in Armenian history. Azerbaijan's oil wealth enabled a political economy of persuasion rather than coercion over the decade-long oil boom of 2006–16, tolerating a politically ineffectual but demonstratively visible opposition (LaPorte 2015). Over time, however, the interests of regime security have been served by an incremental convergence of constitutional and prerogative principles of power. Through the abolition (in 2009) and extension (in 2016) of presidential terms in constitutional referendums, the distance between constitutional and prerogative principles of power has been significantly narrowed (Welt 2014; Altstadt 2017). This has the effect of obviating invocations of the constitution as an alternative and, hence, challenge to prerogative power. In Georgia, again the pattern is substantively different. The realms of intra-elite and government-opposition contestation have converged to a greater extent, generating a pattern of "feckless pluralism": a fluid two-level game, one involving an intra-elite contest to define the power flows within the constitutional state, and the second level engaging the electorate within the contested terms of the constitution (Berglund 2014). Even if itself founded on an unconstitutional power transition in 2003–4, Georgia's constitutional state, if incompletely, contestably, and reversibly so, imposed itself on prerogative power.

These struggles between constitutional and prerogative principles of political authority, wired differently in each case, are symptomatic of the elusive singularity of the South Caucasian state, whose formal institutions fall far short of a monopoly on the patterns and principles of the distribution of power in society. While mediating the salience of vertical fractures within outwardly coherent state structures, the nature of these struggles is also an important determinant of South Caucasian elites' multilateralist calculus and their attitudes toward the kinds of goods or goals that regionalism can deliver.

Hegemonic Regionalisms in the South Caucasus: Profusion and Collision

The construction of sovereign national identities and the impacts of 1990s secessionist conflicts starkly valorized the historical and contemporary roles of external powers in the South Caucasus. There is no consensus on the role of the former metropolitan power, Russia, and no coherent postcolonial regional identity. On the contrary, the postcolonial frame is deeply divisive. Georgia actively embraced a postcolonial identity, opening the Museum of the Soviet Occupation in Tbilisi in 2006, which unequivocally equates Soviet rule with imperialism (for a different perspective, see Scott 2017), and self-identifying with the West. Despite being the region's leading anti-Soviet rebel in the late 1980s, sovereignty, re-exposure to a historically troubled relationship with Turkey, and the need to sustain territorial gains in Nagorny Karabakh reactivated a traditional Armenian proclivity to balancing with Russia for security. In Azerbaijan the initial embrace of a Turcophil postcolonial identity was rapidly tempered by the return to power of the prior Soviet leadership in 1993; since then, Azerbaijan has avoided leveraging a postcolonial identity in the quest for autarchy in a world of competing hegemons.

These fundamentally distinct appreciations of the historical roles of external actors have meshed with a profusion of both local and externally led regional initiatives. Although some of these sought to promote cooperation at a wider regional level, the majority has upscaled the contours of local fracture to the geopolitical plane, constructing an incoherent structure of extraregional linkages reinforcing regional fracture. With the exception of the EU-funded Regional Environmental Center (Ohanyan 2015, 166) and a very small number of initiatives brokered by NGOs, there are no regional formats bringing the three governments, let alone secessionist entities, together. Yet the South Caucasus has been a region of institutional proliferation, with multiple regional initiatives appearing since the early 2000s. What is the logic of this institutional density?

Institutional proliferation has passed through several stages in the post-Soviet South Caucasus. In an initial, residual phase, all three South Caucasian states entered the Russian-led Commonwealth of Independent States (CIS)—Georgia and Azerbaijan under duress at times of deep domestic crises in 1993. After a degree of consolidation of state power had taken place, a second phase of local experimentation began. In 1997 the GU(U)AM group (Georgia, Ukraine, Uzbekistan—which later exited the group, reverting the group's name to GUAM—Azerbaijan, and Moldova) formed as a pro-Western balancing foil to the CIS. The three South Caucasian states were among the founding members of the Organization of the Black Sea Economic Cooperation. The onset of color revolutions augured a new utility to regional cooperation as mutual reinforcement among pro-Western "revolutionary" governments. Post-2005 a "Rose-Orange axis" between Georgia and Ukraine reinvigorated GUAM and yielded a second structure, the Community of Democratic Choice (CDC). Although drawing on the popular legitimacy of color revolutionaries, GUAM and the CDC remained elite-led alliances for mutual reinforcement of small powers, with neither institutional depth nor the involvement of significant outside powers. From the mid-2000s these efforts gave way to a third phase of competitive bloc regionalism, as both the European Union (EU) and a revived Russia increasingly invested in institutionalized regional ties as vehicles for projecting presence and power into the region.

Western initiatives to promote regional cooperation in the South Caucasus were beset by a chicken-and-egg dynamic between a lack of clear strategic vision for the region among Western collective actors and variable receptivity to Western-led regional schemes among local actors. As a result, there is a profusion of Western regional formats and policy platforms present in the South Caucasus, operating at bespoke levels with individual states that embed fracture rather than dilute it through inclusivity. Western policies toward the South Caucasus were slow to develop, given the lack of a unified foreign and security policy and Balkan priorities in the 1990s, and were initially framed as infrastructural initiatives, such as the EU-TRACECA transport corridor. In addition to being members of the Organization for Security and Co-operation in Europe, all three states acceded to the Council of Europe in 1999 (Georgia) and 2001 (Armenia and Azerbaijan). The North Atlantic Treaty Organization (NATO) also promoted cooperation through the three states' inclusion in the North Atlantic Cooperation Council (later renamed the Euro-Atlantic Partnership Council in 1997) and the Partnership for Peace. The EU was slow to conceptualize and activate a regional policy for the South Caucasus (Delcour 2011; Sasse 2013). The region was mentioned only in a footnote in the EU's initial communication of its European Neighbourhood Policy (ENP) in 2003. This was amended in 2004 when the three states were incorporated into the ENP, but the absence of membership perspectives limited the extent to which a "thicker" socialization into a European regional project was possible. This was addressed in the next iteration of EU regional policy in the South Caucasus, the Eastern Partnership (EaP), which included an explicit conditionality component requiring approximation with the EU *acquis* (Tarkhan-Mouravi 2014). In the form of the association agreements, the EU offered a normative regime focused on technical and economic integrations, implying a relatively thick, multisector level of institutionalization, as expressed in compliance with the Deep and Comprehensive Free Trade Area. Central to the EU template for neighboring states to integrate with it was a normative emphasis on identity transformation importing into the South Caucasus a European concept of a liberal security community underpinned by democratization, the rule of law, market liberalization, and security cooperation (Simão 2018).

Russia's linkages and levers by which to pull its peripheries into Russian-led regional initiatives vary by region. In the South Caucasus, Russian-led regionalism has, on the one hand, been contained by South Caucasian elites' concern to preserve sovereignty vis-à-vis Moscow but, on the other, enabled by the desires of the winners of 1990s territorial conflicts to preserve their gains. Several scholars have argued that Russia's position is one of limited structural power (Averre 2009) or "constrained primacy" (Sussex 2012). Rather than thick or genuinely multilateral institutions, Russia has sought weaker associations in combination with more robust bilateral agreements where its leverage can be applied—for example, in the fields of energy and military cooperation. The logic to Russian-led regional institutions, such as the

CIS; the Eurasian Economic Community and its successor, the Eurasian Economic Union (EEU); and the Collective Security Treaty Organization, is not to provide for hard integration but to provide a multilateral gloss to bilateral asymmetries and create bloc-based bargaining power vis-à-vis Western structures. For their members, a key pay-off is protective, sector-specific integration for authoritarian regimes through "virtual regionalism" (Allison 2008b) or the preservation of extant authoritarian political orders through a cooperative but illiberal regionalism (see chapter 6, this volume). Russian-led structures have consequently provided insulation against the good governance agenda in a normatively entrepreneurial form of regionalism compatible with and, indeed, focused on regime security (Popescu 2006b).

The competitive aspect to the EU–Russian dynamic has lent itself to a series of often value-laden dichotomies between "Europeanization" / "sovereignty," benign normative power / malign structural power, "Europe" / "spheres of influence," and so on. While such dichotomies are undoubtedly prone to unhelpful reification (as argued by, e.g., Berg and Mölder 2014), numerous scholars have usefully identified the contrasting qualities of the bloc regionalisms being advanced (Averre 2009; Simão 2018). Put simply, two textures of hegemonic regionalism come into contact in the South Caucasus: a Russian-led variant of institutionally thin, normatively flexible, and sectorally concentrated regionalism, and a European-led regionalism that is institutionally thick, normatively conditional, and sectorally inclusive. This collision has intersected with the outcomes of both 1990s sovereignty wars and domestic struggles between prerogative and constitutional principles of power to entrench and embellish fracture, drawing neighboring states into competing regional blocs and their associated logics of regionalism.

Since the early 1990s Armenia's multilateralist calculus has been confined by the regional isolation resulting from a Turkish–Azerbaijani blockade and the need to maintain the security of the de facto jurisdiction in Nagorny Karabakh. Combined with a strong European outlook and an initially strong commitment to democratization, Armenia developed a demand for multivectored regional integrations. This generated a foreign policy outlook parsed by the Armenian elite as complementarity (Iskandaryan 2013, 6–8) but that could also be interpreted as a reflection of the clashing interests of prerogative and constitutional configurations of power in Armenia. Repeated efforts to reduce Armenia's isolation have been unsuccessful, whether through lobbying for inclusion in infrastructural projects, the failed Turkish-Armenian rapprochement of 2009–2010, or aligning with the EU. In September 2013 President Serzh Sargsyan succumbed in Moscow to a coerced repudiation of an already negotiated association agreement with the EU in favor of joining Russia's rival EEU bloc. This geographically counterintuitive outcome embeds fracture, since Armenia shares no border with any other member of the EEU customs union, while its longest open border is with Georgia, which did sign its association agreement with the EU. Armenian exceptionality within the EEU was also signaled by the identification of nine hundred commodity groups as needing exemptions in early talks (Delcour and Wolczuk 2015, 504). Yet concerns over contiguity and compliance ignore the thin and normatively forgiving nature of Russian-led regional integration; Armenian integration into the EEU is compatible with both a deepening bilateral relationship with Russia and the preservation of the Armenian elite's prerogative power. Deepening domestic fractures count among the costs of Armenia's Eurasian integration, however—notably in the fraught cohabitation between a liberal civil society and an oligarchic economic order played out in repeated confrontations on the streets of Yerevan (see Andreasyan and Derluguian 2015).

On the right side of the international normative consensus against secession, for Georgia, as the only South Caucasian state with access to the open sea and bearing a historically deep European orientation untempered by a narrative of Russia as liberator, participation in Western-led regionalism was a normative, structural, and ideological possibility. But if a European orientation in Georgia has no serious alternatives (Tarkhan-Mouravi 2014, 65), for two decades Europe itself had few policy options, and certainly not membership, to channel it. Georgia's Westernization drive was channeled instead into two other directions: an emphasis on security integration with the West via NATO, and a heavier emphasis on the bilateral relationship with the US (see below). These appeared to offer more than a gradualist relationship with the EU that gave no clear accession perspective and watered down Georgia's commitment to normative regionalism by situating the country within wider rubrics such as the ENP, alongside countries with no credible intent to thicken multilateral ties. The advent of the EaP changed this situation: signing an association agreement in 2013, Georgia had the opportunity to participate in some sectoral EU institutions, heralding a potentially significant scope for modernization and normative penetration. This was tied explicitly to a possible membership perspective at the Riga EaP summit in 2015. To be sure, normative penetration has been uneven—there is evidence that Georgia "cherry-picks" the spheres of accountability that are most compatible with the limited exercise of informal power (Bolkvadze 2016). Yet the margin of Western normative penetration in Georgia is unique in the South Caucasus. Advocates of this penetration make explicit their belief in the connection between rules-based relations and the sovereign survival of small states like Georgia (Sabanadze 2016). But while Georgia may engage its neighbors in bilateral and trilateral frameworks of regional cooperation in sector-specific fields, where the thicker ties of more political regional integration are concerned, the country has no partners in its immediate neighborhood.

Azerbaijan remains the region's outlier in terms of participation in regional initiatives. Internationalization of Azerbaijan's two predominant policy fields, energy development, and the Armenian–Azerbaijani mediation process informed an early rhetorical commitment by the country's elite to a "balanced" foreign policy with a pro-Western tint. Once oil windfalls began to enter the economy, however, the Azerbaijani elite increasingly advocated an "independent foreign policy," effectively avoiding the geopolitics of European or Eurasian alignment. Instead, Azerbaijan demonstrated an interest in plural but shallow memberships of regional cooperation initiatives. In addition to securing numerous memberships, chairs, and roles within the United Nations Security Council; the United Nations Educational, Scientific, and Cultural Organization; the Council of Europe; and the Organization of the Islamic Conference, Azerbaijan acquired full membership of the Non-Aligned Movement in May 2011, applied for observer status at the Shanghai Cooperation Organisation in February 2015 (see Altstadt 2017, 227–28), and the same year began negotiating a strategic partnership agreement with the EU. This strategy substantiates Azerbaijani exceptionalism vis-à-vis multiple normative frames. It moderates the applicability of a Western normativity to Azerbaijan through the consistent message that Azerbaijan is not entirely Western. This allows a flexible strategy of substitution among different normative frameworks and their representatives at key junctures, such as the deployment of "friendly" observation missions at election time. This works both ways, as Azerbaijan is simultaneously able to distance itself from Islamist or Eurasianist discourses when necessary, underlining the utility to regime security of thin, plural memberships resistant to deeper normative, cultural, or geopolitical penetrations. This is reflected in an ever-shifting rhetorical climate, in which different regime figures cultivate essentially pro-Western or pro-Russian policy lines in a discursive pattern continually relativizing Azerbaijan's relationship with any one bloc. As oil rents and the associated political economy of persuasion decline, Azerbaijan would appear to be a candidate for participation in the sort of illiberal regionalism visible in Central Asia: a framework for regional cooperation rooted in authoritarian, not liberal, models of political order (see chapter 6, this volume). But an Azerbaijani path to illiberal regional integration is encumbered by both the lack of partners for such a project in the South Caucasus itself and archrival Armenia's own participation in Russian-led regional schemes.

In sum, regional fracture in the contemporary South Caucasus is reproduced at the meeting point of the domestic politics of regime security, the differing textures of hegemonic regionalism offered or imposed by extraregional actors, and the vested interests sunken into the outcomes of 1990s secessionist conflicts. As a group, the South Caucasian states are able to participate only in the thinnest forms of multilateral initiative. Multiple layers of mutual repulsion—between belligerents in territorial conflicts, between prerogative and constitutional principles of power, between the competing rationales of hegemonic regionalisms, and between normative regionalism and prerogative regimes dependent on discretionary authority—converge and diverge in contingent ways to prevent the emergence of the South Caucasus as a *locally* relevant geopolitical formation.

Alternatives to Regionalism: Bilateralism and Entrepreneurial Fracture

In the absence of a multilateralist calculus advancing regional cooperation, South Caucasian elites have deployed alternative strategies. Two alternatives to a regional fabric have been particularly pronounced over the quarter century since independence: that of "special relationships" in bilateral formats with other states and that of the entrepreneurial fracture of the region's de facto states.

Bilateralism

In place of networked regional ties, it is bilateral special relationships that have dominated South Caucasian linkages and flows. The contours of the Armenian–Russian, Azerbaijani–Turkish, and Georgian–US relationships have differed significantly, cueing variable and inconsistent integrations in distinct, extraregional directions. But in each case, these asymmetrical relationships have been founded on a set of emotive geopolitical storylines situating the geostrategic predicament of the smaller power within broader geopolitical discourses resonant with, and even sponsored by, the larger one. Each of these positive bilateral relationships also interacts with a negative alter ego, the existence and content of which provide foundational narratives in the geopolitical cultures of South Caucasian states and are primal drivers of bilateral attraction. The Georgian–Russian, the Armenian–Turkish, and the Azerbaijani–Iranian relationships constitute orbits of gravitational repulsion—although, again, content and degree differ significantly in each case. These relationships both drive South Caucasian states to seek alternative, extraregional patrons and mire them within the complexities of the evolving relations between their chosen bilateral allies, some of them far from the region and their immediate neighbors.

Armenia's relationship with Russia massively outweighs the country's relations and linkages in any other direction, and, indeed, Armenia's participation in Russian-led integration projects is largely a fictive superstructure to this core bilateral relationship. The relationship is to some extent rooted in the synergy between salient storylines in the geopolitical cultures of each party—that is, great power "rescue fantasies" (Toal 2017, 13, 52) and a buffer state needing "rescue" (Panossian 2006, 117, 189–94; Mirzoyan 2010, 22; Lehman 2011, 502–3). Yet over the course of Armenia's independence, this asymmetry has taken on material reality through Russia's deep penetration of the Armenian military, industrial, and other strategic sectors through debt-for-assets waiver schemes (Mirzoyan 2010, 46–48) as well as the leverage represented by the very substantial Armenian migrant worker population in Russia. An estimated one and a half million Armenians have left the country since independence, more than 90 percent of them to Russia (Hayrapetyan 2017). Crucially, the Armenian–Russian bilateral relationship is so deep as to circumscribe the potentials for Armenia to determine the shape and content of its other bilateral relationships. This is notably the case with Iran, a state with which Armenia has consistently sought to develop a bilateral relationship, yet with ambiguous practical results (Giragosian 2015). Armenian–Russian asymmetry is framed as a necessary evil to "secure" Nagorny Karabakh against a wealthy and re-arming Azerbaijan. Yet the fact that Russia is both the source, as Azerbaijan's primary arms supplier, and salvation from this existential threat attaches a racketeering quality to Russian security guarantees. Russia's security racket may ultimately be self-defeating in that it drives skepticism in many domestic assessments of Armenia's relationship with Russia, especially in the aftermath of the April 2016 escalation of violence in Nagorny Karabakh (Broers 2016b, 13). Rising "Eurasia-skepticism" in Armenia decries and mobilizes against an already "growing conceptual conflict between normative requirements and security needs" (Mirzoyan 2010, 53).

The strongest bilateral relationship, in the sense of being the only one that has generated a multilateral dynamic both independent and reinforcing of it, is that between Azerbaijan and Turkey. In its patterning across a trilateral axis including Georgia, this set of relationships represents the high-water mark of regional cooperation in the South Caucasus. The Azerbaijani–Turkish relationship was initially premised in the early 1990s on a certain euphoria accompanying Turkey's discovery of a Turkic world in the post-Soviet space, reciprocated by the pan-Turkist euphoria of the Azerbaijani national movement. This was expressed in the emotive but obscurantist formula of "one nation, two states," actually uttered by Heydar Aliyev in 1995 when the congruence of the two states' interests was no longer taken for granted (Ismayilov and Graham 2016). Practically, the structural landscape of interaction has been dominated by the energy sector to the detriment of almost all others, resulting in a "gross under-institutionalisation of bilateral contact outside the demands of the energy sector" (Ismayilov 2016, 11). Yet, by its nature, this bilateral agenda necessitated a trilateral approach and was technically inconceivable without Georgia's participation. If trilateralism was initially a transnational outgrowth of Turkish–Azerbaijani ties, it subsequently developed into an autonomous process feeding back into and reinforcing ties between the three states. Trilateralism is now "an organic aspect of the three states' national interests" (Cecire 2016, 77), embodying an economic relationship between energy producer, transit state, and downstream consumer/distributor. Regional infrastructure—notably the Baku–Tbilisi–Ceyhan oil pipeline, the Baku–Tbilisi–Erzurum gas pipeline, and the Baku–Tbilisi–Akhalkalaki–Kars railway—traces this axis but no longer defines its extent. Turkey and Azerbaijan have ranked as two of the most important sources of foreign direct investment in Georgia, Turkish and Azerbaijani citizens topped visitors to Georgia in 2010–11, and Georgian citizens even emerged as a fifth-largest group visiting Turkey in 2010–12 (Cecire 2016, 79). Azerbaijan's State Oil Company (SOCAR) is the largest single investor in Turkey, and its subsidiary in Georgia, SOCAR Georgia Petroleum, became the largest single taxpayer and investor in that country in 2009 (Ismayilov 2014, 85). Turkish–Azerbaijani bilateral ties have expanded beyond the energy sector, embracing education, student exchanges, sponsorship of mosques, business operations, and Turkish media in Azerbaijan (Balci 2013; Ismayilov 2016). These trends are indicative of growing regional interdependency, yet attempts to add geopolitical content, notably through Turkey's 2008 Caucasus Stability and Cooperation Platform, have not taken root. Moreover, even if Turkish–Azerbaijani ties have grown thicker, they are not normatively insulated from vicissitudes in regime dynamics, as the repercussions against various Turkish-sponsored but nongovernmental educational institutes in Azerbaijan following official accusations against "Gülenist" circles in Turkey in 2014–16 show (Bedford 2016).

Although Georgia's Western orientation has been a core moment of consensus in both nation building and foreign policy discourse since the mid-1990s, the weight of the US versus Europe in this orientation has shifted over time. As Gerard Toal argues, the post–Cold War Georgia–US relationship was structured around a set of geopolitical storylines cleverly situating Georgia's territorial fragmentation and geostrategic predicament within broader geopolitical discourses resonant with prominent self-understandings in the US policy community (Toal 2017, ch. 3). Presidents Shevardnadze and Mikheil Saakashvili effectively sold a particular geopoliticization of Georgia to US foreign policy constituencies that reflected (and flattered) the latter's own aspirations, whether these were readings of Georgia as a victim of imperialism, a critical geostrategic pivot, or a beacon of democracy. Extremely successful in procuring US aid and security support, the relationship reached its apogee after 2004 in the heavily personalized chemistry between Presidents Saakashvili and George W. Bush, and the conjunction between the Rose Revolution and the US freedom agenda. The Georgia–US relationship underwent significant adjustment as a result of the August war in 2008 (Mitchell and Cooley 2010), a different personal relationship between Presidents Saakashvili and Barack Obama, and domestic change that brought the still pro-Western but more pragmatic Georgian Dream government to power. Although Georgia–US ties remain close, patron–client bilateralism as the dominant vector in Georgia's Western orientation has given way to other vectors in regional cooperation: association with the EU, cooperation with NATO (which opened a training center in Georgia in 2015), and participation in the Azerbaijani–Turkish axis, all of which can be seen as a maturation from affective to more strategic geopolitics.

Entrepreneurial Fracture: The De Facto States

The existence of three de facto states is the most visible form of fracture in the South Caucasus, and is often exaggerated as its most significant.[5] Rooted in the nested territorialities with which the early Soviet state sought to resolve inherited ethnic conflict, all feature formally institutionalized state political structures (presidencies, parliaments, political parties, and so on) and claim sovereignty as independent states. They form part of an archipelago of exceptional spaces across the former Soviet south and west, including Transnistria, Crimea, Donetsk, and Luhansk (Lynch 2004; Broers 2013; Broers, Iskandaryan, and Minasyan 2015; O'Loughlin, Kolossov, and Toal 2015; Ó Beacháin, Comai, and Tsurtsumia-Zurabishvili 2016). Western actors and intergovernmental agencies have experimented with minimal forms of engagement with these entities under rubrics such as "engagement without recognition." Generally, however, they have been isolated, and informal patterns of engagement—for example, through diasporas—dominate their external relations (Frear 2014).

De facto states sustain and embed fracture in various ways. They physically and demographically fracture the region. Their formation through war in the 1990s involved the destruction of prior social and economic ties that had connected—if not fully integrated—these spaces with their base republics. Previous corridors of connectivity, such as the Enguri River in the south of Abkhazia, the Tskhinvali-Gori Road, and the foothills connecting Karabakh to the plains of central Azerbaijan, were displaced by new configurations of hardened borders, alternative resource flows, and entrepreneurs of fracture in the form of de facto elites (Prelz Oltramonti 2015, 2016). In the case of Abkhazia and especially South Ossetia, entrepreneurs of fracture could also be found among Georgian elites collaborating in criminalized syndicates profiting from the transit of goods across de facto space (Kukhianidze, Kupatadze, and Gotsiridze 2004). With time, Abkhazia and Nagorny Karabakh in particular became progressively more embedded as societies separate from their former base states, reifying new political and human geographies on which they had been built. By the same token, these entities institutionalized the demographic fractures of mass forced displacements in the 1990s (Dale 2001; Toal and Frichova Grono 2011; Conciliation Resources 2011; Lundgren 2016). In South Ossetia a different context prevailed. This entity's spatial context of a patchwork of rival sovereignties populated by intermingled Ossetian and Georgian communities made it more vulnerable to external interventions. These ultimately resulted, in conjunction with a host of other factors, in the August war of 2008 (Welt 2010b; George 2010; Toal 2017).

De facto states, whether directly or indirectly, also provide key entry nodes for the penetration of the region by its most recent hegemon, Russia. The degree of this penetration was by no means inevitable, given that by the late Soviet era the South

Caucasus did not feature substantial ethnic Russian or Slav settler populations, was one of the least russified areas of the former USSR, and had heavily indigenized state bureaucracies. De facto states have compensated for these limitations by providing the theaters for sustained Russian linkages across all spheres in Abkhazia and South Ossetia (Artman 2013; Gerrits and Bader 2016). Russia concluded parallel "association agreements" with both entities in 2014–15, cementing asymmetries and embedding Russian military deployments (RFE/RL 2014; Boden 2014; Kavkazskiy Uzel 2015). Regarding Nagorny Karabakh, sustaining the de facto state in that territory in the context of an oil-rich and re-arming Azerbaijan has mediated Armenian dependence on a deepening security alliance with Russia (Broers 2015a). The presumptive sovereignty of de facto states has in turn enabled Russian norm entrepreneurship to demarcate the post-Soviet space—Russia's so-called near abroad—as "post-Westphalian" consistent with Russian domination (Deyermond 2016).

Finally, although this is a variable phenomenon (whose variability is itself a measure of regional fracture), de facto states in their existence outside of de jure, internationally recognized norms are an important source of the diffusion of informal, prerogative power. To a considerable extent, de facto elites are themselves alternative prerogative regimes on a smaller scale, legitimating their struggle through different discourses they believe will resonate with international audiences (Broers 2014). The extent to which de facto elites cede political space to their own constitutional order is case specific depending on resources, patrons, and geography (Caspersen 2011; Kolstø and Blakkisrud 2008; Broers 2015b). The diffusion of informality from de facto states is most self-evident in Armenia, where natives of Karabakh and veterans of the Karabakh war form core constituencies of the political elite. Armenia's prerogative state is thoroughly interlinked, and thereby legitimated, with the expansive territorial order of "augmented Armenia" (Broers and Toal 2013). This in turn connects the prerogative state with deterritorialized but politically influential and financially significant constituencies in the diaspora (Adriaans 2017). This complex web of connections has allowed the exceptionalism, for example, of US government aid flows, via USAID, reaching the de facto jurisdiction in Nagorny Karabakh. In Georgia under President Shevardnadze, networked elites cooperated across the de jure / de facto divide in profiting from contraband flows through South Ossetia and to a lesser extent Abkhazia, although, to be sure, this was hardly exceptional in pre–Rose Revolution Georgia. As borders hardened in the period after the Rose Revolution, new forms of networked informality took hold. "Outsourcing" of key posts by bringing in nonnatives from Russia, especially in South Ossetia, introduced an accelerated rewiring of the local political elite away from its counterpart in Georgia to Russia (Popescu 2006a).

De facto states, emphatically, do not encompass the range, depth, and embeddedness of South Caucasian regional fracture. It would be a gross simplification to suggest that regional fracture is coextensive with the presumed disjuncture between territorial integrity and national self-determination, and that the resolution of territorial conflict would imply the suturing of fracture. De facto jurisdictions are but one source of informal power among several. In Azerbaijan the nodes and pathways of the prerogative state have other sources and origins. However, what is evident is that settlement of the conflict raises the issue of how rival prerogative states in Armenia and Azerbaijan can be brought into a viable alignment. Both are engaged in struggles with their own constitutional orders, but the discourse of conflict settlement is predicated on legal and institutional frameworks of precisely a constitutional order, invoking formal institutions such as interim government, referendums, or autonomy.[6] It is hard to imagine that the introduction of such modalities would not be seen by the prerogative state in each case as a threat, and that they could be protected from the wider dynamic of subordination of constitutional fabric to prerogative power. This highlights that a securitization of de facto jurisdictions as black holes, zones of chaos, or focal points of transnational disorders is a misdiagnosis. Rather, de facto states are key nodes in wider structures of prerogative power transcending the de facto / de jure divide that are equally resistant to normative incorporation.

The Social Dimension: Fracturing and Suturing Identities

Elite calculations and networks have so far dominated this account. To what extent is the fracture evident at political and institutional levels true of social identities in the South Caucasus? In tandem with debates over the existence and defining parameters of a South Caucasian region, the question of whether and in what form a common Caucasian identity exists lingers with no resolution (Akkieva 2008). Both questions encounter an enduring disjunction between outsider perspectives tracing this regional identity—often for reasons of geographic, narrative, or policy convenience—and insider perspectives denying that such an identity actually exists. Across a range of everyday practices, the deep cultural rhythms of South Caucasian societies exhibit commonalities sufficient for social anthropologists to identify the Caucasus as a world area (Grant and Yalcin-Heckmann 2007). But although scholars in this discipline regularly express frustration at the dominance of conflict in research about the Caucasus, it remains the case that Caucasian commonalities rarely stray beyond social anthropology, linguistics, or cultural history rubrics.

Instead, it is mutually incompatible identity narratives and their associated territorializations that dominate the region's media, policy, and rhetorical spaces as well as (sometimes in regrettably romanticized terms) outsider perspectives. As numerous studies have shown, these narratives are deeply institutionalized, permeating everyday visualizations of territory (Kabachnik 2012; Broers and Toal 2013), school curricula (Vesely 2008; Karpenko 2014), and other theaters of "banal nationalism"

(Billig 1995), even if, as Elisabeth Militz and Carolin Schurr (2016) argue, they may also be challenged by alternative, affective sources of "banal belonging." Opinion polls, especially a group of surveys carried out in the de facto states in 2010–12, indicate that the fractures these entities represent are deeply embedded in the social identities of their populations (O'Loughlin, Kolossov, and Toal 2015). Populations across conflict divides surveyed on their preferred conflict resolution outcomes are predictably polarized.

This apparent image of endemic fracture offers few prospects for advocates of South Caucasian commonalities to appear in the foreseeable future. But this is less a reflection of inveterate South Caucasian nationalisms, and still less the overused straw man of "ancient hatreds," than the exercise of symbolic nationalism as a function of regime building. Whether upscaling local conflict to geopolitical-civilizational frames in Georgia 2004–12, effacing complex borderland histories with ethnic mononarratives in the de facto states, or totalizing the Armenian–Azerbaijani antagonism as the master narrative of Azerbaijani history, incompatible identity narratives have been powerfully enforced through elite discursive strategies. There is nothing inevitable about this process. The Pan-Armenian National Movement of 1989–98, which sought to decouple Armenian foreign policy from the hegemonic narrative of Armenian–Turkish antagonism, and the government of Azerbaijani president Heydar Aliyev (1993–2003), which installed a civic "corrective"—Azerbaijanism—to earlier Azerbaijani ethnonationalism, pursued alternative strategies. In both cases, however, state building subsequently ceded ground to symbolic nationalism in the service of regime building.

Putatively incompatible identities are inseparable from a deep securitization of disruptive counternarratives of interethnic solidarity and empathy and their advocates. Laws on occupied territories have been deployed to legally substantiate the geopolitical upscaling of conflict. Public figures disrupting ethnicized hate narratives, such as Azerbaijani novelist Akram Aylisli, have been harassed and silenced.[7] In the Armenian–Azerbaijani case, the securitization of dialogue precludes social interactions on native soil of almost any kind. Yet, where power fracture has undergone even partial transformation, breezes of revisionism can destabilize and disrupt shibboleths of incompatibility. The impact of Saakashvili's civic nationalism should not be overrated (Berglund 2016), yet change has been tangible. When this author first visited Georgia in 1997, the narrative of the "recent" seventeenth-century arrival and, hence, nonautochthony of Abkhazians in Abkhazia was ubiquitous (see Tuite 2008, 54–65). Twenty years later, however, the Georgian academic and policy establishment has soundly rejected this fallacious theory originally propagated by a literary critic.

A number of scattered and often transient oases of informal regionalism such as the markets at Sadakhlo and (until 2005) Ergneti, the annual summer gatherings of civic and peace activists from across the region in Tekali (the Georgian village closest to the Georgian–Armenian–Azerbaijani border), the cultural and music festivals in Tbilisi and that city's role as a refuge to political émigrés, and the fragile yet durable relationships sustained within NGOs and media engaged in confidence-building all indicate that, in the social dimension, sutures as well as fractures are both imaginable and possible.[8]

Conclusion: Fracture without End?

South Caucasian fracture is so deeply embedded within the practice of power in the region, its material infrastructure, and the pattern of regional alignments that it appears endless. There are very few factors in sight that appear capable of interrupting the reproduction of fracture or of offering an alternative logic of positive-sum multilateralism. This is reflected in the current dearth of ideas for effective regional policies among Western actors, leading some analysts to declare "the end of a region" (Hill, Kirisci, and Moffatt 2015). It is uncertain whether the increased presence of outside actors China and, to an arguable extent, Iran, both free of territorial pretensions in the region, can meaningfully expand the field of multilateral interactions and interdependent interests.

For as long as state power in Armenia and Azerbaijan remains vertically fractured between prerogative and constitutional principles of political authority, this will shape participation in regional initiatives away from thick, normatively configured frameworks. Participation in regional initiatives will instead continue to favor instrumental goals congruent with regime security. As is the case today, this may generate quite distinct patterns—deep but sectorally segmented linkages that further embed power fracture in the case of Armenia, shallow and polyvectoral regional affiliations in the case of Azerbaijan—reflecting the nature of prerogative power in each state. The challenge to Georgia's choice for European integration is for tangible public goods—investment, pluralism, and the long-awaited visa liberalization finally approved by the European Parliament in February 2017 (RFE/RL 2017a)—to decisively seal the country's orientation in the face of its own "Euro-skeptics." Some of the implications of European integration—such as a European concept of tolerance—remain divisive, as the violent dispersal of a lesbian-gay-bisexual-transgender demonstration in May 2013 shows.

It appears likely that the South Caucasus will continue to be a zone of experimentation by both national governments and extraregional actors. Different forms of regionalism will reinforce the distinctive characteristics of the region's different regimes rather than the emergence of a normative game among them. Competing rationalities will continue to prevail, both defiant of comprehensive regional policy formulation by outside actors and contingent on developments elsewhere in the post-Soviet space. Whether Armenia can sustain the incoherence of its plural spatializations of statehood, whether Azerbaijan's prerogative regime can resist political bandwagoning with Russia as normative distance from Western strategic partners grows, and whether Georgia's embrace of normative regionalism can deliver as the EU itself undergoes a period of introspection are critical questions shaping future regional scenarios.

There are precious few indicators of more local determinants of regional cohesion. Two come to mind. First, all of the South Caucasian states have undergone reevaluations of their bilateral "special relationships." Affective geopolitics has ceded ground over time to more pragmatic reviews of bilateral relationships in the light of evolving interests. This is an indication of maturation, even if policy alternatives to these relationships, especially for Armenia, appear few. Second, if uneven and resistant to elevation to a metalevel of public articulation, there is a growing appreciation across the region of the cost of fracture—in underdevelopment, venality, violations of constitutional rule, state violence, institutional decay, policy mediocrity, undiminished insecurity, compromised sovereignty, and families divided by migration—among societies quietly cognizant that their neighbors' problems are also their own.

Notes

I am very grateful to Gia Tarkhan-Mouravi and Anna Ohanyan for extensive comments that significantly improved earlier drafts of this essay. Neither is responsible for any errors of fact or judgment herein.

1. Space does not allow here further exploration of this last theme, on which, see Ratelle and Broers 2018.

2. These were the autonomous republics of Abkhazia and Ach'ara in Georgia and Nakhchivan in Azerbaijan, and the autonomous regions of South Ossetia in Georgia and Nagorny Karabakh (Nagorno-Karabakh) in Azerbaijan.

3. World Bank open data, accessed September 24, 2016, available at http://data.worldbank.org/.

4. Human Development Index 2016, available at United Nations Development Programme, http://hdr.undp.org/en/content/human-development-index-hdi. This index provides a composite ranking of human development based on national data for specific indicators. Cut-off points rank human development scores of 0.800 or more as very high, 0.700–0.799 as high, 0.550–0.699 as medium, and scores below that as low.

5. The proliferation of unrecognized states across the world has been accompanied by a proliferation of the terms used to describe them. In this essay I use the widely used term "de facto state" interchangeably with "de facto jurisdiction," an alternative that avoids the implication that a state-creation impulse drives all such entities. For an overview and definitions of de facto states, see Pegg 2017.

6. Conflicting understandings of the mechanisms and processes envisaged in the current Armenian–Azerbaijani peace proposal, known as the Madrid Principles, have been explored in some depth in a series of briefs produced by the Karabakh Contact Group, a Track-2 initiative supported by peacebuilding NGO Conciliation Resources. These can be found on the Conciliation Resources website, http://www.c-r.org/where-we-work/caucasus/karabakh-contact-group-0.

7. For a collection of essays addressing Akram Aylisli's work and responses to it, see the special section "Dreams in the Black Garden" in *Caucasus Survey* 2, no. 1–2, available with free access at http://www.tandfonline.com/toc/rcau20/2/1-2?nav=tocList.

8. Safety in Tbilisi is not assured. On May 29, 2017, Azerbaijani journalist Afgan Mukhtarli was abducted from outside of his home in Tbilisi and forcibly transferred to Baku, where he was charged with illegal transit and smuggling. "European Parliament Condemns Abduction of Azerbaijani Journalist Afgan Mukhtarli," *EVN Report*, June 15, 2017. https://www.evnreport.com/politics/european-parliament-condemns-abduction-of-azerbaijani-journalist-afgan-mukhtarli.

CHAPTER FIVE

Small States and the Large Costs of Regional Fracture: The Case of Armenia

Richard Giragosian

In the field of materials science and engineering, the concept of "fracture mechanics" focuses on the integrity of structural metals in terms of stress, dislocation, cracks, and collapse. In this engineering context, fracture mechanics is understood to be a result of structural failures arising from the environment, material defects and deficiencies, inadequacies in design, and problematic maintenance (Roylance 2001). In the separate context of geopolitics and political science, the theory of regional fracture shares several fundamental similarities ranging from regional fracture due to the imposition of external stress, in terms of both invasion or war and colonial rule, to structural insufficiencies of regions, states, and societies to withstand such stress. In addition, the capacity to resist or repel such external triggers of stress is also directly related to the degree of local, national, and regional resiliency. By assessing the presence or paucity of several key variables, such as democratic institutions, military metrics, and political economy, the application of the concept of regional fracture offers an insightful analytical model to measure regime resiliency, state security, and territorial stability.

Moreover, in terms of broader stability, fractured regions have clearly emerged as significantly disruptive drivers of instability and conflict. And although fractured regions have served as key arenas for external contest and conquest, marked by both imperial leverage and geopolitical intervention, they have also been subjected to internal stress that has tended to impede democratization and economic development. Throughout much of the last century, for example, the destabilizing nature of territorially fractured regions was most evident in the cases of Africa and the Middle East, exacerbated by the combination of postimperial regional fragility and the impediments inherent in weak or failing states. At the same time, fractured regions have also been defined by more than geography or geopolitics. Rather, regional fracture is also evident in terms of culture, economics, and identity. From this perspective, geographic proximity between states has also been an important driver of regional fracture worldwide, especially in the case of post-Soviet Eurasia. In that example, the geographic proximity between states in fractured regions has fostered conflict over territory and disputed borders, driven largely by the fact that the borders were imposed externally and artificially by the former colonial/imperial powers.

This dynamic also transformed these areas into a "zero-sum" rivalry for limited resources during the initial period of independence. A related challenge for fractured regions stems from the political and economic aftermath of the legacy of colonial/imperial systems, which were based on a center-periphery, or hub-and-spoke, model whereby the fractured regions were consciously subject to policies designed to maintain dependence, prevent the strengthening of statehood, counter nationalist aspirations, and block the development of viable local legitimate institutions.

Demonstrating the powerful burden of that legacy, the countries of the former Soviet Union, or the post-Soviet Eurasian region, have emerged as even more dynamic examples of the potency of fractured regions as drivers of instability and conflict that remain both unresolved and inadequately addressed. In the case of Eurasia, for example, the post-Soviet space has stood out as an arena of competition and a clash of interests among and between larger regional powers, with Russia, Turkey, and Iran each engaged in a contest for power and influence. Moreover, this geopolitical contest has been both encouraged and empowered by the fractured regions of the post-Soviet space, with each newly independent state adopting a coping strategy based on a calculated barter for security from an alignment with one or more of these regional rivals. This barter has been costly, however, and most often came at the sacrifice of sovereignty for security.

The South Caucasus and Central Asia: The Geopolitical Heartland

Within the confines of the post-Soviet space, the sweeping Eurasian "heartland" of the South Caucasus and Central Asia stand out as two regions particularly vulnerable to geopolitical and geographic shifts. Although each region has followed a different trajectory, there is a shared legacy of regional fracture. For the South Caucasus, the region has long served as an arena of competition between the Russian, Turkish, and Persian Empires, further rooted in the geographic proximity of the

Middle East and the gravitational pull of the Arab and Islamic worlds. At the other pole of the non-Slavic Eurasian continent, Central Asia was closely aligned and attracted to Chinese and Southwest Asian influence, notably including neighboring Afghanistan, India, and, more recently, Pakistan.

The strategic importance of Central Asia and the South Caucasus stems largely from the region's geographic position as a vital intersection of regional state powers (China and Russia) and peripheral retrograde states (Afghanistan and Pakistan). In the context of more recent security shifts, especially in the wake of the new post-9/11 landscape, these two regions have garnered a renewed strategic relevance. There is also an underlying geopolitical element that has helped to redefine the strategic significance of both regions, but that has only underlined the presence and power of regional fracture.

This renewed geopolitical relevance of the South Caucasus and Central Asia centers on Sir Halford Mackinder's "heartland" theory (Mackinder 1904), which asserts that control of the Eurasian heartland grants decisive influence, and holds that stability of the Eurasian heartland fosters global security. For Mackinder, the advances in technology were forcing a reevaluation of spatial concepts and military strategies. With the advent of railroads, power projection no longer depended on naval power, as nations could use railroads to move large land armies. Thus, Mackinder believed that the focus of warfare would be shifted from the sea to the hinterland (interiors).

Mackinder's theory represented a significant revision of the concept of sea power, then the dominant spatial theory of power. The sea power concept was developed by Alfred Thayer Mahan in his 1890 work *The Influence of Sea Power upon History* (Mahan 1890), in which Mahan held that because sea power was essential for trade and commerce, power would emanate from the control of the seas. According to this theory, state power is derived from the development of a strong navy as much as from a country's geographic position. Thus, the country with the most power would be the one whose relative location is accessible and connected with a long coastline and good harbors.

For Mackinder, however, the evolution of the strategy included a focus on developing the concept of a "pivot area," comprising the northern and interior parts of the Eurasian continent where the rivers flow to the Arctic or to salt seas and lakes. After the development of railway networks, this area would be pivotal and both easy to defend and hard to conquer. This "pivot area" became known as the "heartland" and, according to Mackinder's heartland theory, argued that "land power" had emerged as the new standard of power. For the "land power" school, Mackinder contended that the emergence of railroads offered the new technological advantage that granted land powers the mobility, agility, and power projection of sea or naval powers.

This concept also reflects an important and fairly novel recognition of the link between globalization and power at that time. Over time, the influence of Mackinder's "heartland theory" was profound, used by a disparate set of later geopolitical strategists and reflected in the theory of Yale University professor Nicholas Spykman's "Rimland" theory (Spykman 1942, 1944). Mackinder also influenced the later US Cold War policy of containment, as developed by George Kennan, and served as a reference point for the strategic thinking of Robert Strausz-Hupé, Colin Gray, and Zbigniew Brzezinski. There is also an interesting parallel between the geopolitics of Mackinder and the realpolitik of Henry Kissinger. His influence has extended even further, with some of his traditional geopolitical concepts adopted in Russia by the "Eurasianists" (Gennady Zyuganov, Aleksandr Dugin, etc.) and reflected in the "near abroad" concept of Yevgeny Primakov as well as in some Chinese strategic theories.

Mackinder Updated?

Given the specific challenges of today's still-evolving system of international security, Mackinder is still somewhat relevant. Generally, his view of a world that has evolved into what he called a "closed system," with little room for expansion, and of a world as one enormous battlefield are both fitting in the context of a global war on terrorism, both in terms of the post-2001 fight against al-Qaeda and the more recent emergence of the Islamic State in Iraq and Syria, or ISIS. More specifically, his heartland concept can be applied to the Central Asian–South Caucasus theater as constituting the "key position" on the battlefield, thereby suggesting that control of the key position would determine global supremacy. Yet there is an interesting new twist to this idea of "key position," as the outlook for security and stability of the heartland now depends on conditions within the littoral periphery—that is, the Rimland.

Further, this theoretical foundation also paved the way for the elaboration of two distinct advances in conceptualizing the link and relationship between geopolitical geography and regional fracture and fragmentation: the diverging classification of a region as pivotal or peripheral (Brzezinski 1997) and the emergence of regional fracture as the basis for buffer zones (Henrikson 2002). There is also a third, related concept that has acquired an enhanced relevance in recent years. This is the concept of "spheres of influence," whereby the powerful gravitational pull of an entrenched yet elastic "sphere of influence" also adds a greater degree of competition that enhances territorial and political fracture, only further exacerbated by cases of more penetrating and permeating "power projection" (Henrikson 2002; Gray 1977).

In modern military terms, however, applying Mackinder is much less relevant. First, the most obvious limitation of Mackinder's nineteenth-century view of the heartland as "the greatest natural fortress" lies in the disparity with modern advances in air power. And although the limits inherent in the sheer scope and scale of the region's natural geography are still formidable, they are still trumped by the projection of air power spanning ever-greater distances. And in military terms, Mackinder's geographical constant has been altered. The necessity of air corridors is increasingly replacing the need for air bases, further clarifying the necessity of a "geopolitical mapping" exercise for regional fracture.

Thus, the strategic significance of Central Asia and the South Caucasus can be seen as Mackinder revisited and updated. But what is needed now is to look for the new dynamic, for the new "railroad" that represents Mackinder's factors of mobility and power projection. This new dynamic is demonstrated by the (re)emergence of Islamist movements in the regions, which have flourished within the degree of state weakness inherent in the sweeping political transition now under way within these regions and are also rooted in a threat defined by a rejection of all technology, in a return to crude asymmetrical warfare, as with the insurgents in Iraq and the resurgent Taliban in Afghanistan—both factors that only enhance the vulnerability to regional fracture.

There are limits to viewing regional fracture through a geopolitical prism, however, as both Central Asia and the South Caucasus are increasingly moving beyond the confines of coherent regional entities. The outlook for true security and stability in these regions in fact depends less on geopolitics and more on economics and politics. The main challenges are increasingly local needs and concerns, especially as the core vulnerability of these states center on the legitimacy of their leaders. This is also demonstrated by the variance in development and trajectory of each state in these regions. Thus, a new set of domestic imperatives has largely replaced geopolitical concerns as the sole driving force for these states' relations with the outside world and its great powers, and these domestic drivers are also directly related to regional fracture.

Imperial "Overreach"

A related aggravating factor has also come in the cyclical trend of power projection leading to "overreach" or "overstretch," whereby the strategic sustainability of such intervention is eroded by fading attention or neglect and undermined by the overextension of force (Kennedy 1987). As states characterized by both geographical proximity and a varying degree of mutual dependence, fractured regions have emerged as significantly disruptive drivers of instability and conflict.

While fractured regions have served as tools for both imperial leverage and geopolitical intervention, they have also tended to impede democratization and economic development. Throughout much of the last century, the destabilizing nature of fractured regions was most evident in the cases of Africa and the Middle

East, exacerbated by the combination of postimperial fragility and the impediments inherent in weak or failing states.

Over the past two decades, however, the countries of the former Soviet Union, or the post-Soviet space, have emerged as even more dynamic examples of the potency of fractured regions as drivers of instability and conflict. In the case of Eurasia, for example, the post-Soviet space has stood out as an arena of competition and a clash of interests among and between larger regional powers, with Russia, Turkey, and Iran each engaged in a contest for power and influence. Moreover, this geopolitical contest has been both encouraged and empowered by the fractured regions of the post-Soviet space and has presented two important subsets:

> *Geographic Proximity*: Too often, and especially in the cases of postimperial regions (Africa, the Middle East, post-Soviet Eurasia are three main examples or case studies), the geographic proximity of fractured regions has fostered conflict over territory and disputed borders (which in most cases were imposed externally and artificially by the former colonial/imperial powers) while also transforming the areas into a "zero-sum" rivalry for limited resources.

> *Mutual Dependence*: The political and economic nature of the colonial/imperial systems were based on a center-periphery, or hub-and-spoke, model whereby the fractured regions were consciously subject to policies designed to maintain dependence, prevent the strengthening of statehood, counter nationalist aspirations, and block the development of viable local and legitimate institutions.

Security Trends and Regional Fracture in the South Caucasus

For the South Caucasus, there are three trends in shifting security. First, Russia now holds a fairly well-entrenched position in the region following a steady reassertion of power and influence. After the incoherence of the Boris Yeltsin period, Russian strategy under Vladimir Putin has been to regain and restore Russia's traditional influence along its southern periphery. This has been largely accomplished through the application of a more sophisticated strategy of exerting influence by using energy as leverage, with economic dependence constituting a new "soft power" over the more traditional Russian "hard power" emphasis on blunt military force or localized, low-intensity conflict.

Second, one of the most active powers in the South Caucasus, Turkey, is currently undergoing its deepest and most historically significant degree of internal change. Arguably as profound and powerful as the birth pains of the modern Turkish state in 1923, the battle in which Turkey is engaged today is with itself—redefining itself and its identity. It is struggling to come to terms with three burdens: its legacy, from the obligation to recognize the Armenian genocide of 1915; its more recent history, regarding its 1974 invasion and continued occupation of the Republic of Cyprus; and its present, as demonstrated in its difficult and damaging approach to its large Kurdish minority. The course of this Turkish transition is particularly important for the region, as it represents both promise and peril in new relations with its large Turkish neighbor. At this point, however, an outright rejection of the Turkish strategic orientation westward suggests a new risk of an overly confident and authoritarian Turkey returning to an aggressive, eastward vision of pan-Turkic and Islamic-based pursuit of power.

The third trend in regional security for the South Caucasus is composed of a set of new dynamics marked by a three-direction trajectory. This three-direction trajectory features Georgia being pulled closer to Europe by the gravitational pull of Ukraine, on a track to closer integration with the EU and even NATO much faster than its two neighbors in the region. Similarly, Azerbaijan is also drawing away from the South Caucasus and moving closer, both in terms of energy and politics, to Central Asia. Both directions in this trajectory leave tiny, landlocked Armenia as a prisoner to the region and, increasingly, as a hostage to its overreliance on Russia. The most serious danger for Armenia is the danger of becoming little more than a Russian garrison state.

Amid this three-trend trajectory, the European Union has also emerged as a major out-of-the-region power, crafting a new role in the South Caucasus as part of its EU Greater Neighborhood policy. It is this Greater Neighborhood policy that reflects a strategic view of the region (and the Mediterranean) as a new security buffer. Without a comprehensive and balanced strategy of engagement, however, this approach to the region as a dangerous periphery may be as shortsighted and self-defeating as the French reliance on the Maginot Line as an integral element of its defensive strategy.

The European Union also holds the key to long-term stability and security in the broader Middle East, but only as long as the EU engages in the region in coordination with, and not in competition with, the United States. It is therefore imperative for the United States to rebuild a more constructive and even more equal partnership with the Europeans in crafting and implementing a common policy toward both the Middle East and the regions of Central Asia and the South Caucasus. A serious European–American rivalry would not only be destructive for both the US and Europe but would also be profoundly destabilizing for these already vulnerable regions.

Against this complicated backdrop of external threats and internal fragility, the three states of the region have pursued a foreign policy based on their differing calculations of national interest and adaptation. The trajectory of the three states' foreign policy orientation has been rooted in a varied combination of national assets and strategic imperatives. And although each state has embarked on a different and at times opposing foreign policy path, all three face a varying degree of external pressure, with Russia's reassertion of power throughout the "near abroad" as the primary driver and division between the countries of the South Caucasus.

Armenia: Geography and Geopolitics

For Armenia, the struggle to overcome a daunting set of challenges, ranging from the inherent limits of its small size and landlocked geography to a virtual "state of war" with Azerbaijan over the unresolved Nagorno-Karabakh conflict, was especially difficult. Equally daunting, Armenia embarked on a difficult path of state building, bolstered by ambitious economic and political reforms. Even well before independence, Armenia was beset by two seminal events: the eruption of the Karabakh conflict and the subsequent outbreak of war with Azerbaijan in February 1988 and a devastating earthquake in December 1989. Against that backdrop, the sudden and unexpected collapse of the Soviet Union left Armenia largely unprepared for the urgency of independence. The infant state also faced a grave and urgent threat to its survival as the Karabakh conflict intensified, leading to an expanded war that disrupted trade and transport routes, cut key energy links, and triggered a near blockade of the country by neighboring Azerbaijan and Turkey.

But as a fundamental factor, Armenia, as the case of all nations, formulates its foreign policy on the basis of the limits of geography and the challenges of geopolitics. And in the case of landlocked Armenia, situated on a well-worn historic crossroads between East and West, the pressure of isolation and closed borders has compelled Armenia to pursue a difficult foreign policy based on geopolitical balancing between competing regional powers. With an area of under 11,500 square miles and a population of roughly three million, the country's geographic vulnerability is compounded by a limited natural resource base, borders and terrain that are difficult to defend militarily, and a demographic crisis, all posing substantial challenges to economic development and security. For Armenian reform, the war years of the 1990s also thwarted early attempts at building democratic institutions and bolstering political reform, and the ongoing state of war shaped an already rigid political discourse, as a new vibrant nationalism crowded out more moderate voices within the Armenian political arena.

And in terms of political developments, two related trends came to dominate and determine the country's political trajectory. First, a downward shift in the level of political discourse and debate was marked by a weakening of moderate politics and a rise of vibrant and at times more militant and xenophobic nationalism. Second, this lowering of political discourse was matched by a second trend involving the transformation of the country's political elite as a new elite from Karabakh gained power and consolidated top leadership positions in Armenia proper, eventually including the Armenian presidency itself when the first president, Levon Ter-Petrosian, was forced from power. Against this backdrop, the cumulative effect of the past decades of independence has actually tended to only deepen greater dependence, especially in terms of the Armenian–Russian relationship, and was further marked by missed opportunities.

Threats of Isolation and Insignificance

From a broader strategic perspective, the most serious threats to Armenia center on the challenges of isolation and insignificance. For a landlocked country limited by its small size in terms of both demography and territory, the threat of isolation stems from the constraints of closed borders, the collapse of regional trade and transport, and an exclusion of all regional development projects. With its borders with Azerbaijan and Turkey closed since the early 1990s, the imperative for Armenia is to overcome the limits of geography. This threat of isolation involves the danger of becoming disconnected from the globalized marketplace and from the technological and economic changes inherent in the process of globalization.

In addition to the relative isolation of the country, Armenia also faces a second, related threat of insignificance, defined by the limits of a small, landlocked country with two of its four borders closed. Most importantly, the threats of isolation and insignificance also pose security concerns. For example, national security depends less on control of territory and natural resources and more on the capacity to integrate with the global economy. And for a country like Armenia, faced with traditional limits of demography and geography, economic issues are increasingly linked to security. Yet this recognition has yet to be fully embraced and reflected by Armenian national security, as the current confines of Armenian nationalism have failed to expand to include the demands of "economic security."

Innovative Foreign Policy

Armenia offers an interesting model of weak-state adaptation stemming from this imperative for foreign policy innovation. Armenian foreign policy over the last decade sought to bridge the inherently conflicting interests of Russia and the West through a foreign policy termed "complementarity," which seeks to incorporate Armenia's strategic imperative of security through a reliance on its strategic alliance with Russia and a positive relationship with Iran while simultaneously conforming to the parameters of its Western orientation. Moreover, this policy of complementarity, although seemingly contradictory, is in fact a natural result of Armenia's historical and geopolitical considerations. The strategic partnership with Russia is rooted in both history and necessity, especially given the implicit threat posed by the isolation and closed borders that impede growth and development. Although these inherently contradictory impulses have at times seemed insurmountable, the Armenian policy of complementarity offers a degree of regional security based on accommodating and exploiting the interests of traditionally competing powers.

For much of the past two decades, Armenia sought to maximize its strategic options based on the imperative to surmount the deeper threat of isolation, exacerbated by the closure of two of the country's four borders. And, for example, in the broader context of foreign policy, Armenia has always pursued a "small state" strategy of pursuing policies designed to maximize its options and expand its room to maneuver amid much larger regional powers. More specifically, for much of the past decade, Armenian foreign policy has successfully bridged the division between its "strategic partnership" with Russia and its deepening of ties and orientation with the West. This particular foreign policy of "complementarity" incorporates Armenia's strategic imperative of security, based on a reliance on its strategic alliance with Russia, while simultaneously expanding its role within Western and Euro-Atlantic security structures.

Thus, in a broader sense, for Armenia, there has been little opportunity for longer-term strategic vision or planning. After more than two decades of independence, however, there is now an obvious imperative for Armenian leaders to recognize and respond to the need for garnering greater strategic options. And despite the burden of unresolved conflict, insufficient democratic institutions, and incomplete economic reform, Armenia is endowed with a significantly wider range of strategic options and greater flexibility in overcoming its isolation. These opportunities are neither immediate nor easy and require political will, vision, and statesmanship. But in light of the country's geographic, economic, and geopolitical isolation, there is no longer any excuse or luxury for failing to recognize the changing regional environment and adopt the dynamic policy initiatives that may be initiated by the Armenian government.

This imperative to regain a degree of strategic balance through a unique foreign policy concept is limited by several challenges, however. First, and most recently, the war in Ukraine has also challenged the Armenian government, especially as it has threatened to only further isolate Armenia as a more subservient Russian supplicant state. Moreover, throughout the crisis, the Armenian government has been especially cautious, largely due to a policy decision to refrain from doing or saying anything that would anger or alienate Armenia's "strategic partner," Russia. At the same time, however, the broader context of the Ukraine conflict has significant implications for Armenia, especially in terms of Russian power and influence in the so-called near abroad.

A second challenge stems from a sudden and unexpected crisis in Armenian–Russian relations. This was sparked by the murder of an Armenian family by a Russian soldier stationed at the nearby Russian military base, triggering a surprisingly intense debate over Armenia's security relationship with Russia. For Armenia, its role as a reliable partner and ally of Russia has never faced any real challenge. Much of this reliance on Russia stems from security and economic ties. Armenia's security reliance on Russia is rooted in the Karabakh conflict and only exacerbated by the absence of "normal" diplomatic relations and a closed border with Turkey. For Armenia, a strategic alliance with Russia is generally accepted as essential for security. And beyond security, Armenia also depends on Russia as a crucial source of remittances sent home by large numbers of Armenians living and working in Russia. Yet there is a surprisingly intense debate now under way within Armenia that seriously questions the Armenian–Russian relationship.

Small State Strategy

Clearly, Armenia has been faced with a rather difficult period of political tension and internal discord over the past two years. Although the most serious crisis—an open confrontation between the Armenian government and the opposition—has dissipated, it has raised several concerns over the future course of the country. While the political tension has revealed a number of deficiencies in both democracy and the rule of law, this recent period of discord has also confirmed the fundamental necessity for forging stability and fostering security in Armenia. To date, however, despite an overly narrow focus on the geopolitical perspective, the strategic challenges to Armenia today are no longer limited to the more traditional threats posed by an external aggressor or rooted in military vulnerability. The current nature of the threat is inherently internal and stems in large part from three fundamental weaknesses: an incomplete democracy, an inequitable economy, and an inconsistent rule of law. Yet all three of these deficiencies must be addressed if Armenia is to achieve its paramount needs for stability and security.

As the traditional geopolitical challenges to Armenian security are largely rooted in its geography, there is no easy path to overcoming the inherent vulnerability of location. Armenia shares this vulnerability with its neighbors in the South Caucasus, as this region has long served as a key arena for the competing interests of the dominant regional Russian, Turkish, and Iranian powers. This historical legacy of external influence and intervention has also been compounded by the region's position as a bridge to much larger regions in terms of both East–West and North–South axes. But while this legacy has generally tended to keep each state in the region weak and insecure, the real source of instability and insecurity now stems more from the internal vulnerabilities of each state.

The pronounced weakness of the region has been further exacerbated by several low-intensity conflicts and the emergence of new security threats, all stemming from a serious deficit of stability and security. But the region's instability and insecurity are actually rooted in more fundamental internal challenges, ranging from incomplete democracy and the related predominance of "strongmen over statesmen" to economic mismanagement and widespread corruption. These factors have significantly impeded the reform efforts in each of these states in transition and have further contributed to a significant erosion of legitimacy. It is this set of internal factors that mandates a new focus in the case of Armenia, however, as the process of state building can never be fully attained without a corresponding process of institution building.

Recommendations: Forging Stability in Armenia

As a case study, there are two specific recommendations to consider for moving beyond the challenge of regional fracture in order to bolster regional security and stability. And in light of the unique Armenian experience and relevance, the key to containing and constraining the negative influence of regional fracture and fragmentation must start locally.

The Importance of Culture

There is another interesting element in the construction of a stable state. The relevance of culture is often underestimated in the course of state building. And especially related to the context of regional fracture and the related weakness and fragility of the state and even state identity, the transformative potential of culture to exert deep influence over the course of nation building is matched by a potential for dynamic change, holding the power as an "agent of change" to sway entrenched policies and move nations to war or peace, to revolution or reform.

Culture may also exert an impressive staying power and can serve as both incentive and impediment to change in society. For the future of Armenia, it is this aspect of culture that must be recognized. Despite the varied characteristics of national pride and cultural wealth, the long, violent history of the Armenians—and that of the entire Caucasus region, for that matter—has seen cycles of brutality, deportation, massacre, and even genocide. Well before the Western use of the term "ethnic cleansing," and even prior to the introduction of the Russian term "pogrom," culture in the Caucasus was deeply ingrained with a historical narrative of suffering and conflict. It is this recognition of an integral historical narrative that must be accepted in order to define Armenia's relations with its neighbors.

But what is needed for the Caucasus, and for many other scarred regions, is the harnessing of the positive power of culture while simultaneously maintaining a vigilant check on the cultural excesses of ethnic nationalism. In this case, the aftermath of ethnic-based violence and a revenge-driven cycle of intransigence fed by unresolved conflict have contributed to a "culture of conflict." The danger, for all sides, is to become too far engulfed by this culture of conflict and miss, or refuse, opportunities for advancing beyond territory-based perceptions of security. A related element of this culture of conflict is the reliance on extreme nationalism as an avenue to power. The nationalist mantle is also used to obscure the internal deficiencies and shortcomings from within the country to redirect critical attention to without. Yet, given the scale of globalization and the relative marginal role of the Caucasus, the priority is to stabilize and secure the nation from within.

For example, in looking at the case of East Asia and its explosive period of postwar economic growth, culture has also marked the emergence of the dynamic "Asian Tigers." While the role of the Asian cultural traditions (such as Confucianism) served as a noteworthy foundation for such rapid regional growth, the more important step was the gradual process of institutionalization, with the development of political institutions and an autonomous legal system culminating in a higher level of stability and security of property rights (due to increasing constraints placed on rulers by the power of the market forces and new political norms). Although the expansion of institutions in the postwar Asian states was unable to prevent the later rise of "crony capitalism" seen in Indonesia and South Korea, it was enough to construct the foundation for stability and economic growth. From a broader perspective, even the nepotism and oligarchic nature of the Asian economies did not necessarily prevent their progress toward fuller democracy and more open markets. The lesson, therefore, is one of degree: institutions are the key, but they must be resilient enough and powerful enough to combat political corruption and economic cronyism.

The Need for a Middle Class

The foundation for both political stability and an open economy rests with the middle class of a society. The middle class is more than the traditional bourgeoisie, however. It is marked by three characteristics: entrepreneurship in economic and commercial activity, activism and participation in politics, and unimpeded mobility in both. But at its core, the most important facet of the middle class is its independence and autonomy from the state.

The development of a middle class is dependent on two important factors, one short term and the other long term. The first prerequisite for the emergence of a vibrant middle class is one of access and opportunity. The structure of the society as a whole, and its economic and political systems in particular, must not be closed or divided between a small wealthy and powerful elite and a much larger impoverished and marginalized majority. This precondition is an immediate need, required for a budding middle class to emerge. But this is also a short-term need because once a middle class is allowed to take hold, it tends to prosper quickly and become far too entrenched to surrender its position in society.

Once in place, a middle class generally represents the interests of society as a whole rather than for any small ruling elite. It is this advocacy role that buttresses political and economic reform and counters economic oligarchs and political demagogues alike. There is also a "trickle-down" effect, with the middle class both serving and strengthening a civil society, a free press, and eventually a responsible political opposition. For Armenia, these needs are more than obvious and more than immediate. The development of middle-class societies in the West has traditionally rested on three elements: employment, with rising wages; education, with expanding access on all levels; and property, through the ownership of homes, businesses, and other properties.

Economic Fragility

A deeper structural impediment to the country's capacity to exploit broader strategic options stems from the discrepancy between the "hidden" and "heavy" hands of Armenian economics. For example, as one of the most profound and long-lasting economic theories, Adam Smith's concept of the "invisible" or "hidden hand" describes the underlying process of market economic forces. In his groundbreaking work *The Wealth of Nations*, Smith contends that the hidden hand of market economics is an inherently self-regulating process whereby an individual pursuing his own self-interest within a market-based economy tends to promote the "public good" of the larger community or society as a whole. For Smith, although the concept of the hidden hand does not necessarily seek a social order or economic justice, it nevertheless benefits the public interest. Despite the profit-driven order of the hidden hand, it is also opposed to monopolies or oligarchic structures as obstacles to free trade and as threats to natural economic development.

But the concept of the hidden hand and its convergence of self-interest with public interest in terms of strengthening national economic growth does not apply to a country like Armenia, for two important reasons. First, there is an absence of an underlying free market, which, in the case of Armenia, has become dominated by powerful commodity-based cartels that have distorted economic growth and disdained market-based competition. Second, the potential of economic individual self-interest has been checked by the emergence of more serious obstacles of corruption and a closed economic system that hinders entrepreneurs and business startups.

In the Armenian model, the concept of the hidden hand has been replaced by the concept of the heavy hand, reflecting the power and interference of oligarchic semi-monopolies and cartels as well as entrenched corruption. The emergence of the heavy hand in all of the post-Soviet states has become one of the defining characteristics of transition economies. Yet, in the case of Armenia, the heavy hand has also become endowed with the destructive role of the state, in terms of both supporting and relying on oligarchic structures. Clearly, the imperative is to weaken the heavy hand of Armenia's oligarchic economics and to look instead to build on the openness and unrestricted economics of Adam Smith's hidden hand.

Conclusion: The Outlook

Although Armenia remains locked in a "region at risk," the country has largely embarked on a new course of seizing opportunities aimed at overcoming the threat of isolation. In a strategic sense, Armenia has succeeded in maximizing its strategic options and is now emerging as the most stable country in the region while also beginning to challenge the nature and asymmetry of its overreliance on Russia as its primary security patron and partner. Moreover, as Armenia's "strategic partnership" with Russia has become steadily one-sided, Yerevan has begun to finally see that, although close relations with Russia are essential over the longer term, the imperative is now to maximize its options and garner dividends from a more concerted embrace of the West.

And within the region, as Georgia's earlier prominence faded and its once prestigious favored position quickly eroded, Armenia has been able to fill the void. By gradually demonstrating its own greater significance by displaying a greater degree of stability and reliability than Georgia, this enhanced significance for Armenia has been further strengthened by a cautious move to replicate Georgia's strategic Western orientation, although in a much more nuanced and subtle embrace of the EU, which concluded a new bilateral agreement with Armenia in 2017. Thus, although it remains far too early to conclude that Armenia has been able to graduate from this "region at risk," the deeper trends clearly suggest a more prudent policy aimed at finally overcoming Armenia's isolation and building a new degree of stability and security, thereby reducing the risk of regional fracture.

CHAPTER SIX

Central Asia: Fractured Region, Illiberal Regionalism

David G. Lewis

Central Asia is a region that lacks meaningful regional institutions, has a weak regional identity, and is beset by a complex litany of political, economic, and social divisions, both within and between states. Tensions among Central Asian states over borders, resources, and security, combined with deep political and social cleavages within states and geopolitical competition across the wider region, all support a view of Central Asia as a prime example of the concept of regional fracture. However, while acknowledging the significance of these underlying fractures, in this chapter I suggest a more complex, multilevel reading of regional interactions in which a focus on the role of shared ideas, norms, and beliefs provides a framework for some limited regional cooperation within a common discourse that is sharply at odds with the liberal norms that underpin most Western theories of regionalism. The result is a form of "illiberal regionalism," which does not offer a resolution of fundamental fractures within and between societies but often provides an effective means to suppress their political articulation.

Central Asia: A Fractured Region

Academic and policy analysis of the Central Asian region has long stressed its potential instability and its fundamentally fractured nature (Lewis 2008; Cummings 2012; Cooley 2012), so much so that critics have warned against framing the region solely through "discourses of danger," external narratives that exaggerate security threats and characterize the region as dominated by Islamist militancy, organized crime, and terrorism (Heathershaw and Megoran 2011). Nevertheless, the region clearly faces severe political and social tensions, including interstate conflicts over resources, water, and borders; intrastate clashes between authoritarian states and restive societies; Islamist movements challenging secular states; and geopolitical tensions between Russia, China, and the West. Against this backdrop, studies of regionalism in Central Asia have tended to answer the ontological question of "what we study when we study regionalism" (Hettne 2005, 543) by highlighting the failures of regional projects and the underlying divisions among states, often dismissing regional organizations as "virtual" or ineffective (Allison 2008b; Collins 2009). Studies of Central Asian regionalism have stressed the failure of Central Asian states to develop their own regional organizations and have highlighted the continuing role of extraregional powers in determining the region's politics and security (Allison 2004; Bohr 2004; Collins 2009; Cooley 2012). Instead of regionalization—"an active process of change towards increased cooperation, integration, convergence, coherence and identity" (Allison 2004, 465)—Central Asian societies became increasingly estranged from each other while their political leaderships united only for brief political summits under the hegemonic tutelage of Russia or China. Although external powers frequently initiated new regional initiatives, they were often ineffective or reinforced the very fractures they were intended to overcome. The result of this breakdown in regional cooperation has been repeatedly identified as imposing heavy social and economic costs on the region (Collins 2009).

The conventional portrayal of Central Asia as a fractured region begins with definitions. Constructivist approaches to the regionalism debate have argued that regions are not predefined entities with clear boundaries but are constructed and deconstructed through discourse, social and economic interaction, and political practice (Hettne 2005; Söderbaum and Shaw 2003; Emerson 2014; Hettne and Söderbaum 2000; Söderbaum 2016). Regions are made and unmade through discursive mechanisms and political practices. Guy Emerson (2014, 560) argues that "the multiple discourses of regionalism, regional identity and the process of region building itself, are constantly being re-defined, with its boundaries and identifying structures the products of continual struggle and therefore reappraisal." Earlier constructivist thought tended to view this process of "imagining" the region as a move that might help to transcend the nation-state and contribute to the development of new, regional identities (Adler 1997), but in many postcolonial contexts it is historical experience and common memory that underlie the idea of the region rather than any common hope for future regional integration. This is certainly the case in Central Asia, where the identification of Central Asia as a region—and therefore a space that is thought by policymakers to require institutionalized cross-boundary cooperation in a form of regional integration—stems above all from a common historical experience and a process of colonial demarcation.

Although the term "Central Asia" is now commonly used in English to portray the five post-Soviet states of Kazakhstan, Kyrgyzstan, Tajikistan, Turkmenistan, and

Uzbekistan, there are many alternative ways to label these territories as a regional entity. Definitions that highlight ethnic and cultural distinctions from the two major civilizations to the north and the east—Russia and China—may include Xinjiang, parts of southern Siberia inhabited by Turkic peoples, Mongolia, and Tibet, in a world sometimes termed "Inner Asia." Soviet-era definitions, on the other hand, used the term "Srednaya aziya" (Middle Asia) to cover only the Tajik, Uzbek, Kyrgyz, and Turkmen Soviet Socialist Republics, but exclude the Kazakh SSR, reflecting a different colonial history and asserting a closer relationship between Kazakhstan and Russia than with the other Central Asian republics. Since 1991 the term "Eurasia" has been widely used in Russia and Kazakhstan to define a more ambiguous region, sometimes encompassing not only Russia and Central Asia but also other former Soviet republics (Laruelle 2008; Gleason 2010). A more expansive notion of "Greater Eurasia" developed by some Russian intellectuals covers much of the continent, including China, Russia, India, Central Asia, and Iran, and has a clear geopolitical agenda to construct a counterbalance to US power (Karaganov 2016). By contrast, another geopolitical construct, the idea of "Greater Central Asia" sought to disconnect Central Asia from Russia and instead reconnect it to Xinjiang, Mongolia, and Afghanistan in alignment with broader US strategy in the region (Starr 2005).

These diverse geographic labels highlight the extent to which social constructedness of regions always emerges from a particular interpretation of history. The current conventional definition of Central Asia derives from frontiers drawn during the period of expansion by imperial powers into the region in the nineteenth and twentieth century. The legacies of imperial history are evident in the most significant geopolitical line of fracture across the region, the frontier of Afghanistan along the Amu Darya river, the fault line introduced in the nineteenth century by Russia and Britain, which carved out Afghanistan as a buffer state between the two expanding Asian empires. Russia's rapid nineteenth-century expansion across Central Asia determined the political content and the boundaries of the region to both south and east for the next 150 years. China's influence in Inner Asia diminished sharply after 1911 but was reasserted in Xinjiang, Tibet, and Inner Mongolia after 1949 (Siegel 2002; Forbes 1986; Frankopan 2015). Soviet border policy, compounded by Sino-Soviet tensions after the 1960s, further hardened these borders and divided the region from historic trade routes and cultural ties to the rest of Asia. Imperialism defined the boundaries of the present-day region but also informed the metaphor of the "Great Game," the Russo-British struggle for influence in the region, which continues to be used as a discursive frame to assert the fractured nature of international relations in the region (Morgan 1973; Becker 2012; Yapp 2001).

A second historical fracture within the region stems from the Soviet process of national territorial delimitation, the creation of the titular Soviet republics that form the basis of today's five nation-states: Kyrgyzstan, Kazakhstan, Tajikistan,

Turkmenistan, and Uzbekistan. Based on Soviet thinking about nationality—defined as a coherent ethnic group with its own territory—Soviet ethnographers and officials divided the region known in the late Tsarist period as Turkestan, which was populated by a very heterogeneous population in terms of ethnicity, language, way of life, and identity, into new territorial formations defined on the basis of a dominant titular nationality. The Soviet state prioritized national identities for a population that had largely self-identified through other categories, whether religious, tribal, nomadic, or settled, rather than the nationality categories to which they were now ascribed (Hirsch 2000, 2005; Edgar 2006). Passportization formalized these new divisions and institutionalized them in bureaucratic structures and symbolic representation.

Although Soviet delimitation policy is sometimes described as facilitating Moscow's "divide and rule," this account is misleading (Hirsch 2000). Border delimitation was based on ethnographic and demographic information, influenced by local political disputes and economic viability rather than attempting to maintain the logic of colonial rule. Nevertheless, there was certainly no exact fit between administrative boundaries and ethnic identity in the Soviet republics. Uzbek ethnicity, in particular, spills over into neighboring states. Uzbek communities in neighboring Kyrgyzstan, Kazakhstan, Tajikistan, and Turkmenistan cause anxieties of national identity in those countries (Fumagalli 2007). Disputes between ethnic Uzbeks and ethnic Kyrgyz over resources, status, and identity fueled interethnic conflict in southern Kyrgyzstan in 1990, and again in June 2010, when hundreds died in violent clashes. Soviet policy also encouraged large-scale migration by Russians and Russian speakers into Central Asia, particularly into Kazakhstan and major cities, such as Tashkent. This influx was partially reversed by an outflow of Russian speakers, primarily to the Russian Federation, in the 1990s. Nevertheless, Russian-speakers still form sizable minorities in Kazakhstan and Kyrgyzstan. In Kazakhstan, the Russian-speaking minority is largely resident in northern regions of the country that some Russian nationalists claim as Russian territory. Other diasporas—Soviet Koreans in Uzbekistan or Chechens in Kazakhstan—are the legacy of Soviet-era forced resettlement programs but have had a lasting impact on societies in the region.

Regional loyalties formed another set of cleavages inside states. After independence Kazakhstan periodically faced centrifugal forces from its northern provinces while oil-producing Western Kazakhstan occasionally proved restive, dissatisfied with the division of benefits with central elites (Cummings 2000). President Nursultan Nazarbayev shifted the capital to the new city of Astana, primarily to assert a new spatial identity for the nation and to overcome regional fracturing (Wolfel 2002). In Kyrgyzstan, a traditional north–south divide is often characterized as dividing the Kyrgyz nation along cultural, religious, and political lines. In reality, other internal fractures—among southern local elites, or between rural and urban areas—are often just as salient (Lewis 2008). Tajikistan's strong regional identities—and forms of political economy associated with different regions—contributed to the civil war that the country experienced in the 1990s. The traditionally dominant northern region of Sughd was sidelined as the southern regions around Kulyab challenged eastern regions for political and economic power in the new state (Heathershaw 2009). In Uzbekistan, political struggles were also often characterized as being among regional elites, with Tashkent and Samarkand groupings dominant for much of the post-Soviet period while elites from Fergana and other regions were marginalized (Collins 2006).

Formally coherent states were also challenged by the informal social structures that asserted alternative spatial imaginaries, challenging the reach of central governments and creating alternative regional networks not dependent on formal interstate relations. Informal social and political networks were formed through genuine and fictive kinship networks and through mutual relations developed through business, informal institutions, and political activism (Collins 2006; Schatz 2004; Tuncer-Kilavuz 2009). In some cases, underlying historical clans played a role. In Kazakhstan, for example, three broad historical clans in Kazakh society, known as *zhus* or "horde," and various subclans appeared to reinforce fractures within the Kazakh nation (Schatz 2004; Junisbai 2010). In many cases, however, substantive political and business networks developed based on long-standing financial, educational, or institutional connections, and these formed both within states and across borders. These networks acted as patron–client systems in which relations of trust and mutual support operate vertically, culminating in a particular patron at the top of a pyramid-type structure (Hale 2015; Radnitz 2010). Although often viewed as weakening the state, in some cases informal networks and patron–client systems functioned in ways that strengthened formally weak post-Soviet states (Lewis 2017). In a similar way, at a regional level, informal networks of political, business, and security elites ensured that some types of regional linkages were maintained even when formal state-to-state relations were weak or dysfunctional. Kathleen Collins (2006) argues that neopatrimonial, authoritarian regimes are resistant to economic regionalism because it often requires liberal reforms that might undermine their domestic political position. However, the informal networks that constitute these states can form transboundary networks in ways that mitigate the lack of formal cooperation. Organized criminal networks—allied with state institutions or powerful political elites—manage effective trade corridors in illicit goods across the region, including opiates smuggled from Afghanistan (Lewis 2014). Smaller-scale smuggling routes were frequently able to ensure that cross-border trade networks continued to function even in situations where cross-border movement was formally halted. Security and intelligence services often maintained informal links, even when political relations between states were poor.

These historical, ethnic, and social cleavages contributed to a crisis of sovereignty for the post-Soviet Central Asian state. In response, state-led nation-building programs promoted a national identity that often denied underlying ethnic differences. Attempts to develop a singular national Uzbek identity, for example, occluded alternative identities, such as the Tajik cultural roots of many residents of Samarkand. Similarly, the Tajik nation-building process was impatient with diverse regional and ethnic identities across Tajikistan: The central government repeatedly intervened to suppress aspirations of autonomy among the Ismaili people of Gorno-Badakhshan in Eastern Tajikistan. They had formed part of the opposition during the 1990s civil war and subsequently faced military interventions in 2012 and 2014 to suppress "warlords" who often received significant local support. Almost inevitably, this imposition of narrow nationalism at home also involved the identification of enemies abroad. Governments often presented the wider region as a source of danger, not as an opportunity for peaceful cross-border trade and social interaction. In Uzbekistan, President Islam Karimov argued, "Uzbekistan is encircled by countries burdened with ethnic, demographic, economic and other problems" (cited in Megoran 2005, 561–62). As a result, according to Nick Megoran, "the 1990s thus witnessed a marked shift in Karimov's sense of the geopolitical identity of Uzbekistan, from a self-confident polity at peace with itself and its neighbours to a besieged island of civilisation in a sea of anarchy that threatened to submerge it" (Megoran 2005, 562). All countries in the region used the experience of Afghanistan as an external threat to demonstrate the need to heighten internal security and as legitimation for authoritarian practices. The Kazakh and Uzbek authorities frequently pointed to political and social unrest in their neighbors, Tajikistan and Kyrgyzstan, as examples of the dangers of liberalization and Islamist radicalism, and often viewed regionalism through a pathological lens that saw cooperation as permitting the infection of political instability to spread across boundaries.

These anxieties over sovereignty and security partly explain the difficult interstate relations experienced in the region during the first twenty-five years of post-Soviet independence. Processes of border delimitation were often strongly contested and in some cases remained uncompleted more than twenty-five years after the collapse of the USSR. At least until the death of President Karimov in 2016, Uzbekistan had poor relations with all its neighbors—intervening in the civil war in Tajikistan in the late 1990s, launching military raids against guerrilla forces in southern Kyrgyzstan in 1999, and imposing severe constraints on cross-border trade and travel with Kyrgyzstan and Tajikistan. Uzbekistan's autarkic economic policy of import substitution further accentuated border disputes, limiting intra-regional trade, people-to-people contacts, and transport links across the region. As a result, Central Asia became one of the least integrated and trade-friendly regions in the world (Cooley 2012). Traveling across borders was often accompanied by tales of harassment, bribery, corruption, and violence. While external powers promoted visions of connectivity and regional trade, the realities of borders in the region became very different (Reeves 2014). Frontiers remained nodes of extreme tension rather than exchange. The Uzbek–Kyrgyz and Uzbek–Tajik borders were heavily mined and fortified and were often closed to travel and trade. Shootings were common. In May 2015 twenty-two-year-old Mansur Makhmudjon Uulu was shot dead when he attempted to cross the Kyrgyz–Uzbek border with potatoes and apricots to sell (Putz 2015b). Uzbek border guards shot dead thirty-six-year-old Kazakh Ualikhan Akhmetov, the father of seven children, when he went out fishing on the Syr Darya River (Putz 2015a). These everyday geopolitical tragedies are stark reminders of the fundamentally fractured nature of the region.

Regional Identity and External Hegemony

An emphasis on national sovereignty and the construction of postcolonial national identities undermined the development of a coherent regional identity. Uzbekistan, for example, which might have assumed the role of regional leader, became an internally focused autarkic state, reluctant to become involved in regional initiatives that might challenge its policies of hard borders and ultrasovereignty. Turkmenistan followed an even more extreme course of self-isolation under the rhetorical protection of a policy of neutrality. Both states pursued active policies of exclusionary nation building, focusing on Uzbek and Turkmen identity to the detriment of any supranational loyalties. Kazakhstan, Kyrgyzstan, and Tajikistan were all open—to varying degrees—to other modes of regional cooperation, but, without Uzbekistan's involvement, there was only limited capacity to develop any genuine regional cooperation. In 2016–17 there were initial signs of a new regional policy emerging in Tashkent, which pursued improved relations with its neighbors and sought to revive trade links within the region, but progress remained slow.

A lack of top-down regional integration, or what has been dubbed "Old Regionalism" (Hettne 2005; Söderbaum 2016), was accompanied by a lack of any indicators of what scholars identified as "new regionalism," defined as "a range of formal/informal mid-level 'triangular' relations among not only states but also non-state actors, notably civil societies and private companies" (Söderbaum and Shaw 2003, 1). New regionalism acknowledged the significance of regional activity in the fields of culture, education, private business, and civil society, with nonstate actors complementing regional organizations and states. It also saw new regional initiatives as more open to globalization and less likely to be influenced by hegemonic powers in determining a sense of "regionness" (Söderbaum and Shaw 2003; Söderbaum 2016). Very few of these attributes of new regionalism could be easily identified in Central Asia. There were almost no regional civil society organizations, business associations, or educational networks, with the exception of those that were externally funded and designed. There was some bilateral trade between countries in the region, but for all countries the main trade links were with extraregional partners—namely, China, Russia, and the EU. Labor migration also had some regional aspects, with both Kyrgyz skilled workers and many Uzbek laborers working in agriculture or trade in Kazakhstan. However, these intraregional flows were outpaced by migration to extraregional states in ways that undermined rather than strengthened a sense of Central Asian regional space. As many as 1 million Kyrgyz, 1.5 million Tajiks, and more than 3 million Uzbek citizens worked as labor migrants in Russia, producing alternative spatial imaginaries constituted by new patterns of settlement and migration. These "bottom-up" flows tended to reinforce hegemonic concepts of regionalism, in which external actors played leading roles in defining the region and shaping regional norms and institutions.

External Powers and Hegemonic Regionalism

In a further distinction from the new regionalism literature, which presumed an end to hegemon-led forms of regionalism in the post–Cold War world, Central Asia has been distinguished by multiple efforts to overcome regional fractures and to induce regional cooperation through externally led regional institutions (Cooley 2012; Lewis 2015). Indeed, almost all post-Soviet regional initiatives have been led by regional powers, primarily Russia and China, but with sporadic proposals also introduced by the US and the EU. Each of these projects explicitly sought to overcome intraregional fractures and promote trade, connectivity, and regional integration. They proposed alternative mechanisms for increased regional cooperation, however, effectively importing a regional identity, a set of norms and values, and a particular discourse that corresponded to the identity projection of the external partner. As a result, geopolitical projects, far from overcoming intraregional divides, have often added a further complex layer of fractured relations on top of existing interstate differences.

The EU promoted regional integration as a central feature of successive EU strategies toward Central Asia, effectively mirroring the EU's own identity in its policy toward the region (Boonstra 2015), but these regional projects usually failed to achieve their objectives. The US initiated the New Silk Road (NSR) project, which sought to build on the wider footprint of US power in the region, particularly in Afghanistan, to overcome historical fault lines in the wider Central and Southern Asian region and to reconnect disparate political entities into a new zone of free trade and connectivity (Kuchins, Sanderson, and Gordon 2009; Laruelle 2015c). The idea was first mooted in 2009, when the US began using Central Asian transport infrastructure to resupply International Security Assistance Force troops in Afghanistan through the Northern Distribution Network. In a 2011 speech in Chennai, US secretary of state Hillary Clinton announced this new strategy designed to link Central and South Asia.

> Historically, the nations of South and Central Asia were connected to each other and the rest of the continent by a sprawling trading network called the Silk Road. Indian merchants used to trade spices, gems, and textiles, along with ideas and culture, everywhere from the Great Wall of China to the banks of the Bosphorus. Let's work together to create a new Silk Road.... That means building more rail lines, highways, energy infrastructure, like the proposed pipeline to run from Turkmenistan, through Afghanistan, through Pakistan into India.[1]

Clinton's speech outlined a lost, mythical world along the Silk Road, characterized by peaceful trade in goods and ideas, and proposed overcoming existing fractures through US-led free trade and infrastructure initiatives. While free trade offered an ideological panacea to overcome the region's divisions, US geopolitical goals nevertheless reinforced new boundaries, effectively constructing a Central Asian region integrated with South Asia, differentiated from the former colonial power, Russia. In reality, the discourse of connectivity along the NSR was undermined by the reality of continued obstacles to trade, including that of corruption, which the military Northern Distribution Network appears to have worsened rather than improved (Lee 2012, 25). An electricity network promoted as part of the NSR—CASA-1000—far from promoting more regional integration, threatened to deepen tensions over water and energy use between Uzbekistan and Tajikistan. Most significantly, a growing strategic interest by the US in the region in the 2000s—and a fear among political elites of what were perceived as Western-backed "color revolutions" in the neighborhood—stimulated counter projects by Russia and China, which intensified geopolitical competition across the region.

Russian-led regional cooperation initiatives in Central Asia were complicated by the colonial past and sensitivities about sovereignty among Central Asian states. The original post-Soviet regional organization set up after the collapse of the USSR—the Commonwealth of Independent States (CIS)—became largely moribund by the mid-1990s as it encountered the new sovereignty projects of independent post-Soviet states. Instead, selective forms of regional cooperation emerged, first in the security sphere and later in trade and economic policy. In security, Russia's Collective Security Treaty Organization (CSTO) brought together Kyrgyzstan, Kazakhstan, and Tajikistan (and, until 2012, Uzbekistan) in a security pact. However, the CSTO had very limited capacity to address security challenges arising from interstate conflicts or from intrastate violence (Lewis 2015). A Russian think tank published a report in 2011 calling for significant reforms to internal decision-making procedures and for capacity to mount peacekeeping-type operations (Yurgens 2011). Yet such pragmatic proposals misunderstood the nature of emerging Russian policy in the region. The failure to develop the CSTO as an effective multilateral regional security organization reflected a very different understanding in Moscow of how regional stability should be achieved in Central Asia. Rather than prioritizing multilateral peacekeeping interventions, Russia preferred to support strong allied regimes in the region through bilateral security and military relationships. In that sense, the CSTO was not a genuine multilateral regional organization but an institutional framework through which Russia could pursue bilateral goals.

Successive regional economic initiatives pursued by Russia in the 1990s and 2000s were ineffective. The Eurasian Economic Union (EEU), a customs union of five members (Russia, Kazakhstan, Kyrgyzstan, Belarus, and Armenia), which began functioning in 2015, was a much more ambitious project that adopted technocratic functionalist ideas to overcome regional fractures and obstacles to regional trade. Technocrats working in its supranational body, the Eurasian Economic Commission, in Moscow referenced the European Union as their institutional model. However, attempts to develop the commission—and a corresponding EEU court in Minsk—as autonomous supranational institutions were stymied by the unwillingness of individual member states to cede sovereignty and their preference for political means to achieve economic goals and to resolve cross-border disputes. Moreover, the EEU was characterized by a duality between a technocratic project, often supported by liberal economists and business (Vieira 2015, 4; Dutkiewicz and Sakwa 2015), and a geopolitical project, aimed at asserting Russia's role both in the region and as a pole in a new multipolar global order (International Crisis Group 2016a). Within the "technocratic" EEU, borders often became easier to negotiate as customs posts were dismantled, but the EEU also produced new fractures defined by the boundaries of the customs union, at which high trade tariffs and new regulatory barriers were enforced. In this way the EEU also created new barriers to cooperation in the region by integrating Kazakhstan and Kyrgyzstan into a Russian-led customs union while Uzbekistan, Tajikistan, and Turkmenistan remained outside, reflecting a further division across Central Asia between states oriented toward Moscow, such as Kazakhstan and Kyrgyzstan, and those that sought to maintain more distance from Russia (Cooley and Laruelle 2013).

Abbott Gleason was among many skeptics who argued that "the unity of post-Soviet 'Eurasia' is fragmentary and fleeting" (Gleason 2010, 31), and that "the positive, attractive power of a 'Eurasian idea' under any kind of Russian hegemony is at present negligible" (Gleason 2010, 32). There was certainly concern in many Central Asian capitals about Russian intentions in the region, but attitudes varied by country and by social group. There was broad support for close relations with Russia among both elites and the wider population in Kyrgyzstan, contrasted with very ambivalent and even hostile positions to more Russian influence among elites in Uzbekistan and Turkmenistan. Attitudes toward Eurasian initiatives also vary within societies. Across the region, opinion polls—although not always reliable—suggested that among all Central Asian societies, regional integration with an orientation toward Russia has quite widespread support (International Crisis Group 2016a). What this means is more ambiguous, however, since the concept of "Eurasia" remains contested and polysemous. The EEU asserts a technocratic and institutional meaning for Eurasia, but the term is used with many other political, economic, and cultural meanings (Laruelle 2015a, 2015b; Smith and Richardson 2017). For far-right Russian nationalists, for example, Eurasia is more ideology than geography, a counterhegemonic idea that unites all those opposed to an "Atlanticist" liberal international order (Dugin 2014). For Kazakhstan, on the other hand, a very different form of Eurasianism offers the possibility to enhance cooperation with Russia while ensuring national sovereignty and openness to the wider world (Kudaibergenova 2016). These diverse meanings have led some to argue that "far from being a significant ideational, geographic, economic and strategic space, Eurasia . . . is an incoherent mess of spaces" (Smith and Richardson 2017, 5). Yet the contested nature of "Eurasia" does not lessen its importance as a geopolitical imaginary. The promise of Russian visions of Eurasia to overcome fractures within the Central Asian region by redefining it through a close relationship with Russia may prove illusory, but the different conceptualizations of Eurasia will continue to have profound impacts on geopolitical thinking in the region.

China's regional initiatives explicitly reject a concept of divisive regionalism, and instead have sought to promote an inclusive vision of connectivity, trade, and cooperation. Chinese foreign policy thinking claims to overcome conflictual international concepts such as "balance of power" or "alliances," seeking instead "win-win" solutions in a harmonious international environment. While Russia's regional initiatives often prioritized spaces and boundaries, China's initiatives have been focused more on the promotion of economic and infrastructure links across the region, linking to the global economy, rather than promoting a conventional form of regional integration (Kaczmarski 2017). Nevertheless, despite an explicit denial of any form of regional hegemony, Chinese initiatives are inevitably characterized by significant asymmetries of economic power and suggest to some the emergence of a new sinocentric form of regional order (Callaghan 2016). China's projects in Central Asia have sought to reconstitute the region by connecting it to China's internal efforts to overcome domestic divisions and the assertion of a new type of Great Power relations in the international system (Godement 2014).

China's first attempt to institutionalize its presence in Central Asia was through the Shanghai Cooperation Organisation (SCO), a regional security club, which included China, Russia, and four of the five Central Asian states (India and Pakistan also joined in 2017). Turkmenistan asserted its long-standing policy of neutrality as a justification for its unwillingness to enter any regional organizations, but that stance did not prevent it from forming an increasingly dependent economic relationship with China, which became the main buyer for Turkmen gas exports. Tajikistan also developed increasingly close economic ties to Beijing, although its reliance on Russia for security ties and as a destination for millions of labor migrants ensured that relations with Moscow remained critical for the regime. The increasing influence of China complicated the geopolitical landscape of Central Asia, ensuring that any Russian vision for overcoming regional fractures through a renewed model of Moscow-centric hegemonic regionalism was unlikely to succeed.

When Chinese president Xi Jinping announced the Belt and Road Initiative (BRI) in 2013, in which Central Asia would play a central role, it opened up new possibilities for enhanced Chinese influence in the region. The BRI was framed as an international extension of the "Chinese Dream," an idea of a China restored to greatness, albeit without threatening any of its neighbors (Callaghan 2016). At a work forum on periphery diplomacy in 2013 Xi called for diplomacy that would "warm the hearts of others so that neighboring countries will become even friendlier" (Heath 2013). The BRI is a central initiative in this new regionalism, in which China's national interests are designed to be complemented by the provision of regional public goods (Sørensen 2015) The BRI aimed to overcome the fractures of disputed borders and complex trade regimes through the construction of new Chinese-funded transport infrastructure and Chinese support for cross-border trade, improved customs procedures, and reduced nontariff barriers. Economic growth and cross-border trade was designed to support a zone of "harmonious societies," pro-Chinese regimes in Central Asia along the BRI. By opening up trade with Central Asia, Beijing also hoped that the BRI would assist in overcoming deep divisions inside China, above all between Han Chinese and ethnic Uighurs inside Xinjiang. However, the grand aims of the BRI to enhance regional cooperation under the aegis of a benevolent Chinese state also risked fueling new fractures in society. Growing Chinese influence encountered historical anti-Chinese sentiment in Kyrgyzstan and Kazakhstan. Chinese investments—particularly plans to lease land to Chinese business—sparked protests in Kazakhstan in May 2016. Chinese business in Kyrgyzstan also faced popular protests and sometimes violent attacks (International Crisis Group 2017). Popular opposition was based not only on traditional xenophobic attitudes toward a powerful neighbor but also on perceptions that Chinese investments involved close relations with predatory elites and were often accompanied by allegations of high-level corruption and malfeasance. As such, foreign investments were frequently portrayed as accentuating already existing class cleavages and disparities between rich and poor (International Crisis Group 2017).

Russian and Chinese projects also aimed to prevent Western powers from achieving a strategic foothold in the region. Tension with US strategic goals has been an inevitable result of both Russian and Chinese regional initiatives, although for the most part the US has viewed the BRI initiative as less threatening to its interests than Russian regional projects. This united stance regarding a Western presence in the region has disguised potential tensions between Russian and Chinese regional projects in the region. In May 2015 in Moscow, Russian president Vladimir Putin and President Xi agreed to coordinate the EEU and the BRI, and there were numerous subsequent negotiations and meetings, but with few tangible results. This does not mean that cooperation is impossible: both sides understand that such talks and agreements effectively paper over incompatibilities between the two projects but construct an important discourse of cooperation that may make such differences less important.

The Eurasian Consensus? Overcoming Fractures through Norms and Discourse

These new institutional projects, primarily focused on regional economic cooperation, have so far failed to overcome the many underlying fractures in the Central Asian region, thereby contributing to the conventional argument that the region is fundamentally divided. In the realm of ideas and discourse, however, some countervailing trends might be identified that nuance or complicate this conclusion. An important recent strand in the regionalism literature focused on "the shared beliefs, norms and rituals that hold a region together," the intersubjective meanings that together serve to constitute a region and underpin a common worldview among states and other regional actors (Emerson 2014). Emerson argues that while military and economic power still plays a central role in region building, the development of particular regional institutions and practices also depends on common understandings or discourse in which actors share a common language and ascribe similar meanings to events and arrive at a common understanding of the world. In Central Asia, it is possible to identify elements of a shared regional discourse that comprises a familiar set of nonliberal norms, including state-led development, the subordination of civil society to the state, a valorization of internal and external sovereignty, and the downplaying of individual rights in favor of the state. Although there are significant differences in political systems across the region, ranging from neototalitarianism in Turkmenistan to the laissez-faire semidemocracy of Kyrgyzstan, many elements in this political discourse are shared by elites across the region. In a neo-Gramscian sense, these ideas form a hegemonic discourse in which there is wide agreement on fundamental meanings and interpretations of social phenomena, even where there is often significant disagreement among actors on specific issues.

Such an approach suggests that by analyzing common discourses among regional elites, we may perceive elements of "regionness" even in a region that is otherwise fractured by political, economic, and geopolitical divides. Some evidence for such a shared set of norms can be found in the founding documents and texts of regional organizations, such as the SCO, which promote a shared set of norms at odds with the liberal principles promoted by Western states and organizations, such as the Organization for Security and Cooperation in Europe (Lewis 2012). Thomas Ambrosio (2008) argued that a "Shanghai spirit" discourse was promoted through the SCO as a framework for a process of norm promotion by China across the region. China used the language of the "three evils" (terrorism, religious extremism, and separatism) and has seen them reproduced in regional forums and official discourse. This discursive formula is repeated in speeches at successive SCO summit meetings but also circulates within member states. For example, in February 2013 the antiterrorism center of the State Committee for National Security of Kyrgyzstan echoed this SCO trope when it announced "it [would] hold explanatory work in government agencies and other interested agencies on threats of international terrorism, religious extremism and separatism in Kyrgyzstan and Central Asia" (Kabar 2013). In this way, contested concepts such as "self-determination" or "minority rights" are given shared meanings that become institutionalized through regional organizations and bilateral relationships and become accepted as "common sense" by regional elites.

One version of this argument is the attempt by Filippo Costa Buranelli (2014a, 2014b) to explain Central Asian regional politics through a reworking of English school theories of international relations, which argue that even in an anarchical international order, states can form an international society based on observance of some common norms and institutions. A rescaling of English school ideas to the regional level opens up a perspective that emphasizes cooperation among Central Asian states rather than division. An analysis of voting patterns and speeches by Central Asian representatives at the UN, for example, demonstrates that they share common positions in many debates on the interpretation of international norms in ways that belie their regional divisions (Costa Buranelli 2014b). This idea of an evolving set of shared norms is more nuanced than notions of "autocracy promotion," which suggest a conscious, linear process of learning, testing, and adopting particular policy ideas from external actors (for discussion, see Ambrosio 2010; Burnell and Schlumberger 2010; Bader 2015; Tansey 2016). Instead, the emergence of a common discourse that references a common set of agreed meanings and interpretations of reality comes through constant processes of social interaction influenced by preexisting historical, cultural, and social norms and practices.

This shared discourse has important consequences for our understanding of a fractured region. First, it partly explains why—despite fundamental fractures between and within states—armed conflict has been relatively rare in the Central Asian region. Second, this intersubjective agreement among actors offers an explanation for the ability of certain hegemons to assert their influence in the region effectively while others are sidelined or marginalized. Russian and Chinese influence in the region is not only the result of security support or economic assistance but also reflects their ability to share normative understandings with states in the region, which are intensified by regular institutional exchange in forums such as the SCO or other multilateral formats. Western attempts to gain traction in the region, on the other hand, have been hampered not only by limited funding and a lack of political commitment but by the absence of a shared set of norms that would underpin broader cooperation. Third, shared discourses permit configurations of geopolitical power that might appear paradoxical when viewed through a neorealist lens. As discussed earlier, the prospects for Sino–Russian relations are often viewed negatively when analysts focus on strategic political or economic interests. But agreement by both powers on the wider normative landscape provides a basis for their ongoing cooperation in the region (Wishnick 2017).

Conclusion

Central Asia remains a deeply fractured region, lacking the most obvious attributes of the new regionalism such as effective regional associations, civil society links, or extensive business cooperation and intraregional trade. Despite these deep fault lines, a multilayered approach to regional fracture suggests that a focus primarily on evidence of regional fracture threatens to overlook important areas of agreement, particularly those evident in the area of norms, ideas, and interpretations of the world. Despite personal, political, and economic differences, regional leaders often share a common discourse and view the world in similar ways. External powers such as China have introduced new normative content into this shared discourse but without significant resistance since their ideas tend to overlap with existing conceptualizations of the nature of the state and its role in relation to society. Even more evident is the extent to which contemporary Russian models of political and economic order, which emphasize counterrevolutionary ideologies and conservative norms, have become central to ideological and political thought across the region. These illiberal ideas, rather than being imposed from outside, have evolved organically through a constant process of discursive interaction among elites in the region. Many of the forums and institutions that served as the platforms for this normative and discursive agreement were dismissed by Western analysts as ineffectual "talking shops." In reality, it may turn out that this role—as discursive forums—served a critical function in developing a shared regional discourse based not on liberal norms or the tenets of the new regionalism but on authoritarian and illiberal ideas of political and social order. Despite the continuing salience of serious political, social, and economic fractures in the region, agreement among elites on shared norms has begun to provide a framework for the emergence of new forms of "illiberal" regionalism in Central Asia.

Note

1. Hillary Clinton, "Remarks on India and the United States: A Vision for the 21st Century," Chennai, India, July 20, 2011, US Department of State, https://2009-2017.state.gov/secretary/2009 2013clinton/rm/2011/07/168840.htm.

PART III

Postcolonial Roots of Regional Fracture beyond the Post-Soviet Space

CHAPTER SEVEN

Stuck in Between: The Western Balkans as a Fractured Region

Dimitar Bechev

In comparison to other areas on the edges of the European Union (EU), the Western Balkans looks rather stable. The EU and the North Atlantic Treaty Organization (NATO) have made inroads into the region, and despite Russia's rising profile in certain countries, it falls short of being a full-blown geopolitical adversary. The threat of war between and within states has receded dramatically since the 1990s. Relations between different ethnic communities are far from harmonious, but power sharing under international tutelage has gone a long way in mitigating the risk of violence on a major scale. There is a clear contrast with the turbulence across Europe's "neighborhood," from Syria to Donbass and from Libya to Nagorno-Karabakh. Challenges in the Balkans have more to do with the perverse aspects of ill-conceived stability. Indeed, stability has become in several cases a cover for democratic erosion, state capture, and economic and social malaise (Bechev 2012).

To be sure, the legacies of Yugoslav disintegration are still haunting the Balkans. The political deadlock in a complex polity such as Bosnia and Herzegovina and the ongoing dispute over Kosovo's independence are not resolved. Relations between Serbia and Croatia, a member of both the EU and NATO, have hit a low point. The Macedonian name issue, straining ties between Skopje and Athens, is far from settled. But what is even more troubling is that the EU, traditionally the anchor of stability and transformation, has been exporting its own internal problems. Balkan economies have been hit badly by the eurozone crisis; recovery to pre-2008 growth levels has not taken place—with all attendant social and political consequences. The 2015–16 refugee crisis when the so-called Balkan route emerged as the main conduit for the mass movement of people from war-torn Syria and Iraq and countries further afield to the core of the EU came as yet another external shock (Dimitrov and Wunsch 2016). To boot, Yugoslavia's successors have been at the forefront of the illiberal wave sweeping across the continent (Gordon, Kmezić, and Opardija-Susnjar 2013; Dolenec 2013; Günay and Džihić 2016; Bieber and Kmezić 2017). With democratic regimes still a long way from consolidation, and in most cases actually backsliding, the countries in question have produced their own versions of Viktor Orbán and Marine Le Pen. That is hardly the fault of the EU, as the region itself has a venerable tradition of nationalism and authoritarian politics (Janos 2000; Fischer 2006; Lampe 2014). Yet the democratic backslide widens the factures between normative aspirations and the grimmer realities on the ground.

This chapter argues that the EU-driven process of region building has been a qualified success. However, the unfinished business of the 1990s together with the democratic and governance deficits weigh heavily on the Western Balkans. The ostensible stability of the status quo (e.g., no more wars over borders) coexists with fragility within states and societies, adding to the fractures that continue to shape the region's politics and societies. This is where Russia comes into the picture. It has managed to exploit the blind spots and weaknesses in order to (re)insert itself in the politics of the region. Indeed, Russia has built alliances with actors in Orthodox-majority countries such as Serbia, Montenegro, Macedonia, and Republika Srpska (part of Bosnia and Herzegovina), allowing it to project influence, obstruct EU policies, and score points in its tug-of-war with the West (Bechev 2015). As elsewhere, regional fractures have worked as a key enabler for a more assertive Russian approach.

Defining the Western Balkans

The Western Balkans, essentially the majority of the Yugoslav successor states plus Albania, ticks most boxes set by the discipline of international relations (IR) as benchmarks for "regionness." It represents a contiguous geographical space that is knit together by multiple linkages at the level of politics, the economy, and, not least, human connections. What is more, the countries that populate the region, with the prominent exception of Albania, were not that long ago part of the same political entity: the Socialist Federative Republic of Yugoslavia. Yet the Western Balkans is also, in a matryoshka-doll fashion, a region within a region within a region. It forms part of Southeast Europe (SEE)—a looser area that also includes EU members such as Croatia, Slovenia, Bulgaria, Romania, Greece, possibly Cyprus, and, with some caveats, Turkey. And, of course, SEE falls within the EU, a macroregion spanning from the North Sea to the Mediterranean and from the Atlantic all the way to the Black Sea and the western boundaries of Turkey, Ukraine, Belarus, and Russia. It is the EU along with its arsenal of norms, institutions, instruments, and policy initiatives that has spearheaded the region-building exercise in SEE, and more narrowly in the post-Yugoslav space, since the early 2000s. Brussels institutionalized the Western Balkans into a political unit, albeit one with shrinking borders considering that Croatia is—formally, at least—no longer part of it since joining the EU. Moreover, the 2007 and 2013 enlargements transformed the region into a territorial enclave surrounded by EU member states, reinforcing the already strong political and economic ties between the EU, on the one hand, and the local countries. It is not an exaggeration that, by virtue of the dense linkages, the Western Balkans is the EU's "near abroad" or, to use a less diplomatic expression, its backyard.

Is the Western Balkans (Still) a Fractured Region?

The principal contention of this volume is that the concept of fractured region provides a superb analytical device to study the international politics of the "gray zones" in Eurasia sandwiched between the West (essentially EU and NATO) and Russia. Fractured regions may differ in fundamental ways from the notion of regionalism and regional integration prevalent in the IR literature since the 1960s, but they are an empirical reality, as acknowledged by researchers from various strands in the discipline (Ohanyan, in this volume). Conflicts and discord between and within states within a given geographical setting tied together by common history and overlapping security concerns are not antithetical to the concept of "regionness." The EU example of a closely integrated region (or a collection of regions) with a tier of supranational institutions underpinned by a legal order that supersedes national laws is one among several modes of being a region. Scholars of comparative regionalism have shed considerable light on the variation of regional orders and integration models, bringing forth examples from Asia, Africa, and Latin America (Hurrell and Fawcett 1996; Acharya and Johnston 2007). Zooming in on Southeast Europe, the Western Balkans were as much a region in the 1990s during the Yugoslav Wars as they are now. What differed back then was the makeup of the glue that connected the various political entities and communities. It was the nature of interlocking conflicts that tended to metastasize across former Yugoslavia along the transnational soft security risks that resulted (cross-border crime and corruption, migration driven by ethnic cleansing and war), not the positive forces of economic integration and policy cooperation. Paradoxically or not, the fractures and cleavages in the region also cement its identity as a political unit. In that regard, the two concepts of "regional complex" and "fractured region" appear, at least in this particular case, to be complementary rather than antithetical.

The question one should ask is what sort of a region is the Western Balkans at present? To what degree do the fractures of the 1990s remain salient? Or, alternatively, is the effort thrown into region building and bringing the Yugoslav successor states into the EU mainstream bearing fruit in terms of cementing a different type of regional order? As the introductory chapter in this volume contends, the two tenets of transition to an integrated regionness would be (1) the consolidation of statehood of the constitutive units and (2) the growing density and depth of institutions operating at the regional level. As we shall see in the sections to follow, those two conditions are largely fulfilled in the Western Balkans, especially when compared to other regions across Eurasia. At the same time, the veneer of stability and integration obfuscates several interlinked fissures that continue to make the politics of the area fragile. They align with the three dimensions mapped out in the introductory chapter in this volume: institutions, values, and power. What comes next is an account of how each of those three dimensions are manifest in the Western Balkans.

Institutional Consolidation: Achievements and Unfinished Business

The Western Balkans is sustained by several layers of intergovernmental institutions invariably linked to the EU. There is, of course, the enlargement track, with each of the six countries bound by Stabilization and Association Agreements and subject to monitoring by the European Commission for compliance with the political, economic, and legal-institutional conditions and benchmarks for membership. It is safe to expect that they will join the Union in the 2020s or soon thereafter. That is even the case of Kosovo, whose status as an independent state is not recognized by five of the EU members (Cyprus, Greece, Spain, Romania, and Slovakia).[1] In addition to the technocratic side of enlargement, there is also the political one—courtesy of the so-called Berlin Process kick-started in August 2014 by the German chancellor, Angela Merkel. The Berlin Process, an annual forum for heads of state and government, brings together the EU, the Western Balkan 6 (Albania, Bosnia, Kosovo, Macedonia, Montenegro, Serbia) and the likes of Slovenia, Austria, Croatia, and Italy, states that are intimately linked to the region (Balfour and Stratulat 2015).[2] The principal mission is to give impetus to the political and economic reforms demanded by the EU as a prerequisite for membership. There are other institutions at play as well: the Sarajevo-based Regional Cooperation Council, heir to the Stability Pact for Southeast Europe of the early 2000s; the Central European Free Trade Agreement (CEFTA), a network of free-trade agreements; and the Southeast European Transport Observatory, among other functional initiatives (Bechev 2011). The Western Balkan 6 also form the core of the EU-sponsored energy community, which also includes Ukraine and Moldova and is to expand to Georgia as well. In sum, this is a regional grouping that is embedded in multiple institutions at both the political and technocratic level and halfway integrated into the EU structures.

The top-down vector of regionalization (Hurrell and Fawcett 1996) matches a bottom-up reality too. Tim Judah, the Balkans correspondent for the *Economist*, has written about the emergence of the "Yugosphere," which is rooted in extensive economic, cultural, and human links running across former Yugoslavia that have resurfaced with the gradual pacification of the region since the early 2000s (Judah 2009). As he adds, the Yugosphere is complemented by another transnational space to consider: the Albanosphere—formed around Albania and Kosovo but also including the Albanian communities in neighbors such as Macedonia, Montenegro, and Serbia.[3]

In a sense, it is all rooted in the economy. The countries of the region, by and large, trade extensively with each other. Although the EU accounts for about two-thirds of the total turnover, the share of intra-CEFTA exports in 2015 stood at 17 percent, while imports were at 10 percent. For a country like Montenegro, the share goes as high as 43 percent for the exports and 38 percent for imports. Serbia, the region's largest economy, sends 21 percent of its exports to the fellow CEFTA members. Those figures concern trade that is reported to national statistics—the actual volumes are higher if one factors in unreported transactions and the gray sector. Importantly, since 2013 there is a positive growth trend with regard to intra-CEFTA trade, after a contraction in 2011–12.[4]

But it is not just trade (in goods and agriculture) that drives regionalization forward. There are other indicators as well, such as the rise of cross-border tourism. Each summer, Croatia, Montenegro, and Albania attract a large number of holiday travelers from neighboring countries, in addition to the ones coming from Western Europe, especially Russians traveling to Montenegro. Second, regional TV channels broadcast in Serbian/Croatian/Bosnian and in Albanian (serving the "Albanosphere"), including the Balkan affiliate of Al Jazeera headquartered in Sarajevo and N1, a twenty-four-hour news channel with studios in Belgrade, Zagreb, and Sarajevo. There are also reality shows with participants from across the Western Balkans. Performers from the Yugoslav era but also from the decades following the collapse of the multinational federation pull the crowds across the region. Protest movements from Belgrade (e.g., Don't Let Belgrade D[r]own / Ne da[vi]mo Beograd, which tackles sore urban development issues and high-level corruption) to Tuzla to Skopje connect and influence one another too.[5] As elsewhere, the internet and the spread of social media facilitate and condition the process of cross-border networking. To cut a long story short, the Western Balkans entity is not just a political construct but a sociological reality as well.

At the same time, institutionalization driven from the outside creates lines of division. As a result, the region itself remains fluid and its boundaries variable. By definition, the region is destined to shrink and wither away as the expansion of the EU rolls on. This is what happened in July 2013 when Croatia became the bloc's twenty-eighth member, effectively leaving the group in formal-institutional (though not in practical) terms. Once Montenegro and even Serbia, in many respects the pivotal state in the area, join the EU (or whatever remains of it) in the 2020s, they will cease to be classified as "Western Balkan." Internal differentiation is already under way since the countries of the region have variable relations with outside anchor organizations. Thus, some have entered NATO (Croatia and Albania in 2009; Montenegro to follow suit in 2017), while others, such as Serbia, are committed to a policy of neutrality and nonalignment. In the same vein, countries vary in terms of their integration into the EU—Montenegro and Serbia are engaged in membership talks, Albania and Macedonia have candidate status (though Macedonia is effectively stuck since 2009 due to the name dispute with Greece), Bosnia is still waiting to be promoted to candidacy, and Kosovo is hobbled by the nonrecognition of five EU member states. An even more important line of division is between those states in the region that still have to deal with sovereignty and constitutional issues—again, Bosnia and Kosovo—and the rest, whose external and internal legitimacy is not put into question. As in any other regional complex, analysts of the Western Balkans explicitly or implicitly engage with the classic theme of how the forces and factors fostering unity and internal diversity/fragmentation combine and feed into one another.

The internal consolidation of statehood, the other element of transformation through EU-driven institutionalization, is even more problematic. There is still unfinished business concerning the cases of Kosovo and Bosnia and Herzegovina. They continue to be the target of peacekeeping operations, although both the EUFOR (European Union Force) and the KFOR (Kosovo Force) have been considerably downsized. Bosnia is still a sort of dual protectorate of the UN and EU since the Office of the High Representative is still in existence, as are the so-called Bonn Powers, allowing the high representative to fire elected officials and pass legislation. Following the unilateral declaration of independence by the Kosovo parliament (February 17, 2008), the legal status of the erstwhile Serbian province remains unresolved. All but five EU members have recognized the new state. In the Western Balkans, it is only Serbia and Bosnia and Herzegovina that refuse to acknowledge the change of status from an international protectorate sanctioned by the UN Security Council Resolution 1244 to full statehood. However, Belgrade has been working, under EU tutelage as a quid pro quo for moving forward in the accession talks, to normalize ties with Prishtina, stopping extending formal recognition. The Brussels Agreement of April 30, 2013, came as a turnaround. Serbia agreed to cooperate in specific sectors, from customs to telecommunications, and, even more important, to reintegrate the northern parts of Kosovo under its control into the formal structures centered in Prishtina. In exchange, the Kosovar leadership accepted the granting of wide-ranging autonomy to local Serbs as well as the establishment of an association of Serbian-majority municipalities, a controversial point with Albanian nationalists. Although the 2013 deal did not solve the dispute regarding sovereignty in Kosovo, it does set the parameters for a future settlement. That does not necessarily mean that Kosovo will be resolved smoothly—or, indeed, that progress is irreversible. There are several spoilers on both the Serbian and Kosovar Albanian side (Bieber 2015). Despite consistent EU pressure, Belgrade and Prishtina have dragged their feet over merging the judiciary in Serb-majority Northern Kosovo (BalkanInsight 2017).

Bosnia, the other legacy item of the 1990s, is in a different spot. Its status as a state is not questioned. Neither Serbia nor Croatia harbor irredentist ambitions at present, a clear departure from the era of Slobodan Milošević and Franjo Tudjman. It is the dysfunctional politics of the complex polity with multiple levels of authority that the Dayton Accords created and the three main communities (Bosniaks, Serbs, and Croats) divided into separate constitutional-legal silos that is bedeviling Bosnia. The leadership of the Serb-majority entity, Republika Srpska (RS), insists their quasi-state has the right to secede from Bosnia and Herzegovina. RS president Milorad Dodik has been resorting to brinkmanship tactics, asserting the right to hold a referendum on secession in order to resist efforts at centralizing power generally favored by the West (Bechev 2016). Meanwhile, in the Federation, the Bosniak and Croat majority part of Bosnia, radical Croat politicians have been pressing on and off for a separate entity. The constant bickering over the common state's constitutional arrangements has deadlocked the policymaking process, holding hostage ordinary citizens. It furthermore diverts attention from mundane governance issues as well as from corruption. Bosnia lags behind its neighbors on the path to the EU as well.

All other countries fare better than Bosnia or Kosovo with respect to the issue of sovereignty. This applies also to multiethnic societies such as Montenegro and especially Macedonia, which has its own power-sharing model following the Ohrid Framework Agreement. Overall, the familiar security agenda related to borders, contested sovereignty, and the threat of organized violence capable of disrupting the political and territorial status quo has been relegated to the past. Where border disputes exist, for example, concerning islets in the river Danube that passes through both Croatia and Serbia, they are consigned to the foreign ministry officials and treated, for the most part, as a technical rather than political matter.

The Values Gap

The "Europeanization" of the Western Balkans has won much praise by politicians and pundits, but the formal adaptation to externally imposed scripts and expectations is at variance with the values held by political elites and a significant portion of their constituents. Many of the root causes that triggered the violent conflicts of the 1990s are still in existence. Nationalism has not lost its appeal; hatchets have not been buried. There is a strong case to be made that neighboring states still see one another as a threat. The rift between the EU normative vision, which on paper still reigns supreme, and the informal principles and values that guide political and social life is the second dimension of regional fracture one should take into account.

Increasingly hostile relations between Croatia and Serbia, the two main players in the region, offer a vivid example. Formally, both subscribe to the EU set of values, including regional cooperation and reconciliation. In practice, governments on both sides have toughened their rhetoric and policies vis-à-vis the neighbor. Croatia's modernization of its armed forces in line with membership in NATO has become a vexing issue in Serbia, with calls for upgrading military capabilities by purchasing fighter jets and antiaircraft missile systems—with help from Russia—to offset the Croats' (perceived) advantage (Milekic 2016). For its part, Zagreb has decided to play hardball and exercise its veto in Serbia's EU accession talks to gain diplomatic advantage. Incidentally, the same strategy was applied to Croatia itself in the late 2000s—by neighboring Slovenia. In the fall of 2015 to spring of 2016, Belgrade and Zagreb also traded some tough words regarding the handling of the refugee crisis. Although escalation is probably not in the cards, Serbian–Croatian relations have gone backward compared to the high point between 2010 and 2012, when Presidents Boris Tadić and Ivo Josipović would fraternize in bilateral summits or international conferences.

Zero-sum thinking prevails in the wider region as well. In Bosnia, RS leaders fuel and exploit their constituents' fears and the memories of war to gain political advantage. Although it is hard to conceive a scenario in which the Serbian entity unravels and is subsumed into a unitary state centered in Sarajevo, the symbolic threat posed by the other is, as ever, an enormous asset to rally popular opinion behind the flag. The same goes for Bosniak political elites who use RS recalcitrance to cement their electoral base, where the trauma of ethnic cleansing and genocide in the 1990s has not been healed. Bosnian Croats repeatedly push for a separate entity to be carved out, which would constitute a major revision of the 1995 Dayton Accords.

Similarly, in Kosovo the implicit threat of a Serbia challenging or subverting the budding state's newly gained sovereignty is a constant leitmotif in domestic squabbles. The association of Serbian municipalities foreseen under the Brussels Agreement is a hot issue as well as heaven-sent for hard-liners who drum up concerns about the threat of subversion through the establishment of a state within a state. To Kosovo's south, in Macedonia, the ruling VMRO-DPMNE (the Internal Macedonian Revolutionary Organization–Democratic Party) has never ceased to capitalize on the resentment against and fear of the Albanian community. Although Prime Minister Nikola Gruevski has stayed in power since 2009 thanks to coalitions with ethnic Albanian parties, he has been aptly using the specter of federalization as a prequel to partition to maximize his support. That is what happened in Macedonia in early 2017, when a political crisis triggered by the allegations of high-level corruption and abuse of power morphed into a dispute about the constitutional role of Albanian language and the rights of the ethnic Albanians.

This all goes to show that nationalism may be contained, adapted to the new realities of the 2010s, and even tamed, but it remains a force to be reckoned with. Political operators have abundant incentives to milk it to their own advantage, just as when Yugoslavia descended into chaos and bloodshed. As much as it is a projection of past conflicts and grudges, nationalism perpetuates regional fractures. The fact that it is often driven and fanned from the top down, not an organic expression of popular will, does not make it less consequential.

At the same time, exclusivist ethnic nationalism, even in its most virulent form, can happily coexist with a commitment to membership in the EU. In contrast to the recent past, value-grounded fractures stop short of causing violence on a significant scale. There are a multitude of reasons as to why this is the case. One indispensable factor worth highlighting is the comprehensive investment in stability by the "international community"—that is, the US and the EU. To fall back on theory, the overlay of external players has anchored political stability, deploying a range of instruments: from brute military force through conditionality tied to economic and political benefits to the soft power of attraction. Intervention and integration have reshaped the regional environment and reconfigured the conditions and incentive structures.

Local elites, even those who have been on the forefront of the wars in the 1990s, have for the most part changed their tune as well. They have adapted to the external overlay and generally prospered under the new status quo. Rather than fight back against the EU and the US, they have learned to talk the talk of democracy, rule of law, and Western values without necessarily walking the walk, at least not all the time. Thus, former (ultra)nationalist parties have reinvented themselves as pro-EU conservatives. That has clearly been the case of the Croatian Democratic Union (HDZ), the party of Tudjman, that, after winning power in late 2003, became a champion of European integration. It was the HDZ government that extradited celebrated generals such as Ante Gotovina, a hero of the so-called Homeland War (1991–95), to the International Criminal Tribunal for former Yugoslavia in The Hague. In much the same way, the Serbian Progressive Party (SNS) of Tomislav Nikolić and Aleksandar Vučić broke from the ultranationalist Radicals and then won power in 2012. Led by Prime Minister Vučić, SNS has overseen the normalization process with Kosovo in tandem with the Socialist Party of Serbia once presided by Slobodan Milošević. What is more, Vučić has opposed the attempts to overhaul the Dayton Agreement in Bosnia and the RS's bid to break apart from the common state.

The trouble in the Western Balkans is that the turn toward the EU has gone hand in hand with a reversal of democratization. The superficial adoption of liberal democratic norms is at odds with informal rules that facilitate state capture and limit elite accountability. Essentially, governments and leaders across the region offer to the West to maintain external stability with the proviso they should be let off the hook when it comes to standards at home. "Stabilitocracy" (see Pavlović 2016) has been on a constant rise in past years, but it was brought to new heights by the refugee crisis of 2015–16 when Macedonia and Serbia emerged as indispensable allies in the effort to curb the influx of asylum seekers from the Middle East. Again, the case of Serbia is very instructive. Prime Minister Vučić has aligned with the EU over Kosovo and even Bosnia on the implicit understanding they would be spared tough questions on issues such as media freedoms, the rule of law, relations with civil society, accountability and transparency in the economy, and the security apparatus. The same goes for Montenegro, which has been governed by the same political force, the Democratic Party of Socialists (heir to the League of Yugoslav Communists) with Milo Djukanović, a one-time ally of Milošević who switched allegiance to the West in 1996–97, serving as either prime minister or president. Another towering figure in the same cohort is Gruevski, who evolved from a technocratic financier into a populist strongman holding a grip on Macedonia's politics and economy from 2006 to 2017. The other names worthy of a special mention are, of course, Milorad Dodik and Hashim Thaçi, the former guerrilla leader who is now the president of Kosovo.

The most salient fracture, therefore, is the one between principles of democracy and rule of law propagated by the West and local practices bending and diluting the latter (Bieber and Kmezić 2017). Balkan "stabilitocrats" subscribe to the basic rules of electoral democracy but make sure there is no level playing field as far as political competitors are concerned. Parties in government use public sector employment and influence in the police, security apparatus, and media to cement their power. The opposition is often marginalized or out of touch with the electorate. EU-mandated judicial and civil service reforms have not stamped out graft and entrenched the rule of law, although frontrunners have scored modest progress. State capture by political elites and special business interests remains pervasive. Media freedom has been the worst-affected area as the economic crisis has made the state the chief source of funding. This dynamic is captured by the indices of watchdogs such as Freedom House (see table 7.1).

In that context, civil society is the only credible corrective to governance dysfunctionality. As elsewhere in the world, the spread of the internet, smartphones, social networks such as Facebook and Twitter, and content-sharing platforms facilitates collective action. A new brand of horizontal civic organizations is on the rise, which differs from the 1990s crop of Western-funded nongovernmental organizations. Since about 2013 street protests have taken place in Bosnia (the Bosniak-Croat

Table 7.1 Freedom House: Democracy Scores 2007 and 2016

	2007	2016	Regime type (2016)
Albania	3.82*	4.14	Hybrid
Bosnia and Herzegovina	4.04	4.50	Hybrid
Kosovo	5.36	5.07	Semi-consolidated authoritarian
Macedonia	3.82	4.29	Hybrid
Montenegro	3.93	3.93	Semi-consolidated democracy
Serbia	3.68	3.75	Semi-consolidated democracy

*1 highest, 7 lowest
Data Source: www.freedomhouse.org.

Federation), Serbia, Macedonia (dubbed "a colorful revolution"), Montenegro, and Kosovo. They have been animated by political grievances (e.g., electoral fraud in Macedonia), socioeconomic issues (workers' rights in Bosnia), and state capture (Don't Let Belgrade D[r]own in Serbia). This type of collective action bypassing formal political institutions is one of the few glimmers of hope that democratization has not run out of steam. Of course, incumbent elites have also learned their lesson. In more than one case, they have done their best to delegitimize civic protests by painting them as driven from murky outside forces (George Soros and his foundation are the usual suspects, as is the US government; in Montenegro, Russia takes the blame.) Through various strategies, for example, through loyalist media, governments have been using protest to polarize the electorate and maximize their own support in the grassroots.

The Power Fracture

The value fracture is reflected into a fracture of power. Formally, the Western Balkans are fully subsumed into the Western sphere of influence. The contrast with other regions across Eurasia, where the geopolitical rivalry between contending powers is the norm, is clear cut. However, the mismatch between the EU-promoted transformational agenda and the institutional legacies and entrenched values within the region opens sufficient space for other players to project influence. That applies, first and foremost, to Russia, which, over the past decade or so, has carved out its niche in the region.

That the Western Balkans gravitate toward the West is hardly surprising. This is due to a combination of factors: geographical contiguity, common historical and political legacies, dense cross-border linkages, and a sense of shared identity—however contested—harking back to the Yugoslav days (again, Albania is the outlier on this count). The collapse of the federation and the wars of the 1990s, starting from the ten-day conflict in Slovenia all the way to the armed standoff between the Macedonian government and the ethnic Albanian National Liberation Army in the spring and summer of 2001, have been the formative experience shaping the politics of the area, as have been several waves of Western military and diplomatic interventions, in stark contrast with the post-Soviet space, which never experienced anything on that scale. Key milestones included NATO's involvement in Bosnia and Herzegovina that ultimately brought about the Dayton Accords of 1995, the Alliance's Operation Allied Force over Kosovo in March–June 1999, the Office of High Representative in Bosnia overseeing postconflict reconstruction in Bosnia and UNMIK in Kosovo, the deployment of peacekeeping missions (IFOR/SFOR superseded in 2004 by EUFOR and KFOR), the ongoing EU-mandated rule-of-law operation in Kosovo, countless humanitarian assistance and economic development initiatives, elections monitors and institution-building programs, and investment into civil society and interethnic reconciliation (Siani-Davies 2003; Keil and Arkan 2015). When it comes to the "international community," there is hardly an intergovernmental organization or global nongovernmental organization that has not been involved in the area, alongside the US and the principal EU states. Few, if any, other regions anywhere in the world have seen such a massive international presence. Although the heyday of external intervention is now long passed and (as we shall see shortly) the EU has taken over from "the international community" writ large, it has left its deep mark on the Western Balkans and contributed to the global recognizability and identity of the region. Starting from the early 2000s, all Western Balkan countries have been included in the EU's policy of enlargement. They already participate in a number of policies and institutions based in Brussels.

Yet, as we have seen in the previous sections looking at institutions and values, the Western Balkans remains halfway integrated: its formal inclusion into the EU-sphere is no cure to local practices that fall short of norms and prescriptions of the external hegemon. Because the Union conceives its foreign policy as one based on the promotion and dissemination of values rather than simply the defense of interests (Manners 2002), the value gap translates into a fracture of *power*. The predicament is made even more complex by the myriad of internal challenges hobbling the EU project from within: the rise of populist and xenophobic parties questioning the legitimacy of supranational integration and calling for the imposition of hard borders, the ultimate departure of the UK ("Brexit"), the eurozone crisis deepening the rift between the "core" and the southern periphery, and the anxiety caused by the 2015–16 migrant crisis (Tsoukalis 2016). The internal strain in the EU impairs both its soft power (that is, attractiveness to outside players) and its ability to project its normative influence.

The value fracture along with the relative weakening of the EU has made it easier for Russia to become more deeply involved in the former Yugoslavia and wider SEE (Bechev 2015). Moscow's policy in the region has gone through several stages. In the 1990s Russia became involved in the Yugoslav Wars in order to safeguard its status as a first-rate player in European security affairs. Most of the time, it tried to partner with Western powers in resolving crises. But other times it also attempted to leverage its relationship with Serbia to balance against the US, notably during the Kosovo crisis of 1998–99. It was not a happy experience overall. Russia did obtain a measure of recognition with its inclusion in the Contact Group, a latter-day version of the Concert of Europe that began work in 1994 in connection with the Bosnian War. But its attempts to play the protector of Bosnian Serbs as well as Milošević ended in frustration with NATO's military interventions in 1995 and especially 1999 (Headley 2008). The second phase, coinciding with Putin's first two terms and Dmitry Medvedev's stint as president, started with the pull-out of the Russian military contingents from Bosnia and Kosovo in 2003. However, Kosovo's unilateral declaration of independence brought Russia back in as Serbia reached out to Moscow as an ally in the international campaign to oppose recognition. The South Stream pipeline project turned the Western Balkans into a critical piece in the Russian strategy to bypass Ukraine as a transit corridor for gas deliveries (Bechev 2017).

What we have now is the third phase of Russian engagement. It came with the crisis in Ukraine and the strain of relations between Moscow and the West. South Stream has been shelved. Tensions with the EU and the US, low energy prices, and scarce resources make it more difficult for Russia to go about co-opting governments. Even friendly countries such as Serbia, which refused to side with the Western sanctions and developed security and defense links to Moscow, are hedging bets and balancing between Russia and the EU. Montenegro, once perceived as a Russian economic enclave, opted for membership in NATO. Accordingly, Russia has been implementing a strategy to exploit weak spots across the region in order to disrupt EU influence and put a spanner in the works of the West. If Western actors meddle in its "near abroad" (Ukraine, Georgia, Moldova, etc.), Russia wants to show it can do mischief in the EU's backyard too.

There are numerous examples. In Bosnia, Russia has provided diplomatic cover for years for Milorad Dodik's obstructionist policies and threats of triggering secession. Playing the patron of local Serbs, Moscow's patronage of Dodik provides incentives for the Bosniak community to reinforce relations with Turkey, perceived as a sort of a kin state on account of extensive diaspora there. In 2014 Russia hinted it could veto the extension of a EUFOR peacekeeping mission in the UN Security

Council. Thus, it instrumentalizes local cleavages to gain advantage in the overall confrontation with Western powers. Moscow has also inserted itself in the domestic politics of Montenegro and Serbia, backing parties and leaders who argue for a radical rupture with the West. In November 2016 Montenegrin authorities accused Russian nationalists connected to the Kremlin of colluding in a coup plot aimed at derailing accession to NATO. In the run-up to the parliamentary elections in Serbia (April 2016), pro-Russian campaigners organized rallies demanding a referendum on NATO. That was an indirect attack against the SNS-led government, which maintains that the neutrality resolution adopted by Parliament in 2007 has settled the issue once and for all. Prime Minister Vučić maintains that Serbia's interest is to develop security ties with both Russia and the West. In Macedonia, Russian media and even Foreign Minister Sergey Lavrov portrayed the antigovernment protests erupting in the spring of 2015 as yet another unfortunate instance of a Western-instigated color revolution.[6] By contrast, in Montenegro, Russia backs the opposition that has also staged street protests. It stresses the duplicity of the Western support for a government marred by corruption. Shockingly, the Russian military intelligence, the GRU, are alleged to have been involved in a failed coup attempt in the minuscule Adriatic republic on the eve of the general elections in October 2016, in league with rogue security operatives from Serbia. The plotters' goal was to derail Montenegro's imminent accession to NATO—which took place on June 5, 2017 (RFE/RL 2017b).

Such disruptive tactics fall short of a concerted policy of rolling back Western influence in the region, let alone replacing the EU as the hegemonic power in the Western Balkans. Yet they make sense in the context of the overall strategy of balancing the West through exploiting fractures and divisions in Europe. As elsewhere, Russia has been playing a weak hand well. It might not have the billions needed to buy Balkan elites' loyalty through lucrative projects such as the South Stream or financial flows commensurate to those coming from Western Europe. But it does have local allies and wields symbolic resources (e.g., the notion of cultural and religious bonds thanks to Eastern Orthodoxy). In countries such as Serbia, RS, Montenegro, and Macedonia, Putin and Russia appeal to considerable segments of public opinion, which holds a grudge against the West that is fueled by the memories of the 1990s. Even if in material terms the West and Russia are not equals, at the symbolic and representational level, they increasingly appear as two rival polls competing for the region. In February 2015 US secretary of state John Kerry famously said that Serbia, Macedonia, Montenegro, and Kosovo all fall within a "firing line"—just like Georgia, Moldova, and Transnistria (B92 2015).

Conclusion

The Western Balkans is a paradigmatic case of "half full, half empty." NATO and EU intervention and expansion has produced a stable regional order. However, the cracks remain visible and are indeed growing bigger as the EU is consumed by overlapping internal crises. In such conditions, the textbook tradeoff between stability and transformation is increasingly resolved in favor of the latter. That has in turn exacerbated the trend toward democratic backslide indicative of a deep-running value fracture between the Western prescriptions and the entrenched norms and informal "ways of doing things" in the region. Russia has found a fertile ground to project influence by exploiting local power fractures. While it is highly unlikely that the Western Balkans could pivot into the Russian sphere of privileged interest, Moscow has carved out a niche in the region and is able to leverage it in its strategic interaction with European powers and the US.

Notes

1. Kosovo was the last state to sign such an agreement in October 2015. The EU signed as a single entity (a right conferred by the 2009 Lisbon Treaty), which was an elegant way for the five nonrecognizer members to avoid the legal implications without obstructing the common policy on Kosovo.

2. The 2015 summit took place in Vienna. Paris hosted the one in 2016, and Rome in 2017.

3. One should also add the large migrant communities of Albanians in Greece and Italy (from Albania) and Austria, Germany, Switzerland, and Sweden (from Kosovo and other parts of ex-Yugoslavia). Members of Yugoslav diasporas also form part of the Serbian/Croatian/Bosnian-speaking "Yugosphere," although nationalist divisions and bitter memories of the 1990s certainly complicate the picture.

4. Data from the CEFTA Trade Statistics Brochure (2015), http://cefta.int/wp-content/uploads/2016/05/CEFTA-Trade-Statistics-Brochure-2015.pdf.

5. For extensive coverage of protests, see the *Balkans in Europe* blog, copublished by the Center for Southeast European Studies at the University of Graz and the European Fund for the Balkans, http://www.suedosteuropa.uni-graz.at/biepag/taxonomy/term/150.

6. The crisis in Macedonia was resolved in May 2017 with the formation of a new government coalition led by the pro-Western Social Democratic Union, replacing the Center-Right VMRO-DPMNE—a party that championed Euro-Atlantic integration when it assumed power in 2006 but then gradually veered into isolationism and flirted with Russia.

CHAPTER EIGHT

Syria and the Middle East: Fracture Meets Fracture

Mark N. Katz

Like the other regions studied in this volume, the Middle East is a region that has been strongly affected by regional fracture. Unlike most of these other regions, though, regional fracture in the Arab states and Israel did not result from Tsarist or Soviet policies but from policies pursued first by the Ottoman Empire and, later, by Western—especially British and French—imperial powers. Both during the Cold War era and the Putin era, though, Moscow sought to take advantage of existing regional fractures to pursue its own aims in the Middle East—especially in Syria.

This chapter examines how Putin has attempted to take advantage of existing regional fractures to reassert Russia as a great power in Syria and elsewhere in the Middle East. Exploiting fractures in this region (as well as exploiting mistrust of the United States) has allowed Moscow to regain some of the influence in the Middle East that it had lost at the end of the Cold War, but these regional fractures have also served to limit what Putin has been able to achieve there so far. Indeed, Russia's increased presence in the Middle East must not be seen simply as being the result of Putin's assertive foreign and military policies but as the result of various Middle Eastern actors wanting Russia as an ally against their regional rivals as well as their loss of confidence in Washington's willingness to play this role. But Putin's efforts to "have it all" and increase Russian influence with all major Middle Eastern actors (excepting the jihadists) has served to limit Russian influence not just with those who oppose Russia's policy in Syria (especially Saudi Arabia) but also those who support it (especially Iran).

Before examining how Putin's policy has interacted with regional fracture in the Middle East, something must be said about how this phenomenon has evolved first in Syria and then the region more broadly. But before this, we need to look at how the theory of regional fracture applies to the Middle East.

Applying Regional Fracture Theory to the Middle East

In chapter 1 in this volume, elucidating the theory of regional fracture, Anna Ohanyan discusses the three dimensions to this phenomenon: (1) the political/power dimension, (2) the institutional dimension, and (3) the social fracture/values dimension. All three of these dimensions are observable in the Middle East's regional fracture.

The political/power dimension of regional fracture in the Middle East has long been present. Different external great powers have exercised predominant influence in the Middle East over the past two centuries, including the Ottoman Empire, the British and French colonial empires, the US and the Union of Soviet Socialist Republics (USSR) during the Cold War, America during the post–Cold War era, and a resurgent Russia under Putin. In each of these cases, the external great power has sought to exercise its influence in partnership with local elites, which have often been minorities. Both sides in this arrangement have benefited: External support has allowed local elites (especially when they are minorities) to obtain resources from abroad, enabling them to exercise a degree of control that they would have found difficult to establish or maintain otherwise. Similarly, external great powers have usually been able to rely on vulnerable local allies who are dependent on them to remain loyal. Usually, but not always, at times of transition when one great power is falling and another rising, the local allies of the former can switch to being allies of the latter. And rising great powers have sometimes allied with the local opponents of a falling great power's vulnerable local allies. These local opponents-turned-rulers have then become the new vulnerable allies, dependent on a great power.

These collaborations between external great powers and vulnerable local allies can be characterized as imperial ventures that are maintained as a result not just of an external great power pushing into a region but of local forces within it pulling a great power in (and acting to keep it there) for their own benefit. Such collaborations, of course, have been made at the expense of the mass of the population and have helped to stunt the development of civil society. With external support, the vulnerable local allies that received it have been able to reduce their vulnerability to any local opposition as well as society as a whole. More concerned about maintaining stability as well as their influence, even democratic great powers have been willing to work with vulnerable local allies that have been willing and able to help them advance and protect their great power concerns. A problem for an external great power can arise, though, when—despite its support—local allies become increasingly vulnerable to domestic opposition. Then a choice must be made between increasing support for a beleaguered ally or attempting to co-opt its rising opponents. Neither strategy is guaranteed to succeed, and both risk the external great power losing its influence and seeing it replaced by that of a rival.

The institutional dimension of regional fracture in the Middle East has been more evident since the countries within it formally became independent in the twentieth century, and most of them established elected legislatures and other institutions that supposedly reflect the popular will but are actually instruments of regime control. This means that democratic institutions are not available to society to bring about evolutionary change. Such change, then, can come about only through revolutionary activity—which of course risks failure and suppression or "success" through replacing one authoritarian regime with another. External great powers helping their vulnerable authoritarian local allies resist such opposition reduces the prospects that these local allies will be replaced by their peaceful, democratic opponents and increases the chances that their violent, authoritarian ones will dominate the political space open to the opposition, if not overthrow the regime.

Similarly, the Middle East's main regional organization—the Arab League—represents the interests of its constituent members: largely authoritarian Arab governments. Unlike the European Union (EU), which seeks to uphold democratic norms among its members, the Arab League basically serves to underpin the existing political dimension of regional fracture in the Middle East.

The social fracture/values dimension of regional fracture in the Middle East has become complicated recently. Perhaps this is not surprising since authoritarian governments are less successful at suppressing the free flow of ideas in the digital age than they are the political movements inspired by them. Still, the existing political and institutional fractures upholding the authoritarian order were clearly not enough to prevent the outbreak of the Arab Spring and its call for democracy. They were, however, strong enough to largely suppress it everywhere. Certain democratic external powers—including the United States and some EU countries—supported the transition to democratization that the Arab Spring initially promised. They did so, though, not just out of the desire to promote democracy but in order to align themselves with what they saw as the rising democratic local forces that were replacing the falling authoritarian ones that they had previously backed. But as these democratic forces proved weak and authoritarian ones reasserted their authority in some states (notably Egypt and Bahrain), the external great powers aligned themselves with the latter—and with the existing pattern of regional fracture they represented. Their willingness to do this was undoubtedly increased by seeing the downfall of the existing pattern of regional fracture leading to chaos in Libya, Yemen, and even Syria (where they called for Bashar al-Assad to step down but did little to bring this about).

The Sunni/Shi'a sectarian split is another example of the complicated nature of the social fracture/values dimension of regional fracture in the Middle East. External great powers and their vulnerable local allies have taken advantage of the

Sunni/Shi'a split (among others) to enforce patterns of regional fracture that benefit them. But in some places—such as Syria and Iraq—this split has become deeply embedded in the popular consciousness and so has intensified to the point that neither external powers nor their local allies can control it. This suggests that the very strength of the social fracture/values dimension of regional fracture can actually undermine its political/power dimension.

With this discussion of how the different dimensions of regional fracture theory apply to the Middle East, we can now turn to an examination of how it has actually developed in Syria and the region as a whole, as well as Russia's role in it.

Pre-Putin: The Evolution of Regional Fracture in Syria

Although sometimes viewed nostalgically as an era of peace, the period of Ottoman rule in what is now Syria witnessed numerous intercommunal and interethnic conflicts—especially over the course of the nineteenth century when these groups saw growing Ottoman vulnerability (Hourani 1991, 277). When the Ottoman Empire collapsed at the end of World War I, France was given control of the territory that became Lebanon and Syria. The French also found local collaborators in establishing and maintaining their rule: Maronite Christians in Lebanon and Alawites in Syria. Now usually described as an offshoot of Shi'ism, the secretive Alawi sect, which was persecuted by the Ottomans, saw the French as protectors against Sunni Arabs, who far outnumbered them. The French recruited Alawites into the lower ranks of their local armed forces (Fildis 2012, 148–56).

Paris's promotion of regional fracture in Syria is succinctly described by Ayse Tekdal Fildis:

> The French policy of divide and rule eroded the ties among Syria's religious and ethnic groups, forging factions within each group and against the others. The French balanced ethnic representation by placing separate ethnicities at the head of different institutional branches of government, allowing one ethnic or religious group to be strongly represented in an institution. As a consequence, the Sunni Arabs were dominant in politics, the officer corps, the gendarmerie and the police, but underrepresented in the military's rank and file. By contrast, the Circassians were overrepresented in the army, but poorly represented in parliament and the police. The Alawites were overrepresented among the soldiers, but poorly represented in politics, the officer corps, the gendarmerie and the police. (Fildis 2012, 149)

After becoming independent at the end of the war, Syria entered a highly unstable phase, during which numerous governments rose and fell, and intercommunal conflict took place. During the 1960s the Alawites, along with other religious minorities in the armed forces, first ousted the highly divided Sunni officer corps and later seized predominant control for themselves. A similar process occurred within what became Syria's Arab Nationalist ruling party, the Ba'ath (Fildis 2012, 150–55).

From the mid-1950s, the USSR was the principal external supporter of Syria's anti-Western regimes, but Syria was definitely less important to Moscow than was Egypt's Gamal Abdel Nasser. But beginning with the rise to power of Hafez al-Assad (an Alawite) as well as the death of Nasser in 1970, which was followed by the deterioration of Soviet–Egyptian relations, Syria became much more important to Moscow during the 1970s and 1980s, although there was also contentiousness in the Soviet–Syrian relationship since Moscow was less anti-Israeli than Damascus and because Moscow supported Syria's neighbor and foe, Iraq (Golan 1990, 140–56).

It must be noted that Moscow did not support what became an increasingly Alawite-dominated regime in Syria because it was Alawite. Moscow supported it instead because it was secular, anti-Western, and pro-Soviet. A regime dominated by any other Syrian minority group, or even the Sunni Arab majority, with similar characteristics might just as well have received Soviet support; in neighboring Iraq, after all, Moscow backed a secular, anti-Western, and pro-Soviet regime dominated by the Arab Sunni minority. Yevgeny Primakov, the longtime Soviet Middle East specialist (and later foreign minister and prime minister under Boris Yeltsin) did note that Moscow saw secular Arab nationalist regimes in Egypt, Syria, and Iraq as bulwarks against the rise of radical Sunni Islamists in these countries (Primakov 2009). Indeed, in a foreshadowing of the revolt against his son's regime that began in 2011, Muslim Brotherhood–led Sunni Arab opposition against the Soviet-armed Hafez al-Assad regime began in 1979 and lasted until its brutal suppression (involving deaths variously estimated from ten thousand to forty thousand) in 1982 (AFP 2012).

Under Yeltsin, Russia largely (but not completely) retreated from the Levant. Putin set out to change this, but his relations with Bashar al-Assad (who became president in 2000 after the death of his father) were quite testy at first due to Putin's insistence that Damascus repay its Soviet-era debt to Moscow. The relationship improved, though, in 2005 in the aftermath of Putin's fears that the West was behind "color revolutions" not just in Georgia (2003) and Ukraine (2004) but also in Lebanon (2005), which resulted in the withdrawal of Syrian forces from that country and fears that the George W. Bush administration might turn its attention to overthrowing Assad. The debt issue was also resolved on terms favorable to Damascus (Katz 2006).

Pre-Putin: The Evolution of Regional Fracture Elsewhere in the Middle East

Space does not permit a detailed discussion of how regional fracture emerged throughout the Middle East. As in Syria, this usually (though not always) began as Ottoman policy and was transformed mainly by the British and French as they gained influence in regions first where the Ottoman Empire was weak and then collapsed. This was followed by British and French cooperation with local collaborators in each of these places to the benefit of both sides (and to the detriment of others), then to power struggles between these collaborators and their internal rivals as the British and French (weakened by World War II) were departing from the region, and finally to alliances between these various groups and either of the newly emergent superpowers—America and the Soviet Union—either to gain or retain power (Lenczowski 1980, 765–73). While the Soviet Union often gained influence from the overthrow of pro-Western regimes (usually monarchies) by anti-Western Arab Nationalist officers, these regime changes usually did not involve a change in the existing pattern of ethnic or sectarian dominance inherited from the colonial era. In Iraq as well as Syria, then, Moscow supported regimes that were anti-Western but that also were dominated by minorities previously favored by the European colonial powers (Alawites in Syria, Sunni Arabs in Iraq).

The most important contribution of British and French imperialism to regional fracture in the Middle East was the redrawing (or confirmation) of Ottoman-era borders between states in it. These borders often put together in an artificially created country groups that were antagonistic to one another—including minorities that were once a majority in a specific region (Burbank and Cooper 2010, 380–86). Despite their intense rivalry during the Cold War, both the US and the USSR supported keeping these borders intact.

One of the most fateful instances of regional fracture in the Middle East—the creation of the Jewish-dominated State of Israel—occurred as a result of British support for Zionist aims toward the end of World War I; British inability to control hostility between indigenous Palestinian Arabs and Jewish migrants; the increase in Jewish migrants to Palestine after the rise of Hitler in Germany; and the retreat from Palestine of a weakened Britain after World War II that gave rise to the Jewish–Arab conflict, resulting in the division of Palestine into three parts: the new Jewish State of Israel, the Jordanian-controlled West Bank, and the Egyptian-controlled Gaza Strip. The United States and the Soviet Union both contributed to this fracture when both extended diplomatic recognition to Israel after its creation. Under Khrushchev, of course, Moscow would switch to supporting various Arab states against Israel. But unlike Arab states, which saw Israel as an illegitimate entity and called (at least initially) for its destruction and transformation into an Arab-ruled Palestine, the Soviet Union continued to recognize Israel's independence—even when Moscow did not have diplomatic relations with it from 1967 until 1991 (Primakov 2009, 253–300).

Another example of regional fracture inherited from the past was the division of the Kurds between the Ottoman and Persian Empires, with European promises of independence for them during World War I not being honored and their continued division among Turkey; Iran; French-ruled, then independent Syria; and British-ruled, then independent Iraq. Moscow was more or less supportive of Kurdish nationalism on various occasions when and where Moscow had poor relations with any of the governments of these four countries. But when it came to choosing between supporting the Kurds or working with these governments, Moscow always came down in favor of retaining existing states and established borders (Primakov 2009, 325–39). It was Washington that would do far more than Moscow to support Kurdish nationalist aspirations in the aftermath of the First Gulf War (1990–91), especially after the US-led intervention in Iraq (2003–11), when the Kurdish Regional Government established de facto rule over Northern Iraq and was dealt with (though not formally recognized) by many states, including Russia (Naumkin 2014).

During the Soviet period, then, Moscow often sought (or just called for) the replacement of pro-Western regimes by anti-Western (and, hence, pro-Soviet) ones, but the USSR acted mainly to uphold, and not challenge, the regional fractures that emerged in the Middle East during the Ottoman, European colonial, and immediate postcolonial eras. Washington did so as well. The one partial exception was that Moscow joined the Arab states in calling for the creation of a Palestinian state. Moscow, though, called for this Palestinian state to be created in the West Bank and Gaza alongside Israel, and not in place of it (Golan 1990, 114).

The one regional fracture that disappeared at the end of the Cold War, the border between North and South Yemen (drawn earlier to demarcate Ottoman and British spheres of influence), occurred as a result of an agreement between the two Yemeni governments leading to their unification in 1990 as the USSR was retreating from the region under Gorbachev. During the Yeltsin era, Moscow largely withdrew from the Middle East. Not only did it not challenge the previously existing regional fractures, it also no longer sought to replace pro-Western governments, as Moscow had done during most of the Cold War (Nizameddin 2013, 37–64).

Putin and the Middle East: 2000–2010

Vladimir Putin has been the most powerful political actor in Russia ever since President Yeltsin appointed him (then Yeltsin's last prime minister) as acting president at the very end of 1999. Putin was subsequently elected president for two four-year terms, in 2000 and 2004; then was prime minister during the presidency of his close associate, Dmitry Medvedev (2008–12), whom Putin had designated as his successor; and finally switched roles with Medvedev in 2012 when Putin decided to run for a third term (but now for six years) as president. Putin was elected to yet another six-year term in 2018. The Medvedev presidency notwithstanding, the Putin era began at the end of 1999 and could well last until 2024—or even beyond.

Since the beginning of the Putin era, Moscow has worked to reassert Russian influence in the Middle East. Moscow has done this mainly through supporting existing governments and, thus, the existing regional fractures upheld by them.

Before the outbreak of the Arab Spring in 2011 (i.e., from 2000 to 2010), Moscow sought to increase its influence in the Middle East through aligning Russia with the existing status quo there. Putin sought to shore up relations with Moscow's traditional anti-American allies in the region: Saddam Hussein in Iraq, Muammar Qaddafi in Libya, and the Assad regime in Syria. Putin also sought to improve relations with the Islamic Republic of Iran (building on one of the few Yeltsin-era initiatives in the region), which, while anti-American, had often had difficult relations with Moscow too. Putin, though, also sought to improve Russian relations with America's traditional allies in the region, including Egypt, the Gulf Arab monarchies, and even Israel. With this latter group, it was not Moscow's aim to displace the US as their major ally but simply to pursue various forms of cooperation with them, including in the realm of trade (Katz 2008).

In addition to established governments, Moscow also sought good relations with three important Arab political movements: Hezbollah, Fatah, and Hamas. While each of these opposed Israel (and Fatah and Hamas opposed each other, while Hezbollah opposed various other parties in Lebanon), each had also become part of the region's status quo, with Hezbollah allying with the Assad regime as well as ruling part of Lebanon, Fatah administering parts of the West Bank, and Hamas seizing control of Gaza from Fatah in 2007 (Nizameddin 2013, 158–62, 217–24).

Under Putin, then, Russia developed good working relations with all the major actors except for al-Qaeda—which did not have good relations with anyone else. Indeed, with its call for the downfall of existing Muslim regimes and the rise of a caliphate across the Muslim world, al-Qaeda sought radical change to the existing regional fractures not just in the Middle East but in the Muslim regions of the former Soviet Union as well as elsewhere (Lawrence 2005, 49). This was quite different from Hezbollah, Fatah, and Hamas, which sought to expand as well as retain political control over specific territories—and which also saw al-Qaeda and other Sunni jihadists as competitors.

Putin's pursuit of good relations with all the major actors in the Middle East was not just aimed at enhancing Russian economic interests or even increasing Russian political influence in the region. He also sought to maximize the degree of support in the Middle East for the existing pattern of regional fracture that Moscow sought to maintain in the former Soviet Union. Middle Eastern (as well as Western) support for the mujahideen forces resisting the Soviet occupation of Afghanistan in the 1980s helped frustrate Soviet efforts to pacify that country (which it withdrew from under Mikhail Gorbachev in 1988–89). Further, Moscow believed that external support from the Middle East had helped fuel the Chechen rebellion in the mid-1990s—something Putin was especially concerned about forestalling after the initiation of another Russian intervention in Chechnya when he was Yeltsin's prime minister in 1999. And in this effort, Putin was largely successful. While some assistance from Middle Eastern governments may have reached the Chechen rebels, Russian intervention in Chechnya did not become a cause célèbre that galvanized Muslim governments and public opinion in the way that the Soviet occupation of Afghanistan had (Trenin and Malashenko 2004, 190–93).

This was partly due to the impact of 9/11, which resulted in most governments throughout the world expressing or even providing support for the US-led intervention in Afghanistan in pursuit of al-Qaeda and the Taliban. It was not just sympathy for the US that motivated this response but fear on the part of other governments—including Russia and many in the Middle East—that al-Qaeda represented a threat to them as well. Further, by giving his blessing for the US-led intervention in Afghanistan as well as the stationing of Western forces in former Soviet Central Asia, Putin elicited a much greater degree of Western "understanding" for Russian intervention in Chechnya—where Moscow claimed it was fighting basically the same enemy as the West was fighting in Afghanistan. Indeed, one of the results of Russian support for the American response to 9/11 was that Washington reportedly pressured Riyadh to curtail Saudi public expressions of sympathy (as well as private sources of material support) for the Chechen rebels (Katz 2004, 3–5).

By contrast, the US-led intervention in Iraq that began in 2003 was widely opposed in the region as well as elsewhere (including Russia). Putin saw the US-led intervention as an attempt to replace a government in Iraq that was friendly to Russia with one that was allied to the US (Nizameddin 2013, 127–52). Further, Russia as well as many Middle Eastern governments opposed the US-led intervention because they (correctly) feared that this action would upset the existing pattern of regional fracture in Iraq and threaten it elsewhere. While Saudi Arabia, Jordan, and other Sunni Arab governments had no love for Saddam, they feared that the replacement of his Sunni Arab minority-dominated regime by a Shi'a Arab majority one as a result of America's democratization effort would result in greatly increased Iranian influence in Iraq (something that Saddam prevented). Further, Turkey feared that American support for Kurdish aspirations in Northern Iraq would not only lead to a de facto independent Kurdish state there but that this would fuel Kurdish nationalism and separatism in Turkey itself. And none of the states in the region, as well as Russia, wished to see democratization actually succeed for fear that this could create unwelcome (to authoritarian governments) pressure for them to democratize as well (International Institute for Strategic Studies 2003, 158–73).

Putin (as well as Turkey and many Arab governments) viewed America as disrupting the status quo as well as existing patterns of regional fracture. Putin portrayed Russia, by contrast, as seeking to protect these and to appeal to governments in the region that viewed the situation similarly. Indeed, while Putin's response to 9/11 was to try to persuade Washington that Saudi Arabia was responsible and was a common threat to Russia and America, Putin's response to the lead-up to and initial US-led intervention in Iraq was to persuade Riyadh that American actions threatened both Russian and Saudi interests (Katz 2004, 9).

Yet, for all of Putin's opposition to the US-led intervention in Iraq, his policy toward Iraq after it occurred and after the US replaced Saddam's regime with one dominated by the Shi'a majority was highly pragmatic. Putin set about establishing improved ties with the new Shi'a leaders in Baghdad—who would soon enough get over their anger at Moscow's having previously backed Saddam, especially as differences between Baghdad and Washington arose over various issues. Moscow was also able to establish good working relations with the Kurdish Regional Government in Northern Iraq (just as Turkey and others did as well). In other words, while Moscow initially sought to preserve the status quo in Iraq (with Saddam and his Sunni Arab minority regime remaining in power), Moscow quickly adjusted to the change in both the status quo and existing pattern of regional fracture (Borshchevskaya 2016, 31–35).

Indeed, Putin was so successful at this that his experience in Iraq may have helped persuade the Obama administration at the outset of the Arab Spring in Syria that even though Putin might express opposition to the downfall of a longtime Russia-approved ruler of a minority-dominated regime in Syria with a new government drawn from that country's majority community, he would quickly adjust to the new situation in Syria just as he had done in Iraq (as a senior officer at a discussion I attended at the Pentagon in September 2012 anticipated). But this, of course, is not what happened.

Putin and the Middle East since the Arab Spring

Prior to 2011 relatively stable authoritarian rule in most Arab countries had persisted for many years or even decades. At the beginning of 2011 massive public protests against long-standing dictatorships spread from Tunisia to Egypt, Libya, Yemen, Bahrain, and Syria (with smaller protests occurring elsewhere). Pro-Western authoritarian rulers were quickly swept from power in both Tunisia and Egypt, with the help of the regimes' own security forces there. Elsewhere, authoritarian rulers resisted their opponents. The pro-Western Bahraini monarchy, which hailed from the nation's ruling Sunni minority, was only able to prevail against opposition from the Shi'a majority with the help of a Saudi-led intervention. In Yemen a settlement seemed to be at hand when the country's longtime president yielded authority to his vice president—but this would later break down when the former president allied with some of his former adversaries against the new president.

More importantly, from Moscow's viewpoint, were the threats that emerged to the pro-Russian regimes in Libya and Syria. Unlike pro-Western rulers in Tunisia and Egypt, the pro-Russian ones in Libya and Syria withstood the initial outburst of opposition, retained control of their armed forces, and moved to forcefully suppress their opponents. Medvedev (who was Russia's president at the time) allowed a UN Security Council Resolution to be approved, creating a no-fly zone in Libya to protect the opposition from Muammar Gaddafi's wrath, but Moscow felt betrayed when several Western and Arab governments went beyond this and gave military assistance to the opposition that resulted, after months of fighting, in their toppling the Gaddafi regime as well as killing Gaddafi himself. When Western and Arab governments began to call for a UN Security Council Resolution authorizing a no-fly zone to protect the Syrian opposition, Moscow refused, claiming that this would be the beginning of an intervention to topple Assad, just as occurred in Libya (Stent 2014, 247–50).

Putin in particular saw the Arab Spring as threatening for several reasons: (1) the Arab Spring was a continuation of the "color revolutions" that had taken place in Georgia (2003) and Ukraine (2004), which he regarded as efforts by America to install pro-American regimes (i.e., the large-scale protests against these regimes were not seen by Putin as resulting from internal causes, but external ones); (2) the impact of successful Arab Spring revolutions (along with the American-led intervention in Iraq earlier) was not the replacement of authoritarian rule by democracy (as Washington claimed it would be) but its replacement by the rise of jihadists and chaos instead; and (3) the ultimate aim of those who promoted the Arab Spring (along with the earlier color revolutions) was for this type of revolution to spread to Russia itself—a view that the eruption of widespread protests in Russia against Putin from late 2011 through mid-2012 (and which Putin publicly declared resulted from a signal sent by Hillary Clinton) only confirmed (Hill and Gaddy 2015, 235).

In response to this apocalyptic vision, Putin sought to portray Russia as the defender of the authoritarian status quo as well as the existing pattern of regional fracture it upheld against American support for its downfall and the rise of conflict that would result. And for many in the Middle East who feared what the overthrow of existing authoritarian regimes there could lead to, Putin's firm defense of the authoritarian status quo was far more reassuring than American criticism of these regimes combined with calls for democratic reform, which they saw as weakening them. Russia and several of America's traditional allies in the Middle East were especially alarmed by what they regarded as the Obama administration's sudden betrayal of America's longtime Egyptian ally, Hosni Mubarak, when widespread opposition to him arose (Stent 2014, 247–48).

In Syria in particular, Putin's efforts to defend the authoritarian status quo were greatly aided by the fact that while Washington was calling for Assad to step down, Obama also made clear that he was not willing either to undertake direct US military intervention or to provide anywhere near the external assistance that Assad's domestic opponents would need to overthrow him. Appalled both by the chaos in Iraq that had resulted from the Bush administration's intervention there and by the chaos that ensued from his own administration's much smaller intervention in Libya, Obama was not willing to countenance another American intervention that would lead to a similar outcome in Syria (Dueck 2015, 84–88). The US, it turned out, was not so willing to see the existing pattern of regional fracture further disrupted in Syria either.

But disrupted it was. For despite receiving support from Russia, Iran, Hezbollah, and other Shi'a militias (and despite limited involvement from the US), the Assad regime lost ground to various groups in Syria, including Islamic State (also known as ISIS), al-Qaeda affiliate Jabhat al-Nusra (which would formally disaffiliate with al-Qaeda), Syrian Kurds, and Sunni Arab and other groups backed by Turkey, Saudi Arabia, and Qatar. Direct Russian military intervention was needed to protect the authoritarian status quo and existing pattern of regional fracture in Syria. Especially ominous from Moscow's viewpoint was that Muslims from the North Caucasus opposed to Russian rule there had come to Syria to fight against Assad—and Putin (International Crisis Group 2016b). Russian military intervention in Syria, then, is protecting not just the existing pattern of regional fracture in Syria but in Russia itself.

While Putin has sought to preserve the existing pattern of regional fracture in Syria since this has meant preserving the Assad regime, he has also supported certain forces arising from the disruption of that pattern through giving some degree of support to Syrian Kurds who oppose both ISIS and the Assad regime. His motive for doing so, perhaps, has been to encourage the Turkish government to reconsider its opposition to the Assad regime in exchange for Russia either not increasing or even reducing its support for the Syrian Kurds whom Ankara fears are linked to the Kurdistan Worker's Party in Turkey (Drwish 2016).

There are other instances of Moscow's acting to support local forces that have arisen from the disruption of existing patterns of regional fracture. In Libya, for example, Moscow has joined Egypt and the United Arab Emirates in giving some support to Gen. Khalifa Haftar in Eastern Libya who opposes the Libyan "unity government" backed by the US (and supposedly the UN) (Reuters 2016). And while Moscow has officially recognized the internationally recognized Yemeni government backed by Saudi Arabia, in late 2016 Russian officials gave some indication of being willing to work with the Iranian-backed Houthi opposition as well as former (and now deceased) president Saleh (Middle East Monitor 2016). Perhaps this was Moscow's way of showing the Saudis that if Riyadh continued to support the opposition to the Russian-backed government in Syria, Moscow could return the favor in Yemen.

Conclusion

Since his rise to power and especially since the outbreak of the Arab Spring, Putin has done much to increase Russian influence in the Middle East through championing not only the region's authoritarian status quo but also its existing pattern of regional fracture. His policy has stood in stark contrast to that of the Bush administration (which threatened existing authoritarian regimes with its grand plan for the democratization of the greater Middle East) and of the Obama administration and other Western governments (which mostly sought to accommodate the Arab Spring's demands for replacing authoritarian regimes). In Syria, in particular, Western calls for democratization would have meant overturning the long-standing pattern of regional fracture through overthrowing Alawite minority rule (which the Assad regime is based on) and replacing it with Arab Sunni majority rule.

Those in the region fearing what the downfall of the Middle East's authoritarian order might lead to have welcomed Putin's support for it. Many even welcomed Moscow's support for the existing regime in Syria (although Saudi Arabia and Qatar did not, since they viewed the contest there as one between Sunni Arabs, on the one hand, and Shi'a Iran and its allies, on the other) (Katz 2015). If nothing else, they saw Putin's support for the status quo after the outbreak of the Arab Spring as useful for putting America and the West on notice that they should return to doing so too for fear of losing influence to Moscow otherwise. This, of course, was similar to the argument that Arab governments in the region had made during the Cold War about how America needed to change its policy toward Israel for fear of losing the Arabs to Soviet influence if it did not—an argument they were unable to make during the Yeltsin and early Putin eras when Russia was not strongly present in the Middle East.

But just because Middle Eastern governments (including Israel) may welcome Russian support for the region's status quo as well as the existing pattern of regional fracture does not mean that they want Russia to become the dominant external power in the Middle East. Even the Assad regime—which is clearly the most dependent on Moscow for its survival—values Russian support partly as a means of lessening its dependence on Iran. Indeed, receiving support from both Moscow and Tehran allows Damascus greater independence from both than if it were totally reliant on only one of them. Assad's continued hard line on Syrian Kurds compared to Moscow's softer one toward them is a case in point (Bozarslan 2016).

Further, while welcome to many authoritarian regimes in the Middle East, Russia's upholding the authoritarian status quo and existing pattern of regional fracture is no easy task for Putin. Although he has intervened militarily to defend the Assad regime, it is highly unlikely that Russia would be able to intervene elsewhere in the

Middle East to defend another beleaguered authoritarian regime. Indeed, it is questionable whether what appears to be Russia's military success in Syria would be possible without the much larger military presence of Iran, Hezbollah, and other Shi'a militias. And while Russia, Iran, and the others have clearly succeeded in propping up the Assad regime and retaking much of the territory it had lost to its opponents, it remains to be seen whether they can actually bring the conflict to closure or will be fighting there indefinitely.

For a larger problem that Russia faces in upholding the authoritarian status quo and the existing pattern of regional fracture is that these have become weaker, especially since the outbreak of the Arab Spring. It will be very difficult for any outside party, including Russia, to restore order wherever it has broken down (such as in Syria, Iraq, Libya, and Yemen). Far from enhancing Russia's ability to do so, America's pulling back from the Middle East under Obama (and which may well continue under Donald Trump) may actually serve to weaken the Middle East's authoritarian status quo and existing pattern of regional fracture. Instead of being an opportunity for Russia to gain influence, then, the downfall of any of America's traditional allies may lead to the rise of a Sunni jihadist regime that is as anti-Russian as it is anti-Western.

It is not at all clear, of course, whether anything like this will happen. The problem that Moscow faces in the Middle East, though, is that, unlike during the Soviet era when Moscow had much greater capacity to preserve the existing patterns of regional fracture when they were stronger, its ability to do so now, at a time when they are weakening, is much less. And should anything happen in Russia that weakens either Putin's rule or the Russian state itself, Moscow will be in a much less favorable position to affect what happens in the Middle East.

Conclusion: Overcoming Regional Fracture

Anna Ohanyan

Moscow's (post)imperial reach has historically extended from its most immediate neighborhoods in the current post-Soviet space to the Middle East and the Balkans, infusing itself in these regions at various depths and densities. This reach has defined grand politics and has affected the daily lives of millions of people in Eurasia for centuries. And the continuity of the imperial engagement in these spaces, from imperial Russia to the Soviet Union, was generally far from evident to most of us, especially to those born and raised with the foundational myths of a "brotherhood of nations," a collective "Communist future," and other grand ideological narratives. This foundational lore portrayed the Soviet experience as distinct and different from all other imperial center-periphery relations that lacked a comparable story and purpose. The exploitative and predatory nature that characterized all other imperial projects was somehow supposedly absent in the case of the Soviet Union.

A resurgent modern Russia has challenged traditional international relations (IR) theories and may well have exposed the paucity of analytical frameworks through which to investigate the post–Cold War period in Eurasia and elsewhere. Contemporary scholarship on Russian foreign policy has generally focused on a range of factors: Putin's leadership style, domestic politics, state weakness and statecraft in Russia, and ideas and political culture in the country, as well as the current structure of the international system, which, some argue, motivates a particularly assertive Russian foreign policy (Götz 2017). A fuller understanding of how domestic and international factors interact and the extent of agency of the Russian state, as well as of the newly independent states in its periphery, has been slow to develop (Götz 2017). Contemporary IR scholarship has also been challenged by the structural effects that characterize the post-Soviet imperial space and that serve to constrain or enable foreign policies in Russia and in the states in its neighborhoods.

The theory of regional fracture developed in this volume and, applied to explain Russia's engagements in its near and far abroad, is one modest step toward addressing this gap in scholarship. Is Russia today an imperial power, and if so, what are the structural effects of its imperial presence on the post-Soviet states as well as the international system? Is it a unique case that transcends established theories of comparative regionalism? How does it fold itself, if at all, into traditional understandings of world order? How does Russia challenge that world order, if it does? These are some of the questions that call for fresh frameworks if one is to garner granular and complex understandings of contemporary Russian foreign policy as well as the newly activated "local" politics within the states in Russia's post-Soviet peripheries.[1]

The theory of regional fracture encompasses Russia's neighborhoods, near and far, in an effort to produce a narrative from the ground up, from the "margins" of the world system and international politics. The view from Moscow of these regions in recent decades has vacillated between benign neglect in the 1990s to hegemonic entitlement (Götz 2017; Clunan 2014). Examining this period through a lens of regional fracture reveals the agency of fractured regions and specifies mechanisms by which they can condition Russian foreign policy. Importantly, and as discussed below, the regional fracture approach illustrates a blind spot in foreign policy circles on both sides of the Atlantic in approaches to a resurgent Russia—namely, the regional fabric and postimperial dimension of Russia's engagement in its neighborhoods.

Alexander Krilov cautions against overestimating the Russian factor in the post-Soviet space, often at the expense of domestic politics in states that are in Russia's foreign policy orbit.[2] As explored in the Middle East chapter of this volume (chap. 8, Katz), external hegemons do have a tendency to "push" into fractured regions; however, the regional states and their governmental elites have developed a habit of "pulling" them in as well. In contrast, other Russian analysts interviewed during recent fieldwork in 2017 were broadly unequivocal that the Soviet Union was indeed a Russian empire.[3] Another perspective rests on the Russia-led Eurasian Economic Union, which one respondent described as a qualitatively new model of Russian engagement with the post-Soviet states, and one that resembles modern regional integration projects that are prevalent the world over, rather than unique to the post-Soviet area.[4]

The regional fracture theory developed in this volume and elaborated in the empirical chapters highlights the finding that a reestablishment of the same tight, predictable, and centralized connections between Moscow and the post-Soviet states is proving to be challenging and is perhaps impossible. What has recently transpired in Russia's neighborhoods requires careful assessment and perhaps revision of traditional theoretical frameworks of IR applied to this context. A prominent Moscow-based analyst points out in an interview that it is time to set aside rather antagonistic debates "as to whose civilization is better, whose history is more ancient, and the like," and instead decide to dedicate our energy to making sense of realities on the ground. In Russia's peripheries, this analyst further noted, there are numerous internal conflicts that are consequential to policy outcomes.[5] Russia is indeed not the only, or even the most important, factor in shaping politics in the post-Soviet world. Understanding the limits, local openings, and opportunities that facilitate Russia's engagement in its neighborhoods, from today's Donbass to Damascus, is one of the primary objectives in this volume.

As I draft this concluding chapter to this edited volume, in the summer of 2017, my school-aged children anxiously await a solar eclipse in North America, eager to see it cover our town in what astronomers have termed its "path of totality." It occurs to me that Russia's persistent presence in its neighborhoods and peripheries, from its imperial to its Soviet eras, can be similarly described as a "path of totality" of sorts; many argue that Russia has overwhelmed these areas with political uniformity, centralization, and a deep bureaucratic embrace that has tied smaller neighbors to Moscow while crippling their capacity to engage with other most immediate and more natural neighbors. Shattered regional neighborhoods with little regional social capital have been one of the most neglected costs of Russian imperialism over the past two centuries. This legacy has been devastating in terms of rendering conflicts around Russia's geopolitical underbelly particularly destructive while at the same time undermining fragile peace processes. Whether capitalizing on regional fracture by default or implementing regional fracture by design as a deliberate foreign policy strategy, Russia's policies toward its neighbors have arguably had a distinct regional dimension. This is in contrast, for example, to a largely bilateral and patchwork nature of engagement with the post-Soviet states as exercised by the United States in the post–Cold War period (de Waal 2002).

Indeed, political, institutional, and economic dependence on Moscow has long been one of the central and centralizing principles of Russia's engagement with the other nationalities and ethnic groups in the Soviet Union. The same approach applied to Russia's connections with East European countries in the Soviet era. Countries in Eastern Europe had only rudimentary links with one another. As Zbigniew Brzezinski wrote in 1989:

> Moscow permitted no real economic cooperation among them. Polish-Czechoslovak plans, developed during World War II, for a genuine federation between the two states were scuttled by the Kremlin, as was the postwar initiative by the communist leaders Tito and Georgi Dimitrov for a confederation between Yugoslavia and

> Bulgaria. Instead, all lines of cooperation ran vertically to Moscow, not horizontally among the regional states. The Warsaw Past and the Council for Mutual Economic Assistance served essentially as instruments of Soviet control. (Brzezinski 1989, 4–5)

Similar attempts at federation between the three countries in the South Caucasus also were unsuccessful under the Russian orbit, dated to the brief period of Transcaucasian federation in 1918 and to one from 1922 to 1936 (de Waal 2012).

With the legacies of two major centralizing imperial projects under its belt, however, Vladimir Putin's "paths of totality"—the concentric rings of projected imperial power from the post-Soviet periphery to Eastern Europe to the Middle East—may be nearing an end. As explored in the empirical chapters of this volume, Moscow's significant influence over its neighborhoods both near and far is becoming heavily compromised. The rise of fragmented publics in these regions, along with a complex array of activists and other nonstate actors, have produced a legitimacy gap between governments and their people, yielding a reality that is more complicated and less manageable than what the Kremlin has been used to over the centuries. Increasingly networked and "hyperconnected" world politics (Ferguson 2017) are also serving to complicate extensive control of these regions by Russia or other actors.

The condition of regional fracture is a key challenge faced by Moscow in its march along a "path of totality." Fragmentation of state authority and capture of regional governance processes by local and external political elites have produced areas that are fractured but that also consolidate intraregional divisions into a coherent, albeit predatory, system. Exercising statecraft in such fractured regions has emerged as a distinguishing challenge among post-Soviet and post-Communist states. In short, a loss of full control by the Kremlin has created regional spaces of fluid and contested politics that evade the full capture of these regions by other external powers. Fractured regions, often otherwise seen as too small to matter for world order, have shown themselves to be big enough to fail and destabilize global security. Understanding the extent of Russia's agency and the states it targets, as well as the power and the limits of postimperial structures that support post-Communist Eurasia and the Middle East, is a research direction that this study puts forth as essential for understanding Russian foreign policy.

Regional Fracture and Imperial Legacies beyond Moscow

Indeed, the geopolitical totality and predictability of policies in Russia's peripheries are no more. The theory of regional fracture applied to various conflict regions around Russia is a fresh, new framework in which to recast Russia and more restive regional neighborhoods and new players contesting its power. In addition to recasting Russia in IR theory, this edited volume also explores the fascinating dynamics of center-to-periphery dynamics in the postimperial settings of the twenty-first century.

The chapters of this volume studying the post-Soviet space explore the extent to which regional fracture is a Soviet legacy. These analyses view regional fracture as, in many ways, path-dependent constructs in Russia's orbit. The chapters on the Western Balkans and the Middle East, in addition to probing Russian involvement in these regions, also seek to assess them in terms of imperial legacies other than the Soviet Union. As such, these chapters help to explore the generalizability of regional fracture theory beyond the Russian and Soviet context, producing early examinations of regional fracture as a postimperial phenomenon. While the Western Balkans has been within the Moscow orbit throughout much of the twentieth century, as a fractured region it was also a constituent and historically contested space within the Austro-Hungarian and Ottoman empires. In addition, partly covered by the European Union, the Western Balkans today is arguably under the Western European regional umbrella; this, as explained by Dimitar Bechev in this volume, has served to reduce Russia's foreign policy choices to mere tactical exploits of division inside the states in the region. Still, the political interethnic conflicts characterizing the Western Balkans remain significant and represent a significant threat to regional instability. Despite its proximity to the European Union and its institutional commitments to European integration, the region has remained remarkably vulnerable to Russian interventions and as such highlights the vulnerabilities of fractured regions to external overlays.

Similarly, the Middle East, considered as a fractured region, is seen to have been vulnerable to great power overlays during the Cold War; as with the Western Balkans, it too is burdened by a legacy of regional fracture from imperial histories. If in the immediate post–Cold War Middle East regional fracture emerged by default, the introduction of Russia and other great powers since has bred regional fracture designed strategically by these outside actors for their own purposes. Russia's military intervention in the Syrian civil war on the side of the incumbent government was, according to many Russian analysts interviewed for this work, a step to prevent state collapse and its capture by extremist and radical forces.[6] Such collapse, the argument goes, would have engendered terrorism in the region and led to its appearance in Central Asia, the South Caucasus, and Russia itself.[7] In addition, Russian state assertions of humanitarian motivations for its Syrian intervention, together with similar reasoning for the annexation of Crimea, served to send the signal that contemporary Russia is a global player, a "modern" actor working within the confines of humanitarian intervention doctrine.[8] The Russian entry into the Syrian civil war is an archetypal case of regional fracture "by design" in that Russia's strategies explicitly and intentionally consolidated conflict structures and cleavages and sharpened intersectarian divisions in the region for its own ends.

In short, relative to Russia, both the Western Balkans and the Middle East region constitute the second "outer ring" of influence from Moscow. While lacking direct and immediate institutional and political connections stemming from the Soviet past, these regions offered different openings for direct and indirect intervention by Moscow. With different imperial legacies and suffering from regional fracture by default as a result, both regions became vulnerable to Russian overlay, albeit via drastically different channels and varied sets of mechanisms. The need for tailored regional approaches to address these conflicts is the key policy recommendation discussed at the end of this chapter.

Imperial legacies are quite powerful in spawning regional fracture. In the cases of both the Middle East and the Western Balkans, the institution of statehood often emerged or was imparted centrally by a retreating imperial power. As such, state formation and nationalism were often at odds; in the case of the Middle East, these developments spanned local tribal structures and intrareligious schisms (Der Matossian 2014). With weak statehoods in their wake, the retreating colonial powers did little to add to the fabric of regional ties between these new state entities. Even within the EU frameworks of engagement with the Balkan countries, region building between the states failed to move beyond rhetoric, lacking solid institutional and financial support (Ohanyan 2016). Whether in the Balkans or the Middle East, the forces of economic globalization and economic liberalism have worked to elevate the primacy of economic integration of these states with the global capitals, producing little incentive for more intimate regional connections between them. Whether it is the EU's Eastern Partnership or Russia's Eurasian Economic Union, the global forces of politics and economy have sought to integrate their peripheries first and foremost rather than nourishing natural regional neighborhoods for greater developmental impact on the local societies (Bartlett 2001).

Fractured regions, even those beyond Russia's vast vicinities, are deeply postcolonial structures. The weakness of the state is perhaps the most visible and unavoidable legacy of a colonial experience as well as a major source of regional fracture. The formal (and often merely physical as opposed to institutional) retreat of an imperial power leaves behind administrative capacities of a new state, and the relevant scholarship on colonialism has documented the various legacy effects of imperial powers on the new successor states. Perhaps a more specific legacy of imperialism pertaining to regional fracture theory is the fact that decolonization processes often have been accompanied by ethnic conflicts of various intensities (Rogan 2015). Recent scholarship has evolved to recognize the complex ways in which ethnic violence and state failure influence one another (Wolff 2011; Patrick 2007; Iqbal and Starr 2008).

Scholars in security studies and conflict management have begun to explicitly document the regional dimension of armed conflict (Diehl and Lepgold 2003;

Crocker, Hampson, and Aall 2011a; Ohanyan 2015) in terms of both sources and enabling factors as well as possible modes of their management and resolution. Wolff (2011) cites studies documenting that state failure has a tendency to develop in regional conflict clusters. Subnational groups and subnational threats to states emanating from across borders are cited as some of the regional factors fueling state failure in the developing world. In such "state failure regions," the regional dimension of conflicts erodes governance capacities of states; similarly, the poor capacities in state governance compromise any prospects of conflict management and peacebuilding in such regions.

The empirical chapters in this edited volume help to identify specific mechanisms of postimperial legacies in producing regional fracture. Postimperial linkages have enabled external hegemonic engagement in such regions at the level of governmental elites, fueling intrastate divisions and schisms within the new states. Fragmentation of state authority inside the states is linked with positional, ideological rivalry between Russia and the West (Chan 2013). Whether election cycles in new states produce pro-Western or pro-Russian governments in the post-Communist world has been pushing and pulling these states in various directions, thereby further eroding chances of more immediate regional connections with their neighbors.

Such transient political affiliations feed into regional fracture but have also proven to be unreliable instruments for external hegemons. In the case of Russia, a respondent noted that it is becoming difficult for Russia in dealing with the former Soviet states because new states' formal bilateral agreements are often not followed and multilateral ones lack consistency in implementation.[9] As such, he further opined that the Russian government is learning not to count on its shared historical past and cultural ties with these new states and is increasingly treating them as it does other countries. Indeed, it is these uncertainties that are further propelling Russia, a former imperial power in the post-Communist world, to engage with the post-Soviet states via institutional links that are deep, institutionalized, and centralized. The Eurasian Economic Union, in the words of a Moscow-based analyst, is a multilateral, modern approach to reengaging with the post-Soviet states and is said to be qualitatively different from the Soviet Union, yet another regional project in and around Russia's territory.[10]

In terms of the social dimension of regional engagement, Moscow-based anthropologist Lyudmila Solovyova noted in an interview that rich cultural capital at a societal level, along with societal experience with coexistence, is also a shared Soviet legacy, offering untapped opportunities of greater regional engagement.[11] And the three-dimensional framework of the regional fracture theory discussed in chapter 1 (power, institutions, and values) reveals regional systems in which societal and institutional forces may pull in opposite directions. It is helpful to delineate regionwide institutional/political connections and to determine which of these connections are politicized and securitized, while regionwide social connections, even small in scale, lay dormant and out of public sight, public mind, and the state media (Krikorian 2017).

The Policy and Politics of Regional Fracture in World Politics

The framework of regional fracture developed in this volume recognizes the regional dimension of armed conflicts and their management. It also holds that fractured regions exhibit systemic features, and their dysfunctionality and destructiveness affect the people living in them. But such regions also have "beneficiaries" and "stakeholders" that gain from such fracture at a regional level. National elites, often with dubious and highly compromised public legitimacy, or criminal groups, trade cartels, and protectionist rings are among the types of actors often able to derive benefit from fracture. Importantly, fractured regions must not be viewed as simply unintegrated regions or foils to more integrated regions. There is significant regionwide trade occurring in such fractured areas, but it is often restricted to very small numbers of individuals or groups at the expense of more broad-based regional ties and interactions. Active fracturing on the side of such groups is a key property of fractured regions.

Indeed, Daron Acemoglu and James Robinson (2012) have recently differentiated between "extractive" and "inclusive" institutions as determinants of poverty and development: "Inclusive economic institutions that enforce property rights, create a level playing field, and encourage investments in new technologies and skills are more conducive to economic growth than extractive economic institutions that are structured to extract resources from the many by the few and that fail to protect property rights or provide incentives for economic activity" (429–30).

Fractured regions are characterized by regionwide economic links that are primarily predatory, extractive, and exclusive, privileging few groups that benefit from regionwide interactions. In such contexts, small and medium enterprises often lack the capacities to reach distant and global markets (Ohanyan 2007, 2015) and are more dependent on the neighboring countries for resources as well as markets (Collier 2008). Yet, in settings of closed borders, only a few groups are able to supply such resources from the neighboring states, typically via alternative routes and political protections they receive at the borders. In contexts of extractive and exclusive regional institutions, connections between societies are still able to sprout on occasion: as case in point, Azerbaijani produce recently found its way to Armenian markets, presumably via such trade, but produced a massive panic in Armenia until the state was pulled in to remove the "illegal" apples.

Within the comparative regionalism scholarship, the benefits of deeply integrated regions and dense neighborhood ties have been widely documented, as have been the potential costs of unintegrated regions and their risks locally and globally.

However, we know less about regions that are "wired" in a way that produces uneven integration or an extractive and exclusive integration, thereby eroding any prospects of broad-based development and sustainable security in the region. It is in such gray areas between fully integrated and fully disintegrated regions in which fractured regions lie and which resisted traditional frameworks of analysis to date.

Regarding Russia, understanding the regional dimension of Russia's foreign policy toward its neighborhoods and its reliance on regional fracture by default and by design is one of the themes of this book. We argue that Russia's use of regional fracture is deliberate and explicit and is varied in its instruments of application. The broader theoretical and policy implications of this work transcend Russia and require closer examination of other postcolonial environments in other parts of the world. While more research on fractured regions in other settings is essential, this study represents a significant analysis of regional fracture as a modern foreign policy tool as practiced by greater powers.

In terms of policy implications, regional fracture constitutes a set of divide-and-conquer policies traditionally practiced by greater powers in their peripheries and former colonies. In contrast to traditional and earlier applications of divide-and-conquer policies, regional fracture is institutionally more complex and multilayered. Comprising domestic schisms inside regional states, regional fracture becomes significantly more complicated to orchestrate and exploit as well as to study. Fractured regions are complex systems: they are defined by the growing number of political actors within states as well as the emergence of external contestants for these geopolitical spaces in the post-American world. Therefore, they defy state-centric theories and classical bilateral policies.

Divide-and-conquer approaches to the exercise of power are perhaps as old as human civilization itself. And much of the Cold War and its variations were applied both by the US as well as the Soviet Union, with proxy wars being their most destabilizing and destructive manifestations. From the American side, the Truman Doctrine shaped the way international development and diplomacy were conceptualized and practiced during the Cold War. However, its bias toward bilateralism, I argue, has had the unintended consequence of eroding the regional fabric in many parts of the world, thereby exacerbating conflicts and failing to recognize diplomatic openings in some of the most charged conflict settings. Russia's engagement in its peripheries, in contrast with and as explored in the present volume, has historically and consistently relied relatively more on fostering internal regional divisions as a foreign policy strategy—designing and exploiting regional fracture.

Moving forward, the previous organizational simplicity in world politics, with its bipolarity, ideological clarity, and Westphalian consensus on state monopoly over violence (Kaine 2017), has been replaced with multipolarity, authoritarian resurgence, and the rise of hybrid regimes and shallow states. The latter signifies politically mobilized publics and governmental legitimacy crises inside states, which have to confront transitional violence and often tend to register strained capacities in their governance. Against this backdrop, American foreign policy, regardless of doctrinal impulses, requires a strong regional dimension, which I discuss below.

On the Perils of Bilateralism and Overcoming Regional Fracture

The regionalization of security management in the post-American world is a frequently voiced policy recommendation within scholarly as well as policy circles. Discussions around that theme tend to translate into calls for greater reliance on regional organizations, despite the significant capacity deficits of such organizations for effective peacekeeping and conflict management. Heightened competition between regional hegemons to control their neighborhoods, and thereby downscale great power competitions to the regional level, has also enjoyed deep support among policymakers and academics. Neither of these developments has been favorable for repairing the fabric of fractured regions. A less radical and more realistic path would be to revise the foreign policy instruments of major powers—the US, in particular—toward engaging with these fractured regions in the modern world.

Consolidation, Not Confrontation or Containment

Much of the policy discourse on recasting the US role in the post–Cold War period calls for confronting or containing rising powers, often drawing historical parallels with World War I and World War II (Mead 2014; Ikenberry 2014; Posen 2014). Among the strategies traditionally considered, various themes recur: the use of military power, self-restraint, trade, democracy, and international institutions and security communities (Jesse et al. 2012). Such approaches rest on the assumption of superiority of American resources and the concentration of American military, economic, and sociopolitical capabilities. But recent research indicates that secondary powers, despite their marginal position in the global hierarchy, are following the great powers' lead less easily and predictably than before. Secondary powers increasingly have a range of tools with which to challenge great powers. The ability of these secondary powers to act in their own interests in turn complicates management of relations among great powers.

A greater regional autonomy of secondary and tertiary states enables them to play great powers against one another. This strategy is more likely in fractured regional neighborhoods than in integrated regions. Regional integration fosters moderation and produces predictability and longer-term stability in world politics. And, as such, investing in region building can help make the relatively more chaotic post–Cold War global political environment less combustible, particularly in a post-Communist world rife with weak democratic institutions and plentiful conflict fault lines.

Against this backdrop the strategy of assisting regional groupings in the developing world to mature into regional structures of their own is more promising than trying to absorb individual states into a Western orbit or decouple them from Russia's or China's influence. Instead of confronting or containing, the West would do better to assist in fostering and consolidating regional arrangements. A regional focus for Western foreign policies can help relieve political polarization associated with bilateral coalition building: a clear case is Ukraine's position between the West and Russia, which precipitated open, armed conflict. Support for genuine region-building projects in the developing world makes states there less vulnerable to geopolitical competition, including that involving rising or revisionist powers such as China and Russia. In particular, a more cohesive South Caucasus or Central Asian region, for example, would be better prepared to withstand unwelcome overtures from Russia or Iran. Steve Chan (2013) has noted astutely that local rivalries are often nested within strategic competition between leading powers, magnifying these rivalries into multilateral affairs. Region building is a clear strategy to break this vicious cycle that has been constraining great powers in such regions.

Region building also allows the West to consolidate its economic presence and normative influence in developing countries because regional integration strengthens private-sector capacities and deepens market structures in regions. Development practitioners and analysts highlight the developmental impact of regionalism for the Global South, which tends to legitimize and strengthen market liberalism among the public in the developing world. In short, region building as a foreign policy strategy can consolidate the position of Western powers while advancing and deepening free trade and market structures.

Give Up Control to Gain Control

Region building as a security strategy also calls for great powers to "give up control to gain control." In the short term, promoting regional integration may appear to weaken great power control over regions and constituent states as it may be viewed to occur at the expense of bilateral ties between great powers and their "client" states. But in the long term, this strategy is a win for Western powers. Championing integrated regions in the developing world directly advances the interests of the West in general and the US in particular. The state-centric tendency in policy circles regarding the developing world obscures the political complexity of these states that experience instability from both regional and internal sources. American foreign policy has a tendency to view political elites as its main interlocutors. However, such elites often turn out to be highly unreliable, with shifting and unsustainable loyalties. Regionally focused foreign policies would allow Western powers to cultivate alliances with nonstate groups, from business associations to civil society. The emergence of new sources in global conflict requires institutionally multilayered and multipronged diplomacy if the US and the EU are to consolidate market liberalism and continue to promote democratic values in the rest of the world.

Deepen and Diversify

Currently, US foreign policy has a dyadic focus. Much energy is expended on winning and building coalitions with a single state, for example, Georgia, Ukraine, or Kyrgyzstan. This approach is poorly suited to address the complexity of regional politics. Region-building strategies would help diversify the potential range of interventions along with potential local interlocutors. Region-building approaches are better matched to the complex, multilevel forms of politics emerging in the developing world.

In addition, by promoting regional integration and deploying distinct regional dimensions in their foreign policies, Western powers will further the liberalizing economic and political reforms that gained momentum after the Cold War. The development community has increasingly called attention to the developmental benefits of South–South regionalism rather than North–South regional arrangements. In a report on intra-Africa trade and development, the United Nations Conference on Trade and Development found that South–South regional agreements bring together partners at a similar level of development.[12] Such regional arrangements offer economies of scale and diversification of production and can help cushion economies from global economic competition in the early stages of industrial development. Such regional integration builds market structures that are more broadly embedded in the fabric of societies rather than exclusively oriented to global markets. Regionalism can also strengthen the capacities of private-sector actors marginalized by globally oriented free-trade policies. These smaller-scale private-sector stakeholders, in turn, have great strategic value in that they tend to favor moderate politics and work against conflict and instability in a given region (Alexander, Gündüz, and Subedi 2009).

In conclusion, the healthy debate on the economic benefits of regionalism versus globalization has failed to be matched by a corresponding political analysis on the promise and perils of region-based strategies toward statecraft and global security. Whether informing policies for engaging Russia or building peace processes for smaller-scale armed conflicts around the world, the regional dimensions of diplomacy and statecraft are long overdue.

Notes

1. Alexander Krilov, interview by Anna Ohanyan, August 11, 2017, Moscow, Russia.

2. Krilov interview, 2017.

3. Masha Lipman, interview by Anna Ohanyan, August 9, 2017, Moscow, Russia; Manana Malkhasyan, interview by Anna Ohanyan, August 10, 2017, Moscow, Russia; and Anya Tkachenko, interview by Anna Ohanyan, August 10, 2017, Moscow, Russia.

4. Anonymous, interview by Anna Ohanyan, August 7, 2017, Moscow, Russia.

5. Krilov interview, 2017.

6. Krilov interview, 2017; Anonymous interview, 2017; and Marat Murtazin, interview by Anna Ohanyan, August 8, 2017, Moscow, Russia.

7. Krilov interview, 2017.

8. Anonymous interview, 2017; and Murtazin interview, 2017.

9. Krilov interview, 2017.

10. Anonymous interview, 2017.

11. Lyudmila Solovyova, interview by Anna Ohanyan, August 8, 2017, Moscow, Russia.

12. "Global Value Chains and South–South Trade: Economic Cooperation and Integration among Developing Countries," UNCTAD, October 2015, http://unctad.org/en/PublicationsLibrary/gdsecidc2015d1_en.pdf.

REFERENCES

Acemoglu, Daron, and James Robinson. 2012. *Why Nations Fail: The Origins of Power, Prosperity, and Poverty*. New York: Random House.

Acharya, Amitav. 2014a. *The End of American World Order*. Polity Press.

———. 2014b. "Global International Relations (IR) and Regional World." *International Studies Quarterly* 58: 647–59.

Acharya, Amitav, and Alastair Iain Johnston. 2007. "Comparing Regional Institutions: An Introduction." In *Crafting Cooperation: Regional International Institutions in Comparative Perspective*, edited by Amitav Acharya and Alastair Iain Johnston, 1–31. New York: Cambridge University Press.

Adler, Emanuel. 1997. "Imagined (Security) Communities: Cognitive Regions in International Relations." *Millennium* 26, no. 2: 249–77.

Adriaans, Rik. 2017. "The Humanitarian Road to Nagorno-Karabakh: Media, Morality, and Infrastructural Promise in the Armenian Diaspora." *Identities: Global Studies in Culture and Power*, August 3. http://dx.doi.org/10.1080/1070289X.2017.1358004.

AFP. 2012. "Syria's Hama: An Uprising Crushed 30 Years Ago." Al Arabiya News, February 3. https://www.alarabiya.net/articles/2012/02/03/192297.html.

Ahmed, Nafeez. 2013. "Syria Intervention Plan Fueled by Oil Interests, Not Chemical Weapon Concern." *Guardian*, February 12. https://www.theguardian.com/environment/earth-insight/2013/aug/30/syria-chemical-attack-war-intervention-oil-gas-energy-pipelines.

Akkieva, Svetlana. 2008. "The Caucasus: One or Many? A View from the Region." *Nationalities Papers* 36, no. 2: 253–73.

Alexander, Lindsey, Canan Gündüz, and D. B. Subedi. 2009. *What Role for Business in Post-Conflict Economic Recovery? Perspectives from Nepal*. London: International Alert.

Allison, Roy. 2004. "Regionalism, Regional Structures and Security Management in Central Asia." *International Affairs* 80, no. 3: 463–83.

———. 2008a. "Russia Resurgent? Moscow's Campaign to 'Coerce Georgia to Peace.'" *International Affairs* 84, no. 6: 1145–71.

———. 2008b. "Virtual Regionalism, Regional Structures and Regime Security in Central Asia." *Central Asian Survey* 27, no. 2: 185–202.

———. 2013. "Russia and Syria: Explaining Alignment with a Regime in Crisis." *International Affairs* 89, no. 4: 795–823.

Altstadt, Audrey L. 2017. *Frustrated Democracy in Post-Soviet Azerbaijan*. Washington, DC: Woodrow Wilson Center Press; New York: Columbia University Press.

Ambrosio, Thomas. 2008. "Catching the 'Shanghai Spirit': How the Shanghai Cooperation Organization Promotes Authoritarian Norms in Central Asia." *Europe-Asia Studies* 60, no. 8: 1321–44.

———. 2010. "Constructing a Framework of Authoritarian Diffusion: Concepts, Dynamics, and Future Research." *International Studies Perspectives* 11: 375–92.

———. 2014. "Beyond the Transition Paradigm." *Demokratizatsiya*, July.

Andreasyan, Zhanna, and Georgi Derluguian. 2015. "Fuel Protests in Armenia." *New Left Review* 95 (September–October): 29–48.

Arbatov, Alexei G. 1993. "Russia's Foreign Policy Alternatives." *International Security* 18, no. 2: 5–43.

Artman, Vincent M. 2013. "Documenting Territory: Passportisation, Territory, and Exception in Abkhazia and South Ossetia." *Geopolitics* 18, no. 3: 682–704.

Asmus, Ronald. 2009. *A Little War That Shook the World: Georgia, Russia and the Future of the West*. New York: St. Martin's Press.

Auer, Stephan. 2015. "Carl Schmitt in the Kremlin: The Ukraine Crisis and the Return of Geopolitics." *International Affairs* 91, no. 5: 953–68.

Averre, Derek. 2009. "Competing Rationalities: Russia, the EU and the 'Shared Neighbourhood.'" *Europe-Asia Studies* 61, no. 10: 1689–1713.

Bachrach, Peter, and Morten S. Baratz. 1962. "Two Faces of Power." *American Political Science Review* 56, no. 4: 947–52.

Bader, Julia. 2015. *China's Foreign Relations and the Survival of Autocracies*. New York: Routledge.

Balci, Bayram. 2013. "Between Secular Education and Islamic Philosophy: The Approach and Achievements of Fethullah Gülen's Followers in Azerbaijan." *Caucasus Survey* 1, no. 1: 107–16.

Balfour, Rosa, and Corina Stratulat, eds. 2015. "EU Member States and Enlargement towards the Balkans." EPC Issue Paper No. 79. European Policy Centre, Brussels.

BalkanInsight. 2017. "Kosovo, Serbia Leaders Pledge to Honour Justice Deal." August 31. https://www.balkaninsight.com/en/article/kosovo-serbia-pledge-to-implement-justice-agreement-08-31-2017/1589/8.

Balmaceda, Margarita. 2008. *Energy Dependency, Politics and Corruption in the Former Soviet Union: Russia's Power, Oligarchs' Profits and Ukraine's Missing Energy Policy (1995–2006)*. London: Routledge.

Barnett, Michael, and Raymond Duvall. 2005. "Power in International Politics." *International Organization* 59: 39–75.

Barnett, Michael, and Martha Finnemore. 2004. *Rules for the World: International Organizations in Global Politics*. Ithaca, NY: Cornell University Press.

Barnett, Michael, and Etel Solingen. 2007. "Designed to Fail or Failure to Design? The Origins and Legacy of the Arab League." In *Crafting Cooperation: Regional International Institutions in Comparative Perspective*, edited by Amitav Acharya and Alastair Iain Johnston, 180–220. Cambridge: Cambridge University Press.

Barrinha, André. 2014. "The Ambitious Insulator: Revisiting Turkey's Position in Regional Security Complex Theory." *Mediterranean Politics* 19, no. 2: 165–82.

Bartlett, David L. 2001. "Economic Development in the Newly Independent States: The Case for Regionalism." *European Journal of Development Research* 13, no. 1: 135–53.

Bartov, Omer, and Eric D. Weitz, eds. 2013. *Shatterzone of Empires: Coexistence and Violence in the German, Habsburg, Russian, and Ottoman Borderlands.* Bloomington: Indiana University Press.

Batalden, Stephen K., and Sandra L. Batalden. 1997. *The Newly Independent States of Eurasia: Handbook of Former Soviet Republics.* Phoenix, AZ: Oryx Press.

Bebbington, A. 2002. "Sharp Knives and Blunt Instruments: Social Capital in Development Studies." *Antipode* 34, no. 4: 800–803.

Bechev, Dimitar. 2011. *Constructing South East Europe: The Politics of Balkan Regional Cooperation.* London: Palgrave Macmillan.

———. 2012. "Periphery of the Periphery: The Western Balkans and the Euro Crisis." Policy brief. August 30. European Council on Foreign Relations. http://www.ecfr.eu/publications/summary/the_periphery_of_the_periphery_the_western_balkans_and_the_euro_crisis.

———. 2015. "Russia in the Balkans: How Should the EU Respond?" European Policy Center, Brussels. http://www.epc.eu/pub_details.php?cat_id=3&pub_id=6018&year=2015.

———. 2016. "Who Is Playing Whom?" *American Interest*, September 25. http://www.the-american-interest.com/2016/09/25/who-is-playing-whom/.

———. 2017. *Rival Power: Russia's Influence in Southeast Europe.* New Haven, CT: Yale University Press.

Becker, Seymour. 2012. "The Great Game: The History of an Evocative Phrase." *Asian Affairs* 43, no. 1: 61–80.

Bedford, Sofie. 2016. "Turkey and Azerbaijan: One Religion—Two States?" In *Turkish-Azerbaijani Relations: One Nation—Two States?*, edited by Murad Ismayilov and Norman A. Graham, 127–49. Abingdon, UK: Routledge.

Beeson, Mark. 2010. "Asymmetrical Regionalism: China, Southeast Asia and Uneven Development." *East Asia* 27, no. 4: 329–43.

Beissinger, Mark. 1993. "Demise of an Empire-State: Identity, Legitimacy, and the Deconstruction of Soviet Politics." In *The Rising Tide of Cultural Pluralism: The Nation-State at Bay?*, edited by Crawford Young, 93–115. Madison: University of Wisconsin Press.

Beissinger, Mark R., and Crawford Young, eds. 2002. *Beyond State Crisis? Post-Colonial Africa and Post-Soviet Eurasia in Comparative Perspective.* Washington, DC: Woodrow Wilson Center Press.

Berg, Eiki, and Martin Mölder. 2014. "When 'Blurring' Becomes the Norm and Secession Is Justified as the Exception: Revisiting EU and Russian Discourses in the Common Neighbourhood." *Journal of International Relations and Development* 17: 469–88.

Berglund, Christofer. 2014. "Georgia between Dominant-Power Politics, Feckless Pluralism and Democracy." *Demokratizatsiya* 22, no. 3: 445–70.

———. 2016. "'Forward to David the Builder!' Georgia's (Re-)turn to Language-Centred Nationalism." *Nationalities Papers* 44, no. 4: 522–42.

Bibilunga, Nikolay V. 2010. "Raspad SSSR I Krizis Moldavskoi Gosudarstvennosti." *Rusin* 4, no. 22: 112–35.

Bieber, Florian. 2015. "The Serbia-Kosovo Agreements: An EU Success Story?" *Review of Central and East European Law* 40, no. 3–4: 285–319.

Bieber, Florian, and Marko Kmezić. 2017. "The Crisis of Democracy in the Western Balkans: Authoritarianism and EU Stabilitocracy." Policy brief. Balkans in European Policy Advisory Group.

Billig, Michael. 1995. *Banal Nationalism*. Thousand Oaks, CA: Sage.

B92. 2015. "Serbia 'in Line of Fire' over Ukraine, Says US Official." February 25. http://www.b92.net/eng/news/world.php?nav_id=93293.

Boden, Dieter. 2014. *The Russian-Abkhaz Treaty: New Tensions in the South Caucasus.* Berlin: Friedrich Ebert Stiftung.

Bohr, Annette. 2004. "Regionalism in Central Asia: New Geopolitics, Old Regional Order." *International Affairs* 80, no. 3: 485–502.

Bolkvadze, Ketevan. 2016. "Cherry-Picking EU Conditionality: Selective Compliance in Georgia's Hybrid Regime." *Europe-Asia Studies* 68, no. 3: 409–40.

Boonstra, Jos. 2015. "Reviewing the EU's Approach to Central Asia." *EUCAM Policy Brief*, no. 34, February 24.

Borshchevskaya, Anna. 2016. *Russia in the Middle East: Motives, Consequences, Prospects*. Washington, DC: Washington Institute for Near East Policy.

Bourdieu, Pierre. 1990. *The Logic of Practice.* Cambridge, UK: Polity Press.

Bozarslan, Mahmut. 2016. "Syria Rejects Russian Proposal for Kurdish Federation." *Al-Monitor*, October 24. http://www.al-monitor.com/pulse/en/originals/2016/10/turkey-russia-mediates-between-kurds-and-assad.html.

Bremer, Stuart A. 2014. "Dangerous Dyads: Conditions Affecting the Likelihood of Interstate War, 1816–1965." In *Conflict, War, and Peace: An Introduction to Scientific Research*, edited by Sara McLaughlin Mitchell and John A. Vasquez, 5–26. Thousand Oaks, CA: CQ Press.

Broers, Laurence. 2009. "'David and Goliath' and 'Georgians in the Kremlin': A Post-Colonial Perspective on Conflict in Post-Soviet Georgia." *Central Asian Survey* 28, no. 2: 99–118.

———. 2013. "Recognising Politics in Unrecognised States: 20 Years of Enquiry into the De Facto States of the South Caucasus." *Caucasus Survey* 1, no. 1: 59–74.

———. 2014. "Mirrors to the World: The Claims to Legitimacy and International Recognition of De Facto States in the South Caucasus." *Brown Journal of International Affairs* 20, no. 2: 145–59.

———. 2015a. "From 'Frozen Conflict' to Enduring Rivalry: Reassessing the Nagorny Karabakh Conflict." *Nationalities Papers* 43, no. 4: 556–76.

———. 2015b. "Resourcing De Facto Jurisdictions: A Theoretical Perspective on Cases in the South Caucasus." *Caucasus Survey* 3, no. 3: 269–90.

———. 2016a. "Diffusion and Default: A Linkage and Leverage Perspective on Nagorny Karabakh Conflict." *East European Politics* 32, no. 3: 378–99.

———. 2016b. *The Nagorny Karabakh Conflict: Defaulting to War*. London: Royal Institute for International Affairs.

Broers, Laurence, Alexander Iskandaryan, and Sergey Minasyan, eds. 2015. *The Unrecognised Politics of De Facto States in the Post-Soviet Space*. Yerevan: Caucasus Institute.

Broers, Laurence, and Gerard Toal. 2013. "Cartographic Exhibitionism? Visualizing the Territory of Armenia and Karabakh." *Problems of Post-Communism* 60, no. 3: 16–35.

Brookes, Peter. 2005. *A Devil's Triangle: Terrorism, Weapons of Mass Destruction, and Rogue States*. Lanham, MD: Rowman & Littlefield.

Brubaker, Rogers. 1994. "Nationhood and National Question in the Soviet Union and Post-Soviet Eurasia: An Institutional Account." *Theory and Society* 23, no. 1: 55–76.

Brzezinski, Zbigniew. 1989. "Post-Communist Nationalism." *Foreign Affairs* 68, no. 5.

———. 1994. "The Premature Partnership?" *Foreign Affairs* 73, no. 2: 67–82.
———. 1997. *The Grand Chessboard: American Primacy and Its Geostrategic Imperatives*. New York: Basic Books.
Burbank, Jane, and Frederick Cooper. 2010. *Empires in World History: Power and the Politics of Difference*. Princeton, NJ: Princeton University Press.
Burnell, Peter, and Oliver Schlumberger. 2010. "Promoting Democracy—Promoting Autocracy? International Politics and National Political Regimes." *Contemporary Politics* 16, no. 1: 1–15.
Buzan, Barry. 1991. *People, States, and Fear: An Agenda for International Security Studies in the Post-Cold War Era*. 2nd ed. Boulder, CO: Lynne Rienner.
Buzan, Barry, and O. Wæver. 2003. *Regions and Powers: The Structure of International Security*. Cambridge: Cambridge University Press.
Byshok, Stanislav, Alexei Kochetkov, and Alexei Semenov. 2014. *Neonazis & Euromaidan: From Democracy to Dictatorship*. Charleston, SC: CreateSpace.
Callaghan, W. 2016. "China's 'Asia Dream': The Belt Road Initiative and the New Regional Order." *Asian Journal of Comparative Politics* 1, no. 3: 1–18.
Casey-Maslen, Stuart. 2014. *The War Report: Armed Conflict in 2013*. Oxford: Oxford University Press.
Caspersen, Nina. 2011. "Democracy, Nationalism and (Lack of) Sovereignty: The Complex Dynamics of Democratisation in Unrecognised States." *Nations and Nationalism* 17, no. 2: 337–56.
Cecire, Michael H. 2016. "The Bilateral Origins of South Caucasus Trilateralism." In *Turkish-Azerbaijani Relations: One Nation—Two States?*, edited by Murad Ismayilov and Norman A. Graham, 72–87. Abingdon, UK: Routledge.
Chan, Steve. 2013. *Enduring Rivalries in the Asia-Pacific*. New York: Cambridge University Press.
Charap, Samuel, and Cory Welt. 2015. "Making Sense of Russian Foreign Policy: Guest Editor's Introduction." *Problems of Post-Communism* 62: 67–70.
Clunan, Anne. 2014. "Historical Aspirations and the Domestic Politics of Russia's Pursuit of International Status." *Communist and Post-Communist Studies* 47, no. 3–4: 281–90.
Collier, Paul. 2008. *The Bottom Billion: Why the Poorest Countries Are Failing and What Can Be Done about It*. New York: Oxford University Press.
Collins, Kathleen. 2006. *Clan Politics and Regime Transition in Central Asia*. New York, Cambridge University Press.
———. 2009. "Economic and Security Regionalism among Patrimonial Authoritarian Regimes: The Case of Central Asia." *Europe-Asia Studies* 61, no. 2: 249–81.
Conciliation Resources. 2011. *Forced Displacement in the Nagorny Karabakh Conflict: Return and Its Alternatives*. London: Conciliation Resources.
Contessi, Nicola P. 2015. "Foreign and Security Policy Diversification in Eurasia: Issue Splitting, Co-Alignment, and Relational Power." *Problems of Post-Communism* 62: 299–311.
———. 2016. "Prospects for the Accommodation of a Resurgent Russia." In *Accommodating Rising Powers: Past, Present, and Future*, edited by T. V. Paul. Cambridge: Cambridge University Press.
Cooley, Alexander. 2012. *Great Games, Local Rules: The New Great Power Contest in Central Asia*. New York: Oxford University Press.

Cooley, A., and M. Laruelle. 2013. "The Changing Logic of Russian Strategy in Central Asia: From Privileged Sphere to Divide and Rule?" PONARS Eurasia Policy Memo No. 261, July 2013. http://www.ponarseurasia.org/memo/changing-logic-russian-strategy-central-asia-privileged-sphere-divide-and-rule.

Cooper, Robert. 2004. *The Breaking of Nations: Order and Chaos in the Twenty-First Century.* London: Groove Press / Atlantic Monthly Press.

Cordesman, Anthony H. 2004. *The Military Balance in the Middle East.* Washington, DC: Center for Strategic and International Studies.

Cordesman, Anthony H., Aram Nerguizian, and Inout C. Popescu. 2008. *Israel and Syria: The Military Balance and Prospects of War.* Washington, DC: Center for Strategic and International Studies.

Cornell, Svante. 2002. "Autonomy as a Source of Conflict: Caucasian Conflicts in Theoretical Perspective." *World Politics* 54, no. 2: 245–76.

Cornell, Svante E., and S. Frederick Starr, eds. 2009. *The Guns of August 2008. Russia's War in Georgia.* Armonk, NY: M. E. Sharpe.

Costa Buranelli, Filippo. 2014a. "The English School and Regional International Societies: Theoretical and Methodological Reflections." In *Regions in International Society: The English School at the Sub-Global Level,* edited by Ales Karmazin, Filippo Costa Buranelli, Yongjin Zhang, and Federic Merke, 22–44. Brno: MUNI Press.

———. 2014b. "May We Have a Say? Central Asian States in the UN General Assembly." *Journal of Eurasian Studies* 5, no. 2: 131–44.

Crocker, Chester A., Fen Osler Hampson, and Pamela Aall. 2011a. "Collective Conflict Management: A New Formula for Global Peace and Security Cooperation?" *International Affairs* 87, no. 1: 39–58.

———, eds. 2011b. *Rewiring Regional Security in a Fragmented World.* Washington, DC: United States Institute of Peace Press.

Croissant, Michael P. 1998. *The Armenia–Azerbaijan Conflict: Causes and Implications.* Santa Barbara, CA: Praeger.

Cummings, Sally N. 2000. *Kazakhstan: Centre-Periphery Relations.* London: Royal Institute of International Affairs.

———. 2012. *Understanding Central Asia: Politics and Contested Transformations.* London: Routledge.

Dahl, Robert A. 1957. "The Concept of Power." *Behavioral Science* 2, no. 3: 201.

Dailey, Erika. 1993. *Human Rights in Moldova: The Turbulent Dniester.* Washington, DC: Human Rights Watch.

Dale, Catherine. 2001. "The Displaced Body and the Body Politic: The Formation of a Bounded, 'Permanently Temporary' Population of Internally Displaced Persons following Internal Conflict in Post-Soviet Georgia." PhD diss., University of California, Berkeley.

D'Anieri, Paul. 1999. *Economic Interdependence in Ukrainian–Russian Relations: Descartes to Kant.* Albany: State University of New York Press.

———. 2010. *Orange Revolution and Aftermath: Mobilization, Apathy, and the State in Ukraine.* Baltimore: Johns Hopkins University Press.

de Waal, Thomas. 2002. "Reinventing the Caucasus." *World Policy Journal* 19, no. 1: 51–59.

———. 2012. "A Broken Region: The Persistent Failure of Integration Projects in the South Caucasus." *Europe-Asia Studies* 64, no. 9: 1709–23.

Delcour, Laure. 2011. "The European Union's Policy in the South Caucasus: In Search of a Strategy." In *Reassessing Security in the South Caucasus*, edited by Annie Jafalian, 177–94. Farnham, UK: Ashgate.

———. 2014. "Faithful but Constrained? Armenia's Half-Hearted Support for Russia's Regional Integration Policies in the Post-Soviet Space." In *Geopolitics of Eurasian Economic Integration*. Edited by David Cadier. London: London School of Economics.

Delcour, Laure, and Kataryna Wolczuk. 2015. "The EU's Unexpected 'Ideal Neighbour'? The Perplexing Case of Armenia's Europeanisation." *Journal of European Integration* 37, no. 4: 491–507.

DeMars, William E. 2005. *NGOs and Transnational Networks: Wild Cards in World Politics.* London: Pluto Press.

Der Matossian, Bedross. 2014. *Shattered Dreams of Revolution: From Liberty to Violence in the Late Ottoman Empire*. Stanford, CA: Stanford University Press.

Deudney, Daniel, and G. John Ikenberry. 2010. "The Unravelling of the Cold War Settlement." *Survival* 51, no. 6: 39–62.

Deutsch, Karl W. 1953. *Nationalism and Social Communication: An Inquiry into the Foundations of Nationality*. Cambridge, MA: Massachusetts Institute of Technology Press.

———. 1954. *Political Community at the International Level.* Garden City, NY: Doubleday.

Deyermond, Ruth. 2016. "The Uses of Sovereignty in Twenty-First Century Russian Foreign Policy." *Europe-Asia Studies* 68, no. 6: 957–84.

Diehl, Paul F., and Joseph Lepgold, eds. 2003. *Regional Conflict Management*. Lanham, MD: Rowman & Littlefield.

Dimitrov, Nikola, and Natascha Wunsch. 2016. "The Migrant Crisis: A Catalyst for EU Enlargement?" Policy brief. Balkans in Europe Policy Advisory Group, June 2016. http://balkanfund.org/publications/the-migrant-crisis-a-catalyst-for-eu-enlargement/.

Dolenec, Danijela. 2013. *Democratic Institutions and Authoritarian Rule in Southeast Europe*. Colchester, UK: ECPR Press.

Donaldson, Robert H., Joseph L. Nogee, and Vidya Nadkarni. 2014. *The Foreign Policy of Russia: Changing Systems, Enduring Interests*. Milton Park, UK: Routledge.

Doyle, Michael. 1986. *Empires*. Ithaca, NY: Cornell University Press.

Dragneva, Rilka, and Kataryna Wolczuk. 2016. "Between Dependence and Integration: Ukraine's Relations with Russia." *Europe-Asia Studies* 68, no. 4: 678–98.

Drezner, Daniel W. 2013. "The Tragedy of the Global Institutional Commons." In *Back to Basics: State Power in a Contemporary World*, edited by Martha Finnemore and Judith Goldstein, 280–312. New York: Oxford University Press.

Drwish, Sardar Mlla. 2016. "Why Syria's Kurds Are Cooperating with Russia." *Al-Monitor*, June 22. https://d2071andvip0wj.cloudfront.net/238-the-north-caucasus-insurgency-and-syria-an-exported-jihad.pdf.

Dueck, Colin. 2015. *The Obama Doctrine: American Grand Strategy Today*. Oxford: Oxford University Press.

Dugin, A. 2014. *Voina kontinentov*. Moscow: Akademicheskii proekt.

Dutkiewicz, P., and R. Sakwa. 2015. *Eurasian Integration: The View from Within*. London: Routledge.

Edgar, Adrienne. 2006. *Tribal Nation: The Making of Soviet Turkmenistan*. Princeton, NJ: Princeton University Press.

Emerson, R. Guy. 2014. "An Art of the Region: Towards a Politics of Regionness." *New Political Economy* 19, no. 4: 559–77.

Eriksson, Mikael. 2011. *Targeting Peace: Understanding UN and EU Targeted Sanctions*. Burlington, VT: Ashgate.

Escobar, Pepe. 2012. "Syria's Pipelineistan War: This Is a War of Deals, Not Bullets." Al Jazeera. August 6. http://www.aljazeera.com/indepth/opinion/2012/08/201285133440424621.html.

Evans, Robert. 2014. "Ukraine Death Toll Rises to More Than 4,300 Despite Ceasefire: UN." Reuters, November 20. http://www.reuters.com/article/2014/11/20/us-ukraine-crisis-un-idUSKCN0J40XC20141120.

Farchy, Jack. 2016. "Russia Senses Opportunity in Nagorno-Karabakh Conflict." *Financial Times*, April 19. https://www.ft.com/content/3d485610-0572-11e6-9b51-0fb5e65703ce.

Farrant, Amanda. 2006. "Mission Impossible: The Politico-Geographical Engineering of Soviet Central Asia's Republican Boundaries." *Central Asian Survey* 25, no. 1–2: 61–74.

Fawcett, Louise. 2004. "Exploring Regional Domains: A Comparative History of Regionalism." 80: 429–46.

Fawn, Rick, and Robert Nalbandov. 2013. "The Difficulties of Knowing the Start of War in the Information Age: Russia, Georgia and the War over South Ossetia, August 2008." In *Georgia: Revolution and War*, edited by Rick Fawn, 57–89. Milton Park, UK: Routledge.

Ferguson, Niall. 2017. "The False Prophecy of Hyperconnection: How to Survive the Networked Age." *Foreign Affairs* 96, no. 5.

Fesenko, Vladimir. 2015. "Ukraine: Between Europe and Eurasia." In *Eurasian Integration: The View from Within*, ed. Piotr Dutkievicz and Richard Sakwa, 126–50. London: Routledge.

Fildis, Ayse Tekdal. 2012. "Roots of Alawite-Sunni Rivalry in Syria." *Middle East Policy* 19, no. 2: 148–56.

Finnemore, Martha, and Judith Goldstein. 2013. "Puzzles about Power." In *Back to Basics: State Power in Contemporary World*. Edited by Martha Finnemore and Judith Goldstein. New York: Oxford University Press.

Fischer, Berndt, ed. 2006. *Balkan Strongmen: Dictators and Authoritarian Strongmen in Southeast Europe*. London: Hurst.

Flint, Colin, and Peter J. Taylor. 2014. *Political Geography: World-Economy, Nation-State and Locality*. Milton Park, UK: Routledge.

Forbes, Andrew. 1986. *Warlords and Muslims in Chinese Central Asia: A Political History of Republican Sinkiang, 1911–1949*. Cambridge: Cambridge University Press.

Fraenkel, Ernst. [1941] 2017. *The Dual State. A Contribution to the Theory of Dictatorship*. With an introduction by Jens Meierhenrich. Oxford: Oxford University Press.

Franke, Anja, Andrea Gawrich, and Gurban Alakbarov. 2009. "Kazakhstan and Azerbaijan as Post-Soviet Rentier States: Resource Incomes and Autocracy as a Double 'Curse' in Post-Soviet Regimes." *Europe-Asia Studies* 61, no. 1: 109–40.

Frankopan, Peter. 2015. *The Silk Roads*. London: Bloomsbury.

Frear, Thomas. 2014. "The Foreign Policy Options of a Small, Unrecognised State: The Case of Abkhazia." *Caucasus Survey* 1, no. 2: 83–107.

Fumagalli, Matteo. 2007. "Ethnicity, State Formation and Foreign Policy: Uzbekistan and 'Uzbeks Abroad.'" *Central Asian Survey* 26, no. 1: 105–22.

Gavrilis, George. 2008. *The Dynamics of Interstate Boundaries*. Cambridge: Cambridge University Press.

George, Julie A. 2010. "The Dangers of Reform: State Building and National Minorities in Georgia." In *War and Revolution in the Caucasus*, edited by Stephen F. Jones, 43–62. Abingdon, UK: Routledge.

German, Tracey. 2012. *Regional Cooperation in the South Caucasus: Good Neighbours or Distant Relatives*. Abingdon, UK: Routledge.

Gerrits, Andre W. M., and Max Bader. 2016. "Russian Patronage over Abkhazia and South Ossetia: Implications for Conflict Resolution." *East European Politics* 32, no. 3: 297–313.

Giles, Keir, Philip Hanson, Roderic Lyne, James Nixey, James Sherr, and Andrew Wood. 2015. *The Russian Challenge*. London: Chatham House, the Royal Institute of International Affairs.

Giragosian, Richard. 2015. "Armenia as a Bridge to Iran? Russia Won't Like It." Al Jazeera, August 30. http://www.aljazeera.com/indepth/opinion/2015/08/armenia-bridge-iran-russia-won-150830063735998.html.

Gleason, Abbott. 2010. "Eurasia: What Is It? Is It?" *Journal of Eurasian Studies* 1, no. 1: 26–32.

Godement, François. 2014. "China Analysis: China's Neighbourhood Policy." European Council on Foreign Relations. http://www.ecfr.eu/publications/summary/china_analysis_chinas_neighbourhood_policy.

Goertz, Gary, Paul F. Diehl, and Alexandru Balas. 2016. *The Puzzle of Peace: The Evolution of Peace in the International System*. New York: Oxford University Press.

Golan, Galia. 1990. *Soviet Policies in the Middle East from World War Two to Gorbachev*. Cambridge: Cambridge University Press.

Goodhand, J., D. Hulme, and N. Lewer. 2000. "Social Capital and Political Economy of Violence: A Case Study of Sri Lanka." *Disasters* 24, no. 4: 390–406.

Gordon, Claire, Marko Kmezić, and Jasmina Opardija-Susnjar, eds. 2013. *Stagnation and Drift in the Western Balkans: The Challenges of Political, Economic and Social Change*. Bern: Peter Lang.

Götz, Elias. 2016. "Russia, the West, and the Ukraine Crisis: Three Contending Perspectives." *Contemporary Politics* 22, no. 3: 249–66.

———. 2017. "Putin, the State, and War: The Causes of Russia's Near Abroad Assertion Revisited." *International Studies Review* 19, no. 2: 228–53.

Grant, Bruce, and Lale Yalçin-Heckmann. 2007. *Caucasus Paradigms: Anthropologies, Histories and the Making of a World Area*. Berlin: Lit Verlag.

Gray, Colin. 1977. *The Geopolitics of the Nuclear Era: Heartland, Rimlands, and the Technological Revolution*. New York: Crane, Russak.

Greenhill, Brian, and Yonatan Lupu. 2017. "Clubs of Clubs: Fragmentation in the Network of Intergovernmental Organizations." *International Studies Quarterly* 61, no. 1: 181–95.

Guixé i Coromines, Jordi, ed. 2016. *Past and Power: Public Policies on Memory: Debates, from Global to Local*. Barcelona: University of Barcelona.

Guliyev, Farid. 2005. "Post-Soviet Azerbaijan: Transition to Sultanistic Semiauthoritarianism? An Attempt at Conceptualization." *Demokratizatsiya* 13, no. 3: 393–434.

———. 2012. "Political Elites in Azerbaijan." In *Challenges of the Caspian Resource Boom: Domestic Elites and Policy-Making*, edited by Andreas Heinrich and Heiko Pleines, 117–30. Basingstoke, UK: Palgrave Macmillan.

Günay, Cengiz, and Vedran Džihić. 2016. "Decoding the Authoritarian Code: Exercising 'Legitimate' Power Politics through the Ruling Parties in Turkey, Macedonia and Serbia." *Journal of Southeast European and Black Sea Studies* 16, no. 4: 529–49.

Hale, Henry E. 2015. *Patronal Politics: Eurasian Regime Dynamics in Comparative Perspective.* Cambridge: Cambridge University Press.

Hanson, Philip. 2008. "The August 2008 Conflict: Economic Consequences for Russia." Chatham House Policy Brief, REP BN 08/06, September. https://www.chathamhouse.org/sites/files/chathamhouse/public/Research/Russia%20and%20Eurasia/0908rep_hanson.pdf.

Hayrapetyan, Garik. 2017. "The Transition of Demographics and the Demographics of Transition." Presentation to the conference Armenia: End of Transition—Shifting Focus, April 10, University of Southern California, www.youtube.com/watch?v=2omhcOJ8haY.

Headley, James. 2008. *Russia and the Balkans: Foreign Policy from Yeltsin to Putin.* London: Hurst.

Heath, Timothy. 2013. "Diplomacy Work Forum: Xi Steps Up Efforts to Shape a China-Centered Regional Order." *China Brief* 13, no. 22. http://www.jamestown.org/programs/chinabrief/single/?tx_ttnews%5Btt_news%5D=41594&cHash=a803315cd93291ad8b1043771111270b#.VxfpaKulb8s.

Heathershaw, John. 2009. *Post-Conflict Tajikistan: The Politics of Peacebuilding and the Emergence of Legitimate Order*. London: Routledge.

Heathershaw, John, and Nick Megoran. 2011. "Contesting Danger: A New Agenda for Policy and Scholarship on Central Asia." *International Affairs* 87, no. 3: 589–612.

Heathershaw, John, and Edward Schatz, eds. 2017. *Paradox of Power: The Logics of State Weakness in Eurasia*. Pittsburgh: Pittsburgh University Press.

Henrikson, Alan. 2002. "Distance and Foreign Policy: A Political Geography Approach." *International Political Science Review* 23, no. 4: 437–66.

Hensel, Paul R. 2000. "Territory: Theory and Evidence on Geography and Conflict." In *What Do We Know about War?* edited by John A. Vasquez, 3–26. Lanham, MD: Rowman & Littlefield.

Hensel, Paul R., and Paul F. Diehl. n.d. "Testing Empirical Propositions about Shatterbelts, 1945–1976." Unpublished manuscript. http://www.paulhensel.org/Research/pgq94.pdf.

Hettne, Björn. 2005. "Beyond the 'New' Regionalism." *New Political Economy* 10, no. 4: 543–71.

Hettne, Björn, and Fredrik Söderbaum. 1998. "The New Regionalism Approach." *Politeia* 17, no. 3: 6–21.

———. 2000. "Theorising the Rise of Regionness." *New Political Economy* 5, no. 3: 457–72.

Hill, Fiona, and Clifford G. Gaddy. 2015. *Mr. Putin: Operative in the Kremlin*, new and exp. ed. Washington, DC: Brookings Institution Press.

Hill, Fiona, Kemal Kirisci, and Andrew Moffatt. 2015. *Retracing the Caucasian Circle. Considerations and Constraints for US, EU, and Turkish Engagement in the South Caucasus.* Washington, DC: Center on the United States and Europe at Brookings.

Hirsch, Francine. 2000. "Toward an Empire of Nations: Border-Making and the Formation of Soviet National Identities." *Russian Review* 59, no. 2: 201–26.

———. 2005. *Empire of Nations: Ethnographic Knowledge and the Making of the Soviet Union.* Ithaca, NY: Cornell University Press.

Hobson, Peter. 2015. "Calculating the Cost of Russia's War in Syria." *Moscow Times*, October 20. https://themoscowtimes.com/articles/calculating-the-cost-of-russias-war-in-syria-50382.

Horowitz, Shale, and Michael D. Tyburski. 2012. "Reacting to Russia: Foreign Relations of the Former Soviet Bloc." In *Beyond Great Powers and Hegemons: Why Secondary States Support, Follow, or Challenge*, edited by Kristen P. Williams, Steven E. Lobell, and Neal G. Jesse, 161–76. Stanford, CA: Stanford University Press.

Hourani, Albert. 1991. *A History of the Arab Peoples*. Cambridge, MA: Harvard University Press.

Hunter, Shireen. 2017. *The New Geopolitics of the South Caucasus*. Boulder, CO: Lexington Books.

Huntington, Samuel. 2011. *The Clash of Civilizations and the Remaking of the World Order*. New York: Simon and Schuster.

Hurrell, Andrew, and Louise Fawcett. 1996. *Regionalism in World Politics: Regional Organization and International Order*. Oxford: Oxford University Press.

Ikenberry, John. 2014. "The Illusion of Geopolitics." *Foreign Affairs* 93, no. 3.

Interfax-Ukraina. 2014. "Ukraine's Defenders Day to Be Observed on October 14, February 23 Celebration Canceled." *Interfax-Ukraina*. Kyiv, October 14.

International Crisis Group. 2016a. *The Eurasian Economic Union: Power, Politics and Trade*. Brussels: International Crisis Group, July 20.

———. 2016b. "The North Caucasus Insurgency and Syria: An Exported Jihad?" Europe Report No. 238, March 16. https://d2071andvip0wj.cloudfront.net/238-the-north-caucasus-insurgency-and-syria-an-exported-jihad.pdf.

———. 2017. *Central Asia's Silk Road Rivalries*. Brussels: International Crisis Group, July 27.

International Institute for Strategic Studies. 2003. *Strategic Survey, 2002/3*. Oxford: Oxford University Press.

Iqbal, Zaryab, and Harvey Starr. 2008. "'Bad Neighbors: Failed States and Their Consequences." *Conflict Management and Peace Science* 25, no. 4: 315–31.

Ishkanian, Armine. 2015. "Self-Determined Citizens? New Forms of Civic Activism and Citizenship in Armenia." *Europe-Asia Studies* 67, no. 8: 1203–27.

Isingarin, Nigmatzhan K. 1998. *Problemy integratsii v SNG* [Problems of integration in the CIS). Almaty: Amatura.

Iskandaryan, Alexander. 2013. "Armenia's Foreign Policy: Where Values Meet Constraints." In *Armenia's Foreign and Domestic Politics: Development Trends*, edited by Mikko Palonkorpi and Alexander Iskandaryan, 6–17. Yerevan: Caucasus Institute and Aleksanteri Institute.

Ismailzade, Fariz, and Kevin Rosner. 2006. *Russia's Energy Interests in Azerbaijan*. London: GMB Publishing.

Ismayilov, Murad. 2014. "Power, Knowledge, and Pipelines: Understanding the Politics of Azerbaijan's Foreign Policy." *Caucasus Survey* 2, no. 1–2: 79–129.

———. 2016. "Together but Apart for Twenty Years: Azerbaijan and Turkey in Pursuit of Identity and Survival." In *Turkish-Azerbaijani Relations: One Nation—Two States?*, edited by Murad Ismayilov and Norman A. Graham, 1–20. Abingdon, UK: Routledge.

Ismayilov, Murad, and Norman A. Graham, eds. 2016. *Turkish-Azerbaijani Relations: One Nation—Two States?* Abingdon, UK: Routledge.

Jackson, Nicole. 2014. "Trans-Regional Security Organizations and Statist Multilateralism in Eurasia." *Europe-Asia Studies* 66, no. 2: 181–203.

Janos, Andrew. 2000. *East Central Europe in the Modern World: The Politics of Borderlands from Pre- to Postcommunism*. Stanford, CA: Stanford University Press.

Jenne, Erin. 2004. "A Bargaining Theory of Minority Demands: Explaining the Dog That Didn't Bite in 1990 Yugoslavia." *International Studies Quarterly* 48, no. 4: 729–54.

Jesse, Neal G., Steven E. Lobell, Galia Press-Barnathan, and Kristen P. William. 2012. "The Leader Can't Lead When the Followers Won't Follow: The Limitations of Hegemony." In *Beyond Great Powers and Hegemons: Why Secondary States Support, Follow, or Challenge*, edited by Kristen P. William, Steven E. Lobell, and Neal G. Jesse, 1–32. Stanford, CA: Stanford University Press.

Judah, Tim. 2009. "Yugoslavia Is Dead: Long Live the Yugosphere." LSEE Papers on South-eastern Europe. London School of Economics. http://www.lse.ac.uk/europeanInstitute/research/LSEE/PDFs/Publications/Yugosphere.pdf.

Junisbai, Barbara. 2010. "A Tale of Two Kazakhstans: Sources of Political Cleavage and Conflict in the Post-Soviet Period." *Europe-Asia Studies* 62, no. 2: 235–69.

Kabachnik, Peter. 2012. "Shaping Abkhazia: Cartographic Anxieties and the Making and Remaking of the Abkhazian Geobody." *Journal of Balkan and Near Eastern Studies* 14, no. 4: 397–415.

Kabar. 2013. "ATC of the State Committee for National Security Conducts Lectures on Threats of Terrorism, Religious Extremism and Separatism." February 17. http://www.kabar.kg/eng/law-and-order/full/6354.

Kaczmarski, Marcin. 2017. "Non-Western Visions of Regionalism: China's New Silk Road and Russia's Eurasian Economic Union." *International Affairs* 93, no. 6.

Kaine, Tim. 2017. "A New Truman Doctrine." *Foreign Affairs*, July/August.

Kamrava, Mehran. 2017. *The Great Game in West Asia*. Oxford: Oxford University Press.

Karaganov, Sergei. 2016. "S Vostoka na Zapad, ili Bol'shaya Evraziya," *Rossisya v globalnoi politike*, October 25.

Karins, Krišjānis. 2014. "EU Consequences of South Stream Closure." *EURANET Plus Network*. December 8. http://euranetplus-inside.eu/south-streams-closure-towards-new-eu-energy-sources-or-eu-division/.

Karpenko, Oksana. 2014. *Problemy i Perspektivy Podgotovki Uchebnikov i Prepodavaniya Istorii na Yuzhnom Kavkaze*. Saint Petersburg: Imagine Center for Conflict Transformation.

Katz, Mark N. 2004. "Saudi-Russian Relations since 9/11." *Problems of Post-Communism* 51, no. 2: 3–11.

———. 2006. "Putin's Foreign Policy toward Syria." *Middle East Review of International Affairs* 10, no. 1: 53–62.

———. 2008. "Comparing Putin's and Brezhnev's Policies toward the Middle East." *Society* 45, no. 2: 177–80.

———. 2015. "Convergent Hopes, Divergent Realities: Russia and the Gulf in a Time of Troubles." Arab Gulf States Institute in Washington. Policy Paper no. 7, November 6. http://www.agsiw.org/wp-content/uploads/2015/11/Katz_ONLINE_edits.pdf.

Katzenstein, Peter. 2005. *A World of Regions: Asia and Europe in the American Imperium*. Ithaca, NY: Cornell University Press.

Kavkazskiy, Uzel. 2015. "Dogovor mezhdu Rossiyskoy Federatsiey i Respublikoy Yuzhnaya Osetiya o soyuznichestve i integratsii." June 30. http://www.kavkaz-uzel.ru/articles/259096/.

Keil, Soeren, and Zeynep Arkan, eds. 2015. *The EU and Member State Building: European Foreign Policy in the Western Balkans.* Abingdon, UK: Routledge.

Kelly, Philip. 1986. "Escalation of Regional Conflict: Testing the Shatterbelt Concept." *Political Geography Quarterly* 5, no. 2: 161–80.

———. 2016. *Classical Geopolitics: A New Analytical Model.* Stanford, CA: Stanford University Press.

Kelly, Robert K. 2007. "Security Theory in the 'New Regionalism.'" 9: 197–229.

Kendall-Taylor, Andrea. 2012. "Purchasing Power: Oil, Elections and Regime Durability in Azerbaijan and Kazakhstan." *Europe-Asia Studies* 64, no. 4: 737–60.

Kennedy, Paul. 1987. *The Rise and Fall of the Great Powers: Economic Change and Military Conflict from 1500 to 2000.* New York: Random House.

Kent, Neil. 2016. *Crimea: A History.* London: Hurst.

Keohane, Robert O., and Joseph Nye. 2012. "Realism and Complex Interdependence." In *The Globalization Reader*, 4th ed., edited by Frank J. Lechner and John Boli, 71–78. Sussex, UK: Wiley-Blackwell.

Khalid, Adeeb. 2007. "Introduction: Locating the (Post-)Colonial in Soviet History." *Central Asian Survey* 26, no. 4: 465–73.

Khanna, Parag. 2008. *The Second World: Empires and Influence in the New Global Order.* New York: Random House.

Kirchner, Emil, and Roberto Domínguez. 2011. "Regional Organizations and Security Governance." In *The Security Governance of Regional Organizations*, edited by Emil Kirchner and Roberto Domínguez, 1–22. New York: Routledge.

Klitschko, Vitali. 2013. Interview by Kseniya Sobchak. "Eto ne moi geroi." *Hromadke.tv.*, December 23.

Kneafsey, Moya. 2000. "Tourism, Place Identities and Social Relations in the European Rural Periphery." *European Urban and Regional Studies* 7, no. 1: 35–50.

Kobolev, Andrei. 2016. Interview by Sonya Koshkina. "Evropeitsy priamo govoriat: 'Gospoda, my v RF zarabatyvaem milliard. V Ukraine tsyvfra poka blizka k nuliu.'" *Levy Bereg*, Kyiv, December 29.

Koehler, Jan, and Christoph Zürcher, eds. 2003. *Potentials of Disorder.* Manchester, UK: Manchester University Press.

Kokcharov, Alex, Alex Melikishvili, and Lilit Gevorgyan. 2016. "Russia's Nagorno-Karabakh Conflict Plan Poses Renewed Armenia-Azerbaijan War Risks," *IHS Jane's Intelligence Weekly*, August 10. https://en.168.am/2016/08/10/10028.html.

Kolstø, Pål, and Helge Blakkisrud. 2008. "Living with Non-Recognition: State- and Nation-Building in South Caucasian Quasi-States." *Europe-Asia Studies* 60, no. 3: 483–509.

Komsomol'skaya Pravda. 2008. "Prinujdenie K Miru: Khronika Voini." August 10. http://www.kp.ru/daily/24143/361264/.

Korolev, Alexander. 2015. "Bringing Geopolitics Back In: Russia's Foreign Policy and Its Relations with the Post-Soviet Space." *International Studies Review* 17: 298–312.

Krause, Keith. 2010. "State-Making and Region-Building: The Interplay of Domestic and Regional Security in the Middle East." *Journal of Strategic Studies* 26, no. 3: 99–124.

Krikorian, Onnik James. 2017. "Unlikely Neighbors." *Stratfor Worldview*, May 7. https://worldview.stratfor.com/article/unlikely-neighbors.

Kuchins, A. C., T. M. Sanderson, and D. A. Gordon. 2009. "The Northern Distribution Network and the Modern Silk Road: Planning for Afghanistan's Future. Report." Washington, DC: Center for Strategic and International Studies, December. http://csis.org/files/publication/091217_Kuchins_NorthernDistNet_Web.pdf.

Kudaibergenova, Diana T. 2016. "Eurasian Economic Union Integration in Kazakhstan and Kyhrgyzstan." *European Politics and Society* 17, sup. 1: 97–112.

Kukhianidze, Alexandre, Alexandre Kupatadze, and Roman Gotsiridze. 2004. *Smuggling through Abkhazia and Tskhinvali Region of Georgia*. Tbilisi: Transnational Crime and Corruption Center.

Kuzio, Taras. 2002a. "ANALYSIS: 'Pro-Ukrainian' or 'Pro-Kuchma'? Ukraine's Foreign Policy in Crisis." *RFE/RL*, May 5. http://www.ukrweekly.com/old/archive/2002/180206.shtml.

———. 2002b. "History, Memory and Nation Building in the Post-Soviet Colonial Space." *Nationalities Papers* 30, no. 2: 242–64.

Lampe, John. 2014. *Balkans into Southeastern Europe: A Century of War and Transition, 1914–2014*. London: Palgrave Macmillan.

Lane, David. 2009. "Coloured Revolution as Political Phenomenon." *Journal of Communist Studies and Transition Politics* 25, no. 2–3: 113–35.

Langhbein, Julia, and Kataryna Wolczuk. 2012. "Convergence without Membership? The Impact of the European Union in the Neighbourhood: Evidence from Ukraine." *Journal of European Public Policy* 19, no. 6: 863–81.

LaPorte, Jody, M. 2015. "Hidden in Plain Sight: Political Opposition and Hegemonic Authoritarianism in Azerbaijan." *Post-Soviet Affairs* 31, no. 4: 339–66.

Laruelle, M. 2008. *Russian Eurasianism: An Ideology of Empire*. Washington, DC: Woodrow Wilson Center Press.

———. 2015a. "Eurasia, Eurasianism, Eurasian Union: Terminological Gaps and Overlaps." *PONARS Eurasia*, no. 366.

———. 2015b. "Russia as a 'Divided Nation,' from Compatriots to Crimea: A Contribution to the Discussion on Nationalism and Foreign Policy." *Problems of Post-Communism* 62: 88–97.

———. 2015c. "The US Silk Road: Geopolitical Imaginary or the Repackaging of Strategic Interests?" *Eurasian Geography and Economics* 56, no. 4: 360–75.

Lawrence, Bruce, ed. and trans. 2005. *Messages to the World: The Statements of Osama bin Laden*. London: Verso.

Lay Hwee Yeo. 2010. "Institutional Regionalism versus Networked Regionalism: Europe and Asia Compared." *International Politics* 47, no. 3: 324–37.

Lee, G. 2012. "The New Silk Road and the Northern Distribution Network: A Golden Road to Central Asian Trade Reform?" New York: Open Society Foundations, October.

Lefebvre, Henri. 2009. *State, Space, World*. Minneapolis: Minnesota University Press.

Lehman, Maike. 2011. "The Local Reinvention of the Soviet Project Nation and Socialism in the Republic of Armenia after 1945." *Jahrbücher für_Geschichte Osteuropas* 59, no. 4: 481–508.

Lenczowski, George. 1980. *The Middle East in World Affairs*. 4th ed. Ithaca, NY: Cornell University Press.

Lepgold, Joseph. 2003. "Regionalism in the Post–Cold War Era: Incentives for Conflict Management." In *Regional Conflict Management*, edited by Paul Francis Diehl and Joseph Lepgold, 9–40. Boulder, CO: Rowman & Littlefield.

Leschenko, Serhiy. 2016. "Leschenko raskryl sgovor Poroshenko and Firtasha po 'pokrytiu' afery so szhyzhenym gazom," NewsOne Press Agency, September 9, https://newsone.ua/news/leshhenko-raskryl-sgovor-poroshenko-i-firtasha-po-pokrytiyu-afery-so-szhizhennym-gazom.htm.

Levitsky, Steven, and Lucan A. Way. 2006. "Linkage versus Leverage: Rethinking the International Dimension of Regime Change." *Comparative Politics* 38, no. 4: 379–400.

———. 2010. *Competitive Authoritarianism: Hybrid Regimes after the Cold War.* New York: Cambridge University Press.

Lewis, David. 2008. *The Temptations of Tyranny in Central Asia.* London: Hurst/Columbia University Press.

———. 2012. "Who's Socialising Whom? Regional Organisations and Contested Norms in Central Asia." *Europe-Asia Studies* 64, no. 7: 1219–37.

———. 2014. "Crime, Terror and the State in Central Asia." *Global Crime* 15, no. 3–4: 337–56.

———. 2015. "Reasserting Hegemony in Central Asia: Russian Policy in Post-2010 Kyrgyzstan." *Comillas Journal of International Relations*, no. 3: 58–81.

———. 2017. "The Contested State in Post-Soviet Armenia." In *Paradox of Power: The Logics of State Weakness in Eurasia*, edited by John Heathershaw and Edward Schatz, 120–35. Pittsburgh: Pittsburgh University Press.

Lieven, Anatol. 1998. *Chechnya: Tombstone of Russian Power.* New Haven, CT: Yale University Press.

Lobell, Steven E. 2016. "Realism, Balance of Power, and Power Transitions." In *Accommodating Rising Powers: Past, Present, and Future*, edited by T. V. Paul, 33–52. Cambridge: Cambridge University Press.

Lundgren, Minna. 2016. "Boundaries of Displacement: Belonging and Return among Forcibly Displaced Young Georgians from Abkhazia." PhD diss., Mid Sweden University.

Lynch, Allen C. 2001. "The Realism of Russia's Foreign Policy." *Europe-Asia Studies* 53, no. 1: 7–31.

Lynch, Dov. 2004. *Engaging Eurasia's Separatist States.* Washington, DC: United States Institute of Peace.

Mackinder, Halford. 1904. "The Geographical Pivot of History." *Geographical Journal* 23, no. 4 (April).

———. 1981. *Democratic Ideals and Reality.* Washington, DC: National Defense University Press. First published in 1919.

Mahan, Alfred Thayer. 1890. *The Influence of Sea Power upon History: 1660–1783.* Boston: Little, Brown.

Manners, Ian. 2002. "Normative Power Europe: A Contradiction in Terms?" *Journal of Common Market Studies* 40, no. 2: 235–58.

Marat, Erica. 2015. "Global Money Laundering and Its Domestic Political Consequences in Kyrgyzstan." *Central Asian Survey* 34, no. 1: 46–56.

Marples, David. 2015. "Open Letter from Scholars and Experts on Ukraine Re. the So-Called 'Anti-Communist Law.'" *Krytyka*, April. https://krytyka.com/en/articles/open-letter-scholars-and-experts-ukraine-re-so-called-anti-communist-law.

Mead, Walter Russell. 2014. "The Return of Geopolitics." *Foreign Affairs* 93, no. 3.

Mearsheimer, John J. 2014a. *The Tragedy of Great Power Politics.* New York: Norton.

———. 2014b. "Why the Ukraine Crisis Is the West's Fault." *Foreign Affairs* 93, no. 5: 77–89.

Megoran, Nick. 2005. "The Critical Geopolitics of Danger in Uzbekistan and Kyrgyzstan." *Environment and Planning D: Society and Space* 23, no. 4: 555–80.

Menon, Rajan. 1998. "After Empire: Russia and Southern 'Near Abroad.'" In *The New Russian Foreign Policy*, edited by Michael Mandelbaum, 100–166. New York: Council on Foreign Relations.

Merabyan, Karen. 2014. "Sovremennaya Politika Rossii Na Yuzhnom Kavkaze." [Modern Russian politics in South Caucasus] *MGIM University Bulletin* 4, no. 37: 92–100.

Middle East Monitor. 2016. "Russia Receives Yemen Houthi Delegation." December 15. https://www.middleeastmonitor.com/20161215-russia-receives-yemen-houthi-delegation/.

Milekic, Sven. 2016. "Defence Expert Plays Down Croatia-Serbia 'Arms Race,'" *Balkan Insight*, December 29. http://www.balkaninsight.com/en/article/croatia-serbia-arms-race-far-from-reality-12-29-2016#sthash.2OxqqynN.dpuf.

Militz, Elisabeth, and Carolin Schurr. 2016. "Affective Nationalism: Banalities of Belonging in Azerbaijan." *Political Geography* 54 (September): 54–63.

Ministry of Foreign Affairs of Russia. 2014. "Zayavleniye MID Rossii po Sobytiyam na Ukraine." August 29. http://www.mid.ru/brp_4.nsf/0/5A4CB5306FC0ABD344257D4300415026.

Mirzoyan, Alla. 2010. *Armenia, the Regional Powers and the West: Between History and Geopolitics*. New York: Palgrave Macmillan.

Mitchell, Lincoln. 2009. *Uncertain Democracy*. Philadelphia: University of Pennsylvania Press.

Mitchell, Lincoln, and Alexander Cooley. 2010. "After the August War: A New Strategy for U.S. Engagement with Georgia." *Harriman Review* 17, no. 3–4, Special Double Issue. New York: Harriman Institute.

Molchanov, Mikhail. 2015. *Eurasian Regionalism and Russian Foreign Policy*. Ashgate, VT: Farnham & Burlington.

Montecinos, Verónica. 1996. "Ceremonial Regionalism, Institutions and Integration in the Americas." *Studies in Comparative International Development* 31, no. 2: 110–23.

Moravcsik, Andrew. 2002. "The Quiet Superpower." *Newsweek*, June 17.

Morgan, Gerald. 1973. "Myth and Reality in the Great Game." *Asian Affairs* 60: 55–65.

Morgan, Patrick M. 1997. "Regional Security Complexes and Regional Orders." In *Regional Orders: Building Security in a New World*, edited by David A. Lake and Patrick M. Morgan, 20–44. University Park: Pennsylvania State University.

Nalbandov, Robert. 2009. "Battle of Two Logics: Appropriateness and Consequentiality in Russian Interventions in Georgia." *Caucasian Review of International Affairs* 3, no. 1: 20–36.

———. 2016. *Not by Bread Alone: Russian Foreign Policy under Putin*. Lincoln: University of Nebraska Press.

Naumkin, Vitaly. 2014. "Russia's Kurdish Dilemma." *Al-Monitor*, January 26. http://www.al-monitor.com/pulse/originals/2014/01/russia-kurdistan-regional-government-iraq.html.

Nechayeva-Yuriychuk, Nataliya V. 2010. "Osobennosti Formirovaniya Moldavskoi Gosudarstvennosti Posle Obreteniya Nezavisimosti." *Rusin* 4, no. 22: 136–44.

Neiromir-TV. 2015. "Politring Strelkov vs. Starikov." January 22. http://neuromir.tv/tsentrsily-silatsentra/.

Nichol, Jim. 2009. *Russia–Georgia Conflict in August 2008: Context and Implications for US Interests*. Washington, DC: Congressional Research Service.

Nizameddin, Talal. 2013. *Putin's New Order in the Middle East*. London: Hurst.

Northrop, Douglas T. 2004. *Veiled Empire: Gender and Power in Stalinist Central Asia*. Ithaca, NY: Cornell University Press.

Nye, Joseph. 1968. *International Regionalism*. Boston, MA: Little, Brown.

Ó Beacháin, Donnacha, Giorgio Comai, and Ann Tsurtsumia-Zurabishvili. 2016. "The Secret Lives of Unrecognised States: Internal Dynamics, External Relations, and Counter-Recognition Strategies." *Small Wars and Insurgencies* 27, no. 3: 440–66.

Obydenkova, Anastassia. 2006. "New Regionalism and Regional Integration: The Role of National Institutions." *Cambridge Review of International Affairs* 19, no. 4: 589–610.

Ogneva, V. V., and L. A. Brysyakina. 2011. "Rossiya I Moldova v Poiske Optimal'nogo Formata Sotrudnichestva." *Scientific Newsletter of the Belgorod State University* 7, no. 102: 1–6.

Ohanyan, Anna. 2007. "On Money and Memory: Political Economy of Cross-Border Engagement on the Politically Divided Armenia-Turkey Frontier." *Conflict, Security and Development* 7, no. 4: 579–604.

———. 2008. *NGOs, IGOs, and Network Mechanisms of Global Governance in Post-Conflict Microfinance.* New York: Palgrave Macmillan.

———. 2009. "Policy Wars for Peace: Network Model of NGO Behavior." *International Studies Review* 11, no. 3: 475–501.

———. 2015. *Networked Regionalism as Conflict Management*. Stanford, CA: Stanford University Press.

———. 2016. "How Deep Is Dayton: Assessing the Regional Impact of the 1995 Dayton Accords." *Wilson Quarterly*. Winter. https://wilsonquarterly.com/quarterly/the-post-obama-world/how-deep-is-dayton/.

O'Loughlin, John, Vladimir Kolossov, and Gerard Toal (Gearóid Ó Tuathail). 2015. "Inside the Post-Soviet De Facto States: A Comparison of Attitudes in Abkhazia, Nagorny Karabakh, South Ossetia and Transnistria." *Eurasian Geography and Economics* 55, no. 5: 423–56.

OSCE. 1994. "Transdnistrian Conflict: Origins and Issues." Background paper, CSCE Conflict Prevention Centre. June 10. http://www.osce.org/moldova/42308.

Oskanian, Kevork. 2013. *Fear, Weakness and Power in the Post-Soviet South Caucasus*. Basingstoke, UK: Palgrave Macmillan.

———. 2016. "The Balance Strikes Back: Power, Perceptions, and Ideology in Georgian Foreign Policy, 1992–2014." *Foreign Policy Analysis* 12, no. 4 (October 1): 628–52. http://dx.doi.org/10.1093/fpa/orw010.

Østby, Gudrun, Ragnhild Nordås, and Jan Ketil Rød Source. 2009. "Regional Inequalities and Civil Conflict in Sub-Saharan Africa." *International Studies Quarterly* 53, no. 2: 301–24.

Özdal, Habibe, Hasan Selim Özertem, Kerim Has, and Turgut Demirtepe. 2013. *Turkish-Russian Relations in the Post-Cold War Period: Current Dynamics—Future Prospects*. Ankara, Turkey: International Strategic Research Organization.

Paasi, A. 1986. "The Institutionalization of Regions: A Theoretical Framework for Understanding the Emergence of Regions and the Constitution of Regional Identity." *Fennia* 164: 105–46.

Panossian, Razmik. 2001. "The Irony of Nagorno-Karabakh: Formal Institutions versus Informal Politics." *Regional and Federal Studies* 11, no. 3: 143–64.

———. 2006. *The Armenians: From Kings and Priests to Merchants and Commissars*. London: Hurst.

Patrick, Stewart. 2007. "'Failed' States and Global Security: Empirical Questions and Policy Dilemmas." *International Studies Review* 9, no. 4: 644–62.

Paul, T. V., ed. 2016. *Accommodating Rising Powers: Past, Present, and Future*. Cambridge: Cambridge University Press.

———. 2017. "Recasting Statecraft: International Relations and Strategies of Peaceful Change." *International Studies Review* 61: 1–13.

Pavkovic, Aleksandar, and Peter Radan. 2011. *The Ashgate Research Companion to Secession*. Burlington, VT: Ashgate.

Pavlović, Srdja. 2016. "Montenegro's 'Stabilitocracy': The West's Support of Đukanović Is Damaging the Prospects of Democratic Change." European Politics and Policy Blog. London School of Economics. December 23. http://blogs.lse.ac.uk/europpblog/2016/12/23/montenegros-stabilitocracy-how-the-wests-support-of-dukanovic-is-damaging-the-prospects-of-democratic-change/.

Pegg, Scott. 2017. "Twenty Years of De Facto State Studies: Progress, Problems, and Prospects." *The Oxford Research Encyclopedia of Politics*. Oxford: Oxford University Press. http://dx.doi.org/10.1093/acrefore/9780190228637.013.516.

Podadera, Pablo Rivera, and Anna Garashchuk. 2016. "The Eurasian Economic Union: Prospective Regional Integration in the Post-Soviet Space or Just Geopolitical Project?" *Eastern Journal of European Studies* 7, no. 2: 91–110.

Popescu, Nicu. 2006a. "'Outsourcing' De Facto Statehood: Russia and the Secessionist Entities in Georgia and Moldova." Centre for European Policy Studies, Policy Brief No. 109, July. Brussels: CEPS.

———. 2006b. *Russia's Soft Power Ambitions*, Centre for European Policy Studies, Policy Brief no. 115, October. Brussels: CEPS.

Posen, Barry R. 2014. *Restraint: A New Foundation for US Grand Strategy*. Ithaca, NY: Cornell University Press.

Potter, Philip B. K. 2016. "Globalization, Interdependence, and Major Power Accommodation." In *Accommodating Rising Powers: Past, Present, and Future*, edited by T. V. Paul, 53–69. Cambridge: Cambridge University Press.

Pouliot, Vincent. 2007. "Pacification without Collective Identification: Russia and the Transatlantic Security Community in the Post–Cold War Era." *Journal of Peace Research* 44, no. 5: 605–22.

Pravda.com.ua. 2016. "Polovyna Ukraintsiv vvazhae rosiyan bratnim narodom." *Ukrainskia Pravda*, December 16.

Prelz Oltramonti, Giulia. 2015. "The Exploitation of Economic Leverage in Conflict Protraction: Modes and Aims: The Cases of South Ossetia and Abkhazia (1992–2008)." PhD diss., Université Libre de Bruxelles.

———. 2016. "Securing Disenfranchisement through Violence and Isolation: The Case of Georgians/Mingrelians in the District of Gali." *Conflict, Security and Development* 16, no. 3: 245–62.

Prieto, Germán Camilo. 2012. "How Does Regionalism Unfold? Discussing the Relationships of Constitution and Causation between Identity and Institutions." *OASIS*, no. 17: 7–37.

Primakov, Yevgeny. 2009. *Russia and the Arabs: Behind the Scenes in the Middle East from the Cold War to the Present*. Translated by Paul Gould. New York: Basic Books.

Prokhanov, Alexander. 2011. "Svyachennie Kamni Imperii" [Sacred stones of the empire], *Zavtra* [newspaper, Moscow].

Putz, Catherine. 2015a. "Kazakh Fisherman Shot by Uzbek Border Guards." *Diplomat*, July 2. http://thediplomat.com/2015/07/kazakh-fisherman-shot-by-uzbek-border-guards/.

———. 2015b. "More Trouble on the Kyrgyz-Uzbek Border." *Diplomat*, May 13. http://thediplomat.com/2015/05/more-trouble-on-the-kyrgyz-uzbek-border/.

Radnitz, Scott. 2010. *Weapons of the Wealthy: Predatory Regimes and Elite-led Protests in Central Asia*. Ithaca, NY: Cornell University Press.

Ratelle, Jean-François, and Laurence Broers, eds. 2018. *Networked Insurgencies and Foreign Fighters in Eurasia*. London: Routledge.

Reeves, Madeleine. 2014. *Border Work: Spatial Lives of the State in Rural Central Asia*. Ithaca, NY: Cornell University Press.

Reinicke, Wolfgang. 1998. *Global Public Policy*. Washington, DC: Brookings Institution Press.

Rekhviashvili, Lela, and Abel Polese. 2017. "Liberalism and Shadow Interventionism in Post-Revolutionary Georgia (2003–2012)." *Caucasus Survey* 5, no. 1: 27–50.

Reuters. 2016. "Libyan General Khalifa Haftar Meets Russian Minister to Seek Help." *Guardian*, November 29. https://www.theguardian.com/world/2016/nov/29/libyan-general-khalifa-haftar-meets-russian-minister-to-seek-help.

RFE/RL (Radio Free Europe / Radio Liberty). 2014. "Russia Strengthens Grip on Abkhazia with New Pact." November 24. http://www.rferl.org/a/georgia-russia-abkhazia/26707329.html.

———. 2017a. "European Parliament Paves Way for Visa-Free Travel for Georgians, Ukrainians." February 13. http://www.rferl.org/a/eu-georgia-ukraine-visa-free-travel/28307248.html.

———. 2017b. "Trial to Resume against Alleged Russian, Serbian Coup Plotters in Montenegro, Radio Free Europe/Radio Liberty." September 7. https://www.rferl.org/a/montenegro-coup-plot-trial-resumes-russia-nato-djukanovic-mandic-knezevic/28719631.html.

Richardson, F. Lewis. 1961. "The Problem of Contiguity: An Appendix to Statistic of Deadly Quarrels." In *Yearbook of the Society for General Systems Research*. Vol. 6, edited by Ludwig von Bertalanffy and Anatol Rapoport, 140–87. Ann Arbor, MI: Society for General Systems Research.

Risse, Thomas. 2013. "Governance under Limited Sovereignty." In *Back to Basics: State Power in a Contemporary World*, edited by Martha Finnemore and Judith Goldstein, 78–104. New York: Oxford University Press.

Roeder, Philip G. 1997. "From Hierarchy to Hegemony: The Post-Soviet Security Complex." In *Regional Orders: Building Security in a New World*, edited by David A. Lake and Patrick M. Morgan, 219–44. University Park: Pennsylvania State University Press.

Rogan, Eugene. 2015. *The Fall of the Ottomans: The Great War in the Middle East*. New York: Basic Books.

Romanenko, Yuriy. 2012. "Perelom: Kak Yanukovich: Likvidiruet Firtasha i drugikh oligarkhov." *Hvylya*, January 24. http://hvylya.net/analytics/politics/perelom-kak-janukovich-likvidiruet-firtasha-i-drugih-oligarhov.html.

Romaniyuk, Yaroslav. 2016. Interview by Viktoria Matola, "Politychni domovlennostiu siogodni perevazhayut pravovi ragumenty." *Levy Bereg*, December 20.

Roper, Steven D. 2002. "Regionalism in Moldova: The Case of Transdnistria and Gagauzia." In *Ethnicity and Territory in the Former Soviet Union: Regions in Conflict*, edited by James Hughes and Gwendolyn Sasse, 101–22. Milton Park, UK: Frank Cass.

Roylance, David. 2001. *Introduction to Fracture Mechanics*. Cambridge, MA: Massachusetts Institute of Technology.

Rozman, Gilbert. 2010. "Post Cold War Evolution of Chinese Thinking on Regional Institutions in Northeast Asia." *Journal of Contemporary China* 19, no. 66: 605–60.

Rubin, Barnett R. 2002. *Fragmentation of Afghanistan*. New Haven, CT: Yale University Press.

Sabanadze, Natalie. 2016. "Georgia Needs Europe's Normative Force." *Clarion*, October 10. http://new.civil.ge/clarion/news/3/1343/eng.

Safiyev, Rail. 2016. "Informality in a Neopatrimonial State: Azerbaijan." In *State and Legal Practice in the Caucasus*, edited by Stéphane Voell and Iwona Kaliszewska, 133–48. London: Routledge.

Sakwa, Richard. 2010. "The Dual State in Russia." *Post-Soviet Affairs* 26, no. 3: 185–206.

———. 2012. "Great Powers and Small Wars in the Caucasus." In *Conflict in the Former USSR*, edited by Matthew Sussex, 64–90. Cambridge: Cambridge University Press.

———. 2013. "Blowback? Chechnya and the Challenges of Russian Politics." In *The Fire Below: How the Caucasus Shaped Russia*, edited by Robert Bruce Ware, 175–202. New York: Bloomsbury.

———. 2015. *Frontline Ukraine: Crisis in the Borderlands*. London: I. B. Tauris.

Samokhvalov, Vsevolod. 2006. "Ukraine and the Orange Revolution: Democracy or Velvet Restoration." *Journal of South-East Europe and Black Sea Studies* 6, no. 2: 257–73.

———. 2015. "Ukraine between Russia and the European Union: Triangle Revisited." *Europe-Asia Studies* 1371–93. doi:10.1080/09668136.2015.1088513.

———. 2016. "Eurasian Regionalism and Russian Foreign Policy." *Europe-Asia Studies* 68, no. 7: 1278–80.

Saparov, Arsène. 2015. *From Conflict to Autonomy in the Caucasus*. London: Routledge.

Sasse, Gwendolyn. 2013. "Linkages and the Promotion of Democracy: The EU's Eastern Neighbourhood." *Democratization* 20, no. 4: 553–91.

Schatz, Edward. 2004. *Modern Clan Politics: The Power of "Blood" in Kazakhstan and Beyond*. Seattle: University of Washington Press.

Schiff, M., and L. A. Winters. 2003. *Regional Integration and Development*. Washington, DC: World Bank.

Schlichte, Klaus. 2017. "The International State: Comparing Statehood in Central Asia and Sub-Saharan Africa." In *Paradox of Power: The Logics of State Weakness in Eurasia*, edited by John Heathershaw and Edward Schatz, 105–19. Pittsburgh: Pittsburgh University Press.

Schwartz, Paul N. 2014. "Crimea's Strategic Value to Russia." Center for Strategic and International Studies, *The Post-Soviet Post* (blog), March 18. https://www.csis.org/blogs/post-soviet-post/crimeas-strategic-value-russia.

Scott, Erik. 2017. *Familiar Strangers: The Georgian Diaspora and the Evolution of the Soviet Empire*. Oxford: Oxford University Press.

Semian, Michal, and Pavel Chromy. 2014. "Regional Identity as a Driver or a Barrier in the Process of Regional Development: A Comparison of Selected European Experience." *Norks Geografisk Tidsskrift-Norwegian Journal of Geography* 68, no. 5: 263–70.

Shahnazarian, Nona. 2016. *"Here Is Not Maida, Here Is Marshal Baghramian": The "Electric Yerevan" Protest Movement and Its Consequences*. PONARS Eurasia Policy Memo.

Shevel, Oxana. 2011. "Russian Nation-Building from Yeltsin to Medvedev: Ethnic, Civic, or Purposefully Ambiguous?" *Europe-Asia Studies* 63, no. 1: 179–202.

Shevel, Oxana, Nuala O'Connor, Lawrence G. Potter, Barbara Crossette, Adekeye Adebajo, Rochelle Davis, Joseph Chamie, and Juan de Onis. 2015. *Great Decisions 2015*. New York: Foreign Policy Association.

Siani-Davies, Peter, ed. 2003. *International Intervention in the Balkans since 1995*. Abingdon, UK: Routledge.

Siegel, Jennifer. 2002. *Endgame: Britain, Russia and the Final Struggle for Central Asia*. London: I. B. Tauris.

Simão, Licínia. 2018. *The EU's Neighbourhood Policy towards the South Caucasus*. Basingstoke, UK: Palgrave Macmillan.

Slade, Gavin. 2017. "Informality as Illegality in Georgia's Anti-Mafia Campaign." *Caucasus Survey* 5, no. 1: 51–64.

Slaughter, Anne Marie. 2017. *The Chessboard and the Web: Strategies of Connection in a Networked World*. New Haven, CT: Yale University Press.

Smith, Alan, ed. 1995. *Challenges for Russian Economic Reform*. Washington, DC: Brookings Institution.

Smith, Hanna. 2016. "Statecraft and Post-Imperial Attractiveness: Eurasian Integration and Russia as a Great Power." *Problems of Post-Communism* 63: 171–82.

Smith, Jeremy, and Paul Richardson. 2017. "The Myth of Eurasia—A Mess of Regions." *Journal of Borderlands Studies* 32, no. 1: 1–6.

Snidal, Duncan. 1996. "Political Economy and International Institutions." *International Review of Law and Economics* 16: 121–37.

Sobják, Anita. 2013. "The Romania–Moldova Gas Pipeline: Does a Connection to the EU Mean a Disconnect from Russia?" *Bulletin of the Polish Institute of International Affairs* 93, no. 546: 1–2.

Söderbaum, Fredrik. 2004. *The Political Economy of Regionalism: The Case of Southern Africa*. Basingstoke, UK: Palgrave Macmillan.

———. 2016. "Old, New, and Comparative Regionalism." *The Oxford Handbook of Comparative Regionalism*. Oxford: Oxford University Press, 2016.

Söderbaum, Fredrik, and Timothy M. Shaw, eds. 2003. *Theories of New Regionalism: A Palgrave Reader*. Basingstoke, UK: Palgrave Macmillan.

Sørensen, Camilla T. N. 2015. "The Significance of Xi Jinping's 'Chinese Dream' for Chinese Foreign Policy: From 'Tao Guang Yang Hui' to 'Fen Fa You Wei.'" *Journal of China and International Relations* 3, no. 1: 53–73.

Spencer, Philip, and Howard Wollman. 2002. *Nationalism: A Critical Introduction*. London: Sage.

Spykman, Nicholas. 1942. *America's Strategy in World Politics: The United States and the Balance of Power*. New York: Harcourt, Brace.

———. 1944. *The Geography of the Peace*. New York: Harcourt, Brace.

Starr, S. F. 2005. "A Partnership for Central Asia." *Foreign Affairs* 84, no. 4: 164–78.

Stati, Vasiliy. 2012. "Mejdu Russkimi I Ruminami." *Rusin* 1, no. 27: 130–36.

Stent, Angela E. 2014. *The Limits of Partnership: U.S.-Russian Relations in the Twenty-First Century*. Princeton, NJ: Princeton University Press.

Subtelny, Orest. 2009. *Ukraine. A History*. 4th ed. Toronto: University of Toronto Press.

Suny, Ronald G. 1998. *The Soviet Experiment: Russia, the USSR, and the Successor States*. New York: Oxford University Press.

———. 2010. "The Pawn of Great Powers: The East–West Competition for Caucasia." *Journal of Eurasian Studies* 1: 10–25.

Sussex, Matthew. 2012. "The Shape of the Security Order in the Former USSR." In *Conflict in the Former USSR*. Edited by Matthew Sussex. Cambridge: Cambridge University Press.

Swietochowski, Tadeusz. 1995. *Russia and Azerbaijan: A Borderland in Transition*. New York: Columbia University Press.

Tansey, Oisín. 2016. "The Problem with Autocracy Promotion." *Democratization* 23, no. 1: 141–63.

Tarkhan-Mouravi, Gia. 2014. "Georgia's European Aspirations and the Eastern Partnership." In *The Making of Modern Georgia, 1918–2012*, edited by Stephen F. Jones, 49–73. Abingdon, UK: Routledge.

TASS News Agency. 2015. "Rol' Rossii V Uregulirovanii Vooruzhennogo konflikta v Sirii, Dos'ye." August 30. http://itar-tass.com/info/889036.

Tickner, Ann J. 2016. "Knowledge Is Power: Challenging IR's Eurocentric Narrative." *International Studies Review* 18, no. 1: 157–59.

Toal, Gerard. 2017. *Near Abroad: Putin, the West and the Contest over Ukraine and the Caucasus*. Oxford: Oxford University Press.

Toal, Gerard, and Magdalena Frichova Grono. 2011. "After Ethnic Violence in the Caucasus: Attitudes of Local Abkhazians and Displaced Georgians in 2010." *Eurasian Geography and Economics* 52, no. 5: 655–78.

Tolstrup, Jakob. 2014. *Russia vs. the EU: The Competition for Influence in Post-Soviet Space*. Boulder, CO: Lynne Rienner.

Trenin, Dmitri V., and Aleksei V. Malashenko. 2004. *Russia's Restless Frontier: The Chechnya Factor in Post-Soviet Russia*. Washington, DC: Carnegie Endowment for International Peace.

Tsheola, J. 2010. "Global 'Openness' and Trade Regionalism of the New Partnership for Africa's Development." *South African Geographical Journal* 92: 45–62.

Tsoukalis, Loukas. 2016. *In Defence of Europe*. Oxford: Oxford University Press.

Tsukanova, Ol'ga V. 2010. "Rol' Rossii V Processe Uregulirovaniya Moldovo-Prindnestrovskogo Konflikta." *Problems in the Russian Legislature*, 4: 294–97.

Tsygankov, Andrei P. 2013. *Russia's Foreign Policy: Change and Continuity in National Identity*. Lanham, MD: Rowman & Littlefield.

Tuite, Kevin. 2008. "The Rise and Fall and Revival of the Ibero-Caucasian Hypothesis." *Historiographia Linguistica* 35, no. 1–2: 23–82.

Tuncer-Kilavuz, Idil. 2009. "Political and Social Networks in Tajikistan and Uzbekistan: 'Clan,' Region and Beyond." *Central Asian Survey* 28, no. 3: 323–34.

Tymoshenko, Yulia. 2007. "Containing Russia." *Foreign Affairs*, May–June. https://www.foreignaffairs.com/articles/russia-fsu/2007-05-01/containing-russia.

Umbach, Frank. 2016. "The Energy Dimensions of Russia's Annexation of Crimea." *NATO Review*, December 9. http://www.nato.int/docu/review/2014/NATO-Energy-security-running-on-empty/Ukraine-energy-independence-gas-dependence-on-Russia/EN/index.htm.

van Langenhove, Luk. 2003. *Theorising Regionhood*. Tokyo: United Nations University Comparative Regional Integration Studies.

Vanin, Grigorii, and Alexander Zhilin. 2014. "Pochemu Tak Stremitel'no Reshalsya Vopros O Prisoedinenii Krima K Rossii." *REX Information Agency*, May 5. http://www.iarex.ru/articles/47561.html.

Vervisch, Thomas, Kristof Titeca, Koen Vlassenroot, and Johan Braeckman. 2013. "Social Capital and Post-Conflict Reconstruction in Burundi: The Limits of Community-Based Reconstruction." *Development and Change* 44, no. 1: 147–74.

Vesely, Lubos, ed. 2008. *Contemporary History Textbooks in the South Caucasus*. Prague: Association for International Affairs.

Vesti TV Channel. 2014a. "Lavrov: Pridnestrov'ye Mozhet Stat' Nezavisimym, Esli Moldaviya Izmenit Svoy Vneblokoviy Status." October 20. http://www.vesti.ru/doc.html?id=2060323.

———. 2014b. "Putin: Rossiiskiy Medved' Nikomu Ne Otdast." October 24. http://www.vesti.ru/doc.html?id=2071417.

Vieira, A.V.G. 2015. "Eurasian Integration: Elite Perspectives before and after the Ukraine Crisis." *Post Soviet Affairs* 32, no. 6: 566–80.

Vinokurov, Evgheni, and Alexey Libman. 2012. *Eurasian Integration: Challenges of Transcontinental Regionalism*. Basingstoke, UK: Palgrave Macmillan.

Vladisavljević, Nebojša. 2014. "Popular Protest in Authoritarian Regimes: Evidence from Communist and Post-Communist States." *Southeast European and Black Sea Studies* 14, no. 2: 139–57.

Wegner, Stephen K. 2012. *Return to Putin's Russia: Past Imperfect, Future Uncertain*. Lanham, MD: Rowman & Littlefield.

Welt, Cory. 2004. "Explaining Ethnic Conflict in the South Caucasus: Mountainous Karabagh, Abkhazia, and South Ossetia." PhD diss., Massachusetts Institute of Technology.

———. 2010a. "Georgia's Rose Revolution: From Regime Weakness to Regime Collapse." In *Democracy and Authoritarianism in the Postcommunist World*, ed. Valerie Bunce, Michael McFaul and Kathryn Stoner-Weiss, 155–88. Cambridge: Cambridge University Press.

———. 2010b. "The Thawing of a Frozen Conflict: The Internal Security Dilemma and the 2004 Prelude to the Russo-Georgian War." *Europe-Asia Studies* 62, no. 1: 63–97.

———. 2014. "In the Shadow of Revolution: A Decade of Authoritarian Hardening in Azerbaijan." Working paper. George Washington University.

Wendt, Alexander. 1992. "Anarchy Is What States Make of It: The Social Construction of Power Politics." *International Organization* 46, no. 2: 391–425.

Wheatley, Jonathan. 2005. *Georgia from National Awakening to Rose Revolution*. Aldershot, UK: Ashgate.

Wheatley, Jonathan, and Christoph Zürcher. 2008. "On the Origin and Consolidation of Hybrid Regimes: The State of Democracy in the Caucasus." *Taiwan Journal of Democracy* 4, no. 1: 1–31.

White, Stephen, and Valentina Feklyunina. 2014. *Identities and Foreign Policies in Russia, Ukraine and Belarus: The Other Europes*. Basingstoke, UK: Palgrave.

Williams, Kirsten P., Steven E. Lobell, and Neal G. Jesse. 2012. *Beyond Great Powers and Hegemons: Why Secondary States Support, Follow, or Challenge*. Stanford, CA: Stanford University Press.

Wilson, Andrew. 1994. "Modern Ukrainian Nationalism and Nationalist Parties in Ukraine, 1988–1992." PhD diss. London: University of London.

———. 2005. *Ukraine's Orange Revolution*. New Haven, CT: Yale University Press.

———. 2014. *The Ukraine Crisis: What the West Needs to Know*. New Haven, CT: Yale University Press, 2014.

Wishnick, Elizabeth. 2017. "In Search of the 'Other' in Asia: Russia–China Relations Revisited." *Pacific Review* 30, no. 1: 114–32.

Wolfel, Richard L. 2002. "North to Astana: Nationalistic Motives for the Movement of the Kazakh(stani) Capital." *Nationalities Papers* 30, no. 3: 485–506.

Wolff, Stefan. 2011. "The Regional Dimensions of State Failure." *Review of International Studies* 37: 951–72.

Wolff, Stefan, and Oya Dursun-Ozkanca. 2012. "Regional and International Conflict Regulation: Diplomatic, Economic and Military Interventions." *Civil Wars* 14, no. 3: 297–323.

Wood, Elizabeth A., William E. Pomeranz, Merry E. Wayne, and Maxim Trudolyubov. 2016. *Roots of Russia's War in Ukraine*. New York: Columbia University Press.

World Economic Forum. 2014. *Scenarios for the South Caucasus and Central Asia*. Geneva, Switzerland: World Economic Forum.

Yapp, Malcolm. 2001. "The Legend of the Great Game." *Proceedings of the British Academy* 111: 179–98.

Yaz'kova, Alla. 2009. "Rossiya I Nezavisimie Gosudarstva Kavkaza," *Caucasus and Globalization* 3, no. 1: 25–32.

Yurgens, I., ed. 2011. *ОДКБ: Ответственная безопасность*'. Moscow: INSOR, August 2011, http://www.insor-russia.ru/files/ODKB.pdf.

Zarembo, Kateryna. 2012. *EU–Ukraine DCFTA: What Do Oligarchs Think?* Policy brief. Kyiv: Institute of World Policy.

Zdravomislov, Andrey. 1997. *Mezhnatsionalnye Konflikty v Postsovetskom Prostranstve*. Moscow: Aspekt Press.

Zhungzhi, Sun, and Zhao Huirong. 2012. "Chinese Views of the Russia–Georgia Conflict and Its Impact." In *Eurasia's Ascent in Energy and Geopolitics: Rivalry or Partnership for China, Russia and Central Asia?*, edited by Robert E. Bedeski and Niklas Swanström, 199–213. Milton Park, UK: Routledge.

Zimmerbauer, K., and A. Paasi. 2013. "When Old and New Regionalism Collide: Deinstitutionalization of Regions and Resistance Identity in Municipality Amalgamations." *Journal of Rural Studies* 30: 31–40.

Zimmerman, William. 2002. *The Russian People and Foreign Policy: Russian Elite and Mass Perspectives, 1993–2000*. Princeton, NJ: Princeton University Press.

Zürcher, Christoph. 2007. *The Post-Soviet Wars*. New York: New York University Press.

CONTRIBUTORS

Dimitar Bechev is a research fellow at the Center for Slavic, Eurasian, and East European Studies at the University of North Carolina at Chapel Hill as well as nonresident senior fellow at the Atlantic Council. He is the author of *Rival Power: Russia in Southeast Europe* (Yale, 2017). Dr. Bechev has held fellowships at Harvard's Center for European Studies, the London School of Economics and Political Science, and St. Antony's College, Oxford. Previously, he headed the Sofia office of the European Council on Foreign Relations, where he had been a senior policy fellow. Bechev has written extensively on the politics of Turkey and the Balkans, EU external affairs, and Russian foreign policy. Bechev received his DPhil in international relations from Oxford University in 2005.

Laurence Broers is a research associate at the School of Oriental and African Studies in London, and coeditor-in-chief of the triannual journal *Caucasus Survey*. He is also affiliated to the Russia and Eurasia Programme at the Royal Institute of International Affairs at Chatham House as an associate fellow. He has written articles and reports on the territorial conflicts of the South Caucasus and has coedited *The Unrecognised Politics of De Facto States in the Post-Soviet Space* (Caucasus Institute, 2015) and *Networked Insurgencies and Foreign Fighters in Eurasia* (London: Routledge, 2018).

Richard Giragosian is the founding director of the Regional Studies Center, an independent think tank located in Yerevan, Armenia (www.regional-studies.org), and serves as both a visiting professor at the College of Europe's Natolin Campus and a senior expert at Yerevan State University's Centre for European Studies. From 2002 to 2006, Giragosian served as a guest lecturer for the US Army Special Forces and, for nine years, as a professional staff member of the Joint Economic Committee of the US Congress. He has also worked as an analyst for Abt Associates Inc., a social science consulting firm, and was a research consultant for the New America Foundation and the Center for National Policy in Washington. He has written for the Centre for European Policy Studies, the European Council on Foreign Relations, the Center for Strategic and International Studies, *Moscow Times*, the London School of Economics, Al Jazeera, *Turkish Daily*, and *Asia Times*, among others, in addition to authoring articles in academic journals. He has also been regularly quoted in and cited by the *Washington Post, Wall Street Journal, New York Times*, and *International Herald Tribune* as well as by *Le Figaro, Economist, Newsweek*, Radio France Internationale, and the BBC, Reuters, and Bloomberg news agencies.

Mark N. Katz (PhD, MIT) is a professor of government and politics at the George Mason University Schar School of Policy and Government. He has written primarily about Moscow's relations with the Middle East (especially the Persian Gulf and Arabian Peninsula) for over thirty-five years. During 2017 he was a visiting scholar first at the Arab Gulf States Institute in Washington (January–March) and then at the Finnish Institute of International Affairs in Helsinki (April–September). In 2018 he is a Fulbright Scholar at the School of Oriental and African Studies in London (January–March) and then a Sir William Luce Fellow at Durham University (late April–late June).

David G. Lewis is a senior lecturer in politics at the University of Exeter, UK. David previously worked as senior research fellow in the Department of Peace Studies at the University of Bradford. He was director of the Central Asia Project of the Brussels-based think tank the International Crisis Group in 2001–5 and established a crisis group project in Sri Lanka in 2006–7. He also worked as a political risk consultant in the private sector, in London and Moscow, and as a consultant to numerous government bodies and international organizations. He has published extensively in the fields of international politics and peace and conflict studies, with a regional focus on the politics, security, and international relations of Russia and Eurasia.

Robert Nalbandov received his PhD in political science from the Central European University, Budapest, in 2008; an MA in international relations from the Fletcher School of Law and Diplomacy, Tufts University; an MPA from the Georgian-American Institute of Public Administration; and a BA in linguistics from the Tbilisi Foreign Language Institute. He has authored four books as well as numerous articles on international security, terrorism, and global conflict. His most recent book is *Not by Bread Alone: Russia's New Foreign Policy* (Potomac Press, 2016). Dr. Nalbandov is currently an adjunct professor at the US Air Command and Staff College.

Anna Ohanyan is a Fulbright Scholar (2012–13) and the Richard B. Finnegan Distinguished Professor of Political Science and International Relations at Stonehill College in Massachusetts. Her latest book is *Networked Regionalism as Conflict Management* (Stanford University Press, 2015), and she has authored numerous articles on global governance, security studies, and conflict management in various academic and policy journals. Her research has been supported by the Kennedy School of Government at Harvard University, the Woodrow Wilson International Center for Scholars, the German Marshall Fund, the US State Department, and the Eurasia Foundation, among others. Professor Ohanyan has also consulted for a range of organizations such as the UN Foundation, the World Bank, the National Intelligence Council Project at Maryland University, the US Department of State, the Carter Center, and

USAID. Her work has taken her across the globe, from Northern Ireland to the Balkans, the South Caucasus, and, most recently, to Russia.

Vsevolod Samokhvalov is Marie-Curie Lecturer at the University of Liege and an adjunct professor at the Vesalius College (Free University of Brussels). Vsevolod obtained a BA in international relations (Odessa, Ukraine), an MA in South-East European Studies (Athens), and a PhD in international relations (Cambridge). In 2002–6 he worked as a research and policy officer at the International Center for Black Sea Studies and the European Union Institute for Security Studies. As a journalist he worked as a BBC correspondent for Greece and Cyprus and as a Eurasian affairs analyst for *New Europe Weekly* (Brussels). He currently runs a research project on Eurasian integration and Ukraine's transformation in Liege and teaches in Brussels, Liege, and Maastricht. Vsevolod's articles on political developments in the post-Soviet space, identity and foreign policy, and Russia–EU relations in the Balkans and the Black Sea region have been published in *Europe-Asia Studies*, *Contemporary Politics*, *Journal of South-East Europe*, and *Black Sea Studies*. His recent books include *Russian-European Relations in the Balkans and Black Sea Region: Great Power Identity and the Idea of Europe* (Palgrave, 2017) and *Eurasian Project and Europe: Regional Discontinuities and Geopolitics* (Palgrave, 2015).

INDEX

www.ingramcontent.com/pod-product-compliance
Lightning Source LLC
LaVergne TN
LVHW041111090826
844660LV00057B/172

* 9 7 8 1 6 2 6 1 6 6 1 9 6 *